Black Freethinkers

Critical Insurgencies

A Book Series of the Critical Ethnic Studies Association

Series Editors: Jodi A. Byrd and Michelle M. Wright

Critical Insurgencies features activists and scholars, as well as artists and other media makers, who forge new theoretical and political practices that unsettle the nation-state, neoliberalism, carcerality, settler colonialism, Western hegemony, legacies of slavery, colonial racial formations, gender binaries, and ableism, and challenge all forms of oppression and state violence through generative future imaginings.

About CESA The Critical Ethnic Studies Association organizes projects and programs that engage ethnic studies while reimagining its futures. Grounded in multiple activist formations within and outside institutional spaces, CESA aims to develop an approach to intellectual and political projects animated by the spirit of decolonial, antiracist, antisexist, and other global liberationist movements. These movements enabled the creation of ethnic studies and continue to inform its political and intellectual projects.

www.criticalethnicstudies.org

Black Freethinkers

A History of African American Secularism

Christopher Cameron

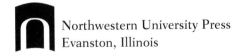

Northwestern University Press
Evanston, Illinois

Northwestern University Press
www.nupress.northwestern.edu

Copyright © 2019 by Northwestern University Press. Published 2019.
All rights reserved.

Printed in the United States of America

10 9 8 7 6 5 4 3 2 1

ISBN 978-0-8101-4079-0 (cloth)
ISBN 978-0-8101-4078-3 (paper)
ISBN 978-0-8101-4080-6 (e-book)

Cataloging-in-Publication data are available from the Library of Congress.

CONTENTS

ACKNOWLEDGMENTS

.

I am incredibly grateful for the encouragement and advice I've received from my colleagues at UNC Charlotte. In particular, I'd like to thank John David Smith, Christine Haynes, Robert McEachnie, Dan Dupre, Jurgen Buchenau, Carmen Soliz, Gregory Mixon, Aaron Shapiro, and Cheryl Hicks for reading and commenting on chapter drafts in our department's Brown Bag seminars. I also want to thank the participants in the Charlotte Area Historians Seminar who read and commented on three of the four chapters in this book. Special thanks go to Joseph Moore for his incisive critiques and support from the inception of this project.

Since I founded it in 2014, the African American Intellectual History Society (AAIHS) has been an incredibly supportive intellectual community. I am grateful to all those who read and commented on my blog posts on black freethought and for those people who emailed me sources, videos, and writings of any black atheists they came across. Many thanks as well to the participants in AAIHS's first two symposiums who read and gave me feedback on two chapter drafts, including Guy Emerson Mount, Phil Sinitiere, Brandon Byrd, Ashley Farmer, Kami Fletcher, Emily Owens, Greg Childs, Keisha Blain, and Reena Goldthree. Mississippi State University's history department and the Africana Studies department at the University of Pennsylvania likewise deserve recognition for funding these gatherings.

I have received generous financial support for this project from a number of sources. A short-term fellowship from Emory University's Stuart A. Rose Manuscript, Archives, and Rare Books Library allowed me to conduct research for chapter 3 and the afterword. Faculty Research Grants from UNC Charlotte supported two summers of work on this book. A Reassignment of Duties Leave from the College of Liberal Arts and Sciences at UNC Charlotte allowed me to research and draft chapter 2, while a Cotlow leave from the history department allowed me to draft chapter 3.

This book would not have been possible without the pioneering work of freethought scholars such as Anthony B. Pinn, Michael Lackey,

Christopher Grasso, and Sikivu Hutchinson. Pinn's work pointed me to many of the sources that comprise this study and is an example of the highest quality of scholarship. Chris Grasso generously shared some work in progress from his book *Skepticism and American Faith*, including the vignette that opens this book. Hutchinson's scholarship pushed me to focus on women and the intersection of gender and freethought in every chapter. And I probably never would have thought of this project were it not for the important work of contemporary black freethinkers such as Debbie Goddard, Mandisa Thomas, Kimberly Veal, and others. I appreciate being welcomed into the freethought community and am glad to be able to share this work with you all.

Last but not least, I am incredibly grateful for the support of my family. My sister Sophie Walrond, my brother Reggie Walrond, and my in-laws Tom and Regina Jones provided crucial child care while I worked on the book. Special thanks go to my wife, Shanice Cameron. As a believer herself, I'm sure she gets tired of hearing me talk about black atheists all the time. She has nevertheless supported this project from the start and encouraged me every step of the way. She has watched my siblings while I've been off on research trips, taken on greater child care responsibilities with our three children, and sacrificed her time and energy to see this project to its completion. I could not have written this book without her love and support.

INTRODUCTION

In his 1842 book *The Religious Instruction of the Negroes*, Charles Colcock Jones, a slaveholder and Presbyterian minister from Georgia, noted the widespread presence of religious skepticism among slaves. "He who carries the gospel to them," Jones pronounced, "encounters depravity, intrenched in ignorance, both real and pretended. . . . He discovers deism, skepticism, universalism." Jones claimed that many slaves perverted the gospel. According to him, many enslaved people upheld common arguments against God's existence. This latter point especially surprised him because he contended that most atheist arguments were "peculiar only to the cultivated minds, the ripe scholarship and profound intelligence, of *critics and philosophers*." As a missionary to slaves, Jones had a vested interest in highlighting instances of irreligiosity to convince his fellow slaveholders to be more attuned to their slaves' spiritual state. Most significantly, his statement reveals his assumption that freethought, including atheism, agnosticism, and nontraditional religious views such as deism, was the preserve of educated or cultivated minds belonging to philosophers—that is, white people.[1]

The assumption that atheism and other forms of nonbelief are the preserve of whites has caused most historians and scholars of religion to ignore or downplay their existence among African Americans. *Black Freethinkers* challenges this trend by arguing that atheism, agnosticism, and secular humanism have been central components of black intellectual and political life since the nineteenth century. The influence of nonbelief on black life can be seen during many times and among key black thinkers. Black freethinkers run the gamut from the antireligious (atheists or agnostics) to those who believed in private or unconventional faiths (such as deism) that were at odds with traditional religious beliefs. This latter group includes figures such as Frederick Douglass, who was the most prominent black abolitionist of the nineteenth century. Moving into the 1900s, black freethinkers such as Zora Neale Hurston, Nella Larsen, and Langston Hughes made significant contributions to Harlem Renaissance literature. A. Philip Randolph, Grace P.

Campbell, Louise Thompson Patterson and W. E. B. Du Bois, all free-thinkers, were central figures in labor organizing and black radical leftist politics during the period between the two world wars. Additionally, atheists such as James Forman, Lorraine Hansberry, and Huey Newton played important roles in the civil rights, Black Power, and black arts movements of the 1960s and 1970s. In contemporary America, individual black freethinkers including Alice Walker remain prominent in movements ranging from feminism to prison reform to the abolition of sex trafficking. And since 1990, the black freethought movement has become institutionalized and grown significantly, witnessing the creation of groups such as Black Atheists of America and African Americans for Humanism that count thousands among their members. So, while black freethinkers have constituted a small segment of the overall black population, they have nevertheless had a significant impact on African American life and culture in a variety of ways.

One reason for the lack of attention to the history of black free-thought is the assumption that black people are naturally religious and that the black church has always been at the center of the black community. This former belief has its roots in the early nineteenth-century abolitionist movement. In his influential 1835 work *Slavery*, Unitarian minister William Ellery Channing noted of southern slaves, "Of all the races of men, the African is the mildest and most susceptible of attachment. He loves, where the European would hate. He watches the life of a master, whom the North-American Indian, in like circumstances, would stab to the heart. The African is affectionate." The primary reason for this supposedly loving and affectionate nature of African Americans, in Channing's view, was that "the colored race are said to be peculiarly susceptible of the religious sentiment." As Curtis Evans notes in *The Burden of Black Religion*, both abolitionists and proslavery thinkers alike appropriated Channing's argument. This reasoning reinforced the nineteenth-century view that blacks were naturally religious and has continued to influence perceptions of African American religiosity since his time. Freethinkers during the late 1800s echoed Channing's view; one 1883 article by Eugene Macdonald, editor of the *Truth Seeker*, noted in similar language that "there is no class of people in the world more religious than the negroes. Their fervent African temperament makes them peculiarly susceptible to religious sentiment."[2]

Notions of blacks as naturally religious likewise persisted into the twentieth and twenty-first centuries. From March 21 to 26, 1953, for example, Langston Hughes testified before Joseph McCarthy's

Permanent Subcommittee on Investigations regarding the atheist and communist themes in his 1932 poem "Goodbye, Christ." At one point during the testimony, Senator Everett Dirksen of Illinois wanted to know whether Hughes thought the "Book is dead" (referring to the Bible) and whether or not "Goodbye, Christ" could be considered an accurate reflection of African American religious values. Dirksen noted that he was familiar with African Americans and knew them to be "innately a very devout and religious people." More than sixty years later, in a 2014 survey by the Pew Forum for the Study of Religion, nearly 90 percent of African Americans affirmed belief in God, while 75 percent noted that religion was very important in their lives. These numbers are well above the national averages for other ethnic groups and, when combined with the prominence of religious figures in the civil rights movement and the ubiquity of religious discourse in black political thought, tend to reinforce Dirksen's statement that African Americans are naturally religious.[3]

This notion of the innate religiosity of black people has had significant ramifications for scholarship on African American religion. The overwhelming focus of works on slave religion has been on variants of Protestant Christianity and their intersection with African religious traditions. During the early eighteenth century, most scholars note, the Society for the Propagation of the Gospel attempted to Christianize the slave population but was unsuccessful because of resistance from masters, language barriers, and an emphasis on religious education that precluded many illiterate slaves from converting. The efforts to convert African Americans to Christianity became more successful during the First Great Awakening and accelerated during the Second Great Awakening of the nineteenth century; sects including the Methodists and Baptists deemphasized religious education and posited the primacy of the conversion experience. Rituals such as baptism by immersion were similar to African traditions and thus also appealed to Southern slaves. Scholars such as Edward Curtis IV, Michael Gomez, and Yvonne Chireau have added to this picture by demonstrating the importance of alternate faiths such as Islam and conjure throughout slave communities. Yet the assumption still remains that some form of religiosity was endemic to the enslaved population and that few if any slaves became religious skeptics and freethinkers.[4]

Some scholars have recently challenged the assumptions about black religiosity, especially enslaved people's adherence to Protestant Christianity during the slavery era. In *Slavery, Civil War, and Salvation*, for example, Daniel Fountain argues that while Christianity was a significant component of slaves' religious worldview, most slaves were not Christians. We have come to believe that a majority of slaves were Christians because of the ubiquity of comments about slaves' religious practice. But, according to Fountain, these comments were so frequent because religion was the most visible form of public behavior for blacks in the South. While Fountain's argument leaves the door open for other forms of religiosity, including adherence to traditional African religions, it also includes the likelihood that many slaves were religious skeptics. Anthony Pinn has explored this latter point in depth since 1998, noting the presence of humanism among slaves in his works, including *Varieties of African American Religious Experience, Introducing African American Religion*, and *The End of God-Talk*. While Pinn's scholarship has been less historically focused and geared more toward the creation of black humanist theology as a field, his works have included significant and original explorations of humanism and secularism among slaves. This study builds off Pinn's work, as well as that of contemporary black freethinkers such as Norm Allen Jr., Sikivu Hutchinson, Donald Barbera, and Candace Gorham, to offer the first history of African American freethought from the early nineteenth century to the civil rights era.[5]

Greater recognition of skepticism and unbelief among Southern slaves challenges the major thrust of the scholarship on early American freethought. Most of this scholarship posits that freethought stemmed from Enlightenment philosophy and Newtonian science and was most prevalent in the North. Scholars also focus almost exclusively on white freethinkers. However, examining slaves who rejected prevailing religious beliefs demonstrates an alternative origin to freethought in early America: the brutality of the institution of slavery itself. The constant presence of physical violence, sexual assault, hunger, and breakup of families, among other facets of American slavery, pushed many slaves to question not only Christianity but also the very idea of God. While James Turner argues in his seminal work *Without God, Without Creed* that atheism "seemed almost palpably absurd" before the American Civil War, this view does not reflect that of some slaves. This group of African Americans did not need to justify rejecting God; slavery provided the necessary foundation for them to deny prevailing theodicies and to embrace nonbelief.[6]

Scholars have long used slave narratives to document the rich and textured religious worldview of Southern slaves, but these sources also provide a window into the growth of religious skepticism and nonbelief in disparate slave communities, as we will see in chapter 1. The narratives of individuals such as Austin Steward, Henry Bibb, Harriet Jacobs, Frederick Douglass, Charles Ball, and William Wells Brown all speak to the presence of nonbelief and religious skepticism on Southern plantations. Proslavery religion and the hypocritical religious professions of their masters were two central reasons that slaves came to deny not only the "truth" of Christianity but also the idea of God. Also, when contemplating their lives in bondage, many slaves believed that there could not be a just and benevolent God who cared about them. These professions of nonbelief among slaves can also be gleaned from travelers such as the black minister Daniel Payne and from whites such as Charles Colcock Jones, the minister and slaveholder whose account opened this introduction. Taken together, they provide compelling evidence for the existence of African American freethought during the antebellum period.

Chapter 1 also explores those free blacks who became freethinkers during the nineteenth century. Frederick Douglass expressed deistic and agnostic views at times and was a religious liberal and humanist. In the 1880s, he became vice president of the Free Religious Association, an organization aimed at promoting the separation of church and state, and he was friendly with white freethinkers such as Robert Ingersoll. And individuals such as David Cincore, Lord A. Nelson, and R. S. King participated in national freethought conventions and wrote letters to the *Truth Seeker*, the leading freethought journal of the day. They all recognized the paucity of black atheists in the country and saw their role as freethought ambassadors to the black community. While African Americans were largely ignored or marginalized in the freethought movement, these individuals' writings and speeches laid the foundation for a more robust presence during the twentieth century.

The Harlem Renaissance provided ideal conditions for many black writers to express their critiques of Christianity, as described in chapter 2. The Great Migration that precipitated the explosion of black arts and letters meant that many blacks found themselves in large urban areas for the first time. Here they encountered diverse people open to new ideas, including atheism and agnosticism. Writers such as Zora Neale Hurston, Alain Locke, Claude McKay, Langston Hughes, and Nella Larsen all produced works that undermined orthodox Christianity and displayed their diverse freethought perspectives, including deism, agnosticism, atheism, and an adherence to the Baha'i faith without monotheism. Some had come to doubt Christianity and the idea of God while living in the rural South, but moving to the city and participating in the Harlem Renaissance provided a sense of community that allowed them to express their ideas in print, including poems, scholarly essays, novels, and memoirs.

Many scholars view secularism as arising directly from industrialization and urbanization. Technology and modern science reduce the need for religion, in this formulation, leading to more widespread articulations of freethought perspectives and a lessened role of religion in public life. Jonathan Kahn and Vincent Lloyd's recent work *Race and Secularism in America* challenges this framework. Looking at the diversity of religion that arose in northern cities during the Harlem Renaissance, they claim that "the encounter with modernity seems to have broken the secular management of the religious that led white elites to tolerate sleepy southern churches." My study takes a middle path between these two frameworks. While I do not argue that industrialization and urbanization caused black secularism, I do argue that urbanization and northern migration helped foster black freethought by providing conditions whereby African Americans felt comfortable openly expressing their critical religious perspectives.[7]

Women writers of the Harlem Renaissance also included significant explorations of feminism in their work that drew from their perspective as freethinkers. Nella Larsen began this trend with her novella *Quicksand*, which explores the life of a woman named Helga Crane who marries a Baptist preacher from Alabama and settles down into a miserable life of domesticity. Throughout the work, Larsen, herself a freethinker, critiques the pretensions to respectability among the black middle class in both the North and the South. She likewise attacks the idea of marriage and domestic life providing happiness for black women and notes the prevalence of patriarchy among black men. Zora Neale Hurston's *Their Eyes Were Watching God* similarly critiques notions of marriage and material comfort and implies that women can be happy either on their own or with much younger men. Their works inaugurated the literary ties between feminism and black freethought and would profoundly shape the writings of future black women freethinkers such as Alice Walker and Sikivu Hutchinson.[8]

Chapter 3 examines the period between World War I and World War II, a time when many black freethinkers became involved in radical leftist politics. Indeed, as national freethought organizations and publications started to fold, participation in the Socialist and Communist

Parties became a key outlet for freethinkers, white and black, to express
their social and political activism. Individuals such as Hubert Harrison,
A. Philip Randolph, W. E. B. Du Bois, Harry Haywood, and Richard
Wright all became socialists or communists because of these parties'
critique of power relations in American society, anticolonialism, and
support of black nationalism. The Communist Party was especially
irreligious and thus appealed to freethinkers. Publications such as
Randolph's *Messenger* magazine and the *Crusader*, the organ of the
African Blood Brotherhood, contained articles critical of Christianity
and opposing American racism, imperialism, and capitalism. For those
black freethinkers who embraced socialism and communism, religion
was simply a tool of oppression black people would be better off without. Judith Weisenfeld notes that throughout American history, African
Americans have viewed white Christianity as "at the very least, deeply
skewed and even bankrupt" because of its support for slavery and Jim
Crow. Despite this view, most black people embraced their own version of Christianity. Black freethinkers of the 1920s and 1930s were
singular in their opposition not only to white Christianity but to black
Christianity as well.[9]

Black women freethinkers were also drawn to the Communist
Party and, like both Nella Larsen and Zora Neale Hurston, combined
a critique of religion with a feminist perspective. Individuals such as
Audley Moore, Grace P. Campbell, Elizabeth Hendrickson, and Louise Thompson Patterson joined the Communist Party because they
believed the party was the best vehicle for bringing about both gender
and racial equality. Leadership positions in the Communist Party were
open to women, and the party likewise engaged in relief efforts that
helped black women stave off eviction and hunger. By participating in
Communist Party politics, black women freethinkers also challenged
traditional ideas of proper womanhood and respectability, especially
through their roles as soapbox orators on the streets of Harlem. Eric
McDuffie posits that these women articulated a philosophy of intersec-
tional oppression nearly half a century before the emergence of black
feminism. Freethought thus played a key role in one of the most important intellectual and political developments in twentieth-century black
life.[10]

Black freethinkers were also central theorists and activists in the civil
rights and Black Power movements that are the subject of chapter 4.
Leaders of the Student Non-Violent Coordinating Committee such as
James Forman and Stokely Carmichael were atheists who pushed the

organization away from its early focus on nonviolent demonstrations toward an embrace of Black Power. And the founders and early members of the Black Panther Party for Self-Defense, including Huey Newton, Eldridge Cleaver, and David Hilliard, were likewise nonbelievers who rejected the nonviolence of Christian civil rights leaders such as Martin Luther King Jr. and instead embraced a focus on self-defense, black pride, black self-determination, and anti-imperialism. One of the main slogans of the Black Panther Party, "All Power to the People," developed as a humanist response to the perceived otherworldliness of black Christian churches. The party's many social service programs, including free breakfast, medical clinics, and schools, were likewise secular humanist endeavors aimed at motivating black people to take control of their own communities. The official organ of the party, the *Black Panther*, also served at times as a freethought publication by including poems and essays attacking both the black church and the idea of God.

Black freethought was also prevalent among some of the most well-known writers, artists, and intellectuals of the civil rights era. Lorraine Hansberry, James Baldwin, and Sarah Webster Fabio, among others, used their plays, novels, essays, and poetry to explore atheism's place in black culture. An examination of their writings makes it clear that they were not just writers who happened to be freethinkers but that their nonbelief played a crucial role in shaping their identities and their literary productions. The philosopher William R. Jones's work likewise made an important contribution to the freethought movement with his critique of black theology and his call for black thinkers to adopt a "humanocentric theism" that downplayed the power of God in determining the course of life on earth. The work of these writers and intellectuals was a corollary to the political activism of organizations such as the Black Panther Party and further demonstrates the significance of freethought in the civil rights movement.[11]

Finally, the afterword briefly examines the literary career of black freethinker Alice Walker. Walker, a pagan and nontheist, has been active in a range of social and political causes from the mid-1960s to the present. In 1997, the American Humanist Association honored her as its Humanist of the Year, making her the first black woman to win that award. I then turn to Anthony Pinn's work from the mid-1990s to the present because his body of scholarship has helped bring attention to the vibrant tradition of black humanism. This study ends by looking at the most significant development in black freethought during the late twentieth and early twenty-first centuries—namely, its institutionalization. Black Atheists of America, African Americans for Humanism, and Black Nonbelievers are just a few of the organizations created specifically to foster freethought in black communities across the country. These organizations provide support, fellowship, and programming to help make atheism more appealing to African Americans. And they have likewise critiqued the narrow focus on scientism and the separation of church and state prevalent among "New Atheists" to proffer a more expansive, humanist vision for the freethought movement, one that sees it as a duty of freethinkers to combat homophobia, racism, and sexism in American society.

Black Freethinkers

Slavery and Reconstruction

Shortly after the abolition of slavery in New York in 1827, Nathaniel Paul, a black minister and abolitionist in Albany, gave a speech claiming that slavery was contrary to the laws of God and that "in whatever form we behold it, its visage is satanic." This statement would not have been controversial among antislavery activists, but Paul went even further than most abolitionist writers might have, noting that if he did not have hope that slavery would someday end, "I would deny the superintending power of divine providence in the affairs of this life; I would ridicule the religion of the Saviour of the world, and treat as the worst of men the ministers of the everlasting gospel." Indeed, if he did not think slavery would soon be abolished, "I would at once confess myself an atheist, and deny the existence of a holy God." Paul eventually assured his audience that "slavery will cease, and the equal rights of man will be universally acknowledged." For Paul, speaking the day after slavery had been abolished in New York, it was easy to be optimistic. But for countless African Americans still toiling in bondage, all such hope seemed false, and Paul's theoretical embrace of atheism did not seem like such a bad idea.[1]

Black freethought had its roots partially in the Second Great Awakening, a major nineteenth-century religious movement that increased evangelicals' outreach to slaves. This period of religious fervor also brought to the fore what many observers saw as not only the hypocritical nature of Christian masters' owning slaves but also of the way their masters treated them. Some slaves told themselves that their masters were not true Christians and looked forward to the day when God would deliver them from bondage, as he did Moses and the Israelites. Some turned to Islam or derivatives of African religions such as conjure and voodoo, while many moved back and forth between various religious beliefs. However, others came to reject the idea of

God altogether, reasoning that a just and benevolent deity would not leave them in bondage. While it is unclear just how many did so, travel accounts, slave narratives, and writings by former slaves demonstrate that nonbelief was present in disparate slave communities and was more prominent than previous scholars have realized.

In addition to slave communities, African American freethought was present among free blacks in the North. For individuals such as Frederick Douglass and William Wells Brown, freethought meant more than just an articulation of skepticism or nonbelief. It was instead a way of life and a worldview that influenced political ideologies and social engagement. Sometimes black freethinkers posited a belief in God and used religious language, but their conceptions of the deity, like white freethinkers, were unorthodox and posed strong challenges to prevailing religious ideas and institutions. So, while the origins of black and white freethought might have been different, their ultimate function could at times be strikingly similar—namely, to bring about a more democratic society by advocating causes that included political rights for blacks, women's equality, and the abolition of slavery.

One of the most powerful arguments that black activists deployed in the antebellum antislavery movement was that slavery led to infidelity and religious skepticism. This argument was true of religious abolitionists such as Harriet Jacobs but was also a common theme in the writings of black freethinkers such as Douglass and Brown. This latter group pointed to the many ways that slavery was harmful to the spread of Christianity, including the reluctance of many slaveholders to convert their slaves, the perverted portrayal of Christianity present in the sermons of white ministers, and the hypocrisy of slaveholders' religious professions. In tying together these two themes, black freethinkers advanced the cause of abolition while also contributing to the growing freethought movement in the mid-nineteenth century.

Liberal Religion and Deism

Before delving into the rise of black freethought, it will be useful to briefly examine the growth of freethought among whites in colonial America. While freethinkers in the twenty-first century would be most likely to self-identify as atheist, agnostic, spiritual but not religious, or some similar term indicating lack of religious belief, early American freethinkers usually still identified themselves as religious, professed a belief in God, and for some, even called themselves Christians. Free-thinkers in the eighteenth century were usually deists who believed in a benevolent and loving God who set up the universe to run according to natural laws (both physical and moral), laws that human beings could discern through the use of reason. Deism in America grew out of a liberalization of American Protestantism that was in itself a by-product of Enlightenment science, political theory, and epistemology. New conceptions regarding the nature of the universe and the relation of individuals to the state precipitated a challenge to orthodox Puritanism in the mid-1700s that laid the foundation for the rise of American secularism.

In early eighteenth-century New England, liberal theologians began to undermine the once dominant ideology of Calvinism with increasing ferocity. By midcentury, the battle between the two sides was in full swing. A group of Arminian ministers, including Charles Chauncy, Ebenezer Gay, and Jonathan Mayhew, challenged orthodox Calvinist ideas regarding original sin, the covenant of grace, and the very nature of God. At its most basic level, Arminianism, the idea that people could in some way affect their spiritual state, represented a fundamental shift among theologians in New England and throughout the Atlantic World in notions about human capacity, and it proffered a new vision for the type of religion best suited to a civil society.

Jonathan Mayhew became an early proponent of Arminianism in colonial America. Jonathan had grown up on Martha's Vineyard, where his father, Experience Mayhew, was a missionary to the Wampanoag Indians. Over the years, Experience Mayhew slowly drifted toward Arminianism, and Jonathan followed suit. Having attended Harvard during the height of religious revivalism and bitter church disputes in New England, Jonathan Mayhew ascended to the pulpit of Boston's West Church in 1747 and quickly made his challenge to orthodox Calvinism known. "Men have naturally as clear a conception of the general difference betwixt moral good and evil," he proclaimed, "antecedent to all consideration of human laws and compacts, yea, to the consideration of the will of God himself, as they have of the difference betwixt light and darkness." Rejecting the notion that human beings were inherently depraved sinners who could do no good, Mayhew painted a more optimistic portrait of human nature. To be sure, he was not saying human beings are good by nature, but in Mayhew's estimation they do possess a natural, moral sense that they could use when determining ethical questions.[2]

Mayhew also took exception with the Calvinist doctrine of original sin and the conception of God as anything less than a wise, benevolent ruler. In regard to the former, he claimed that "the doctrine of total ignorance, and incapacity to judge of moral and religious truths, brought upon mankind by the apostasy of our *first parents*, is without foundation." Mankind was not doomed to a life of ignorance and sin because of the actions of Adam and Eve. And in addressing the nature of God, Mayhew posited, "were God a malevolent Being; were he an unreasonable Tyrant; were he an hard master; were he an implacable and revengeful being; instead of a merciful and faithful creator; a compassionate parent; a gentle master, a righteous Judge; we might well think of him with horror and dread; and even with a period put to his existence." For Mayhew, the theological positions of the orthodox were more likely to promote atheism than religious devotion and observance. Thus, he posited that it was absolutely essential for people to see God as rational and just, attributes he believed did not square with predestination, original sin, and human depravity.[3]

The principal tenets of Arminian ministers such as Mayhew, Gay, and Chauncy—God's reasonable and benevolent nature, the rational design of the universe, humans' ability to influence their own spiritual state through willpower and reason—would profoundly influence the rise of deism and early American freethought. While few individuals in the American colonies openly espoused deism before the 1770s, there were some notable converts earlier in the century, including Benjamin Franklin, who wrote that at the age of fifteen, "some books against Deism fell into my Hands. They were said to be the Substance of Sermons preached at Boyle's lectures. It happened that they wrought an Effect on me quite contrary to what was intended by them: For the Arguments of the Deists which were quoted to be refuted, appeared to me much Stronger than the Refutations. In short I soon became a thorough Deist." Franklin's experience would not be an uncommon one, as the opponents of deism were so prolific and outspoken that they unintentionally introduced countless readers to the very ideas they were trying to undermine.[4]

What were the arguments of the deists to which Franklin refers? According to Henry May, "deists believed God bound by definition to act in an orderly, moral, and rational manner." They further posited that faith could not run contrary to reason. Anything in the Bible, for instance, that was either unreasonable or immoral did not come from God. As such, most deists accepted the sufficiency of natural religion

over revealed religion, an emphasis that distinguished them from Arminians such as Ebenezer Gay, who always maintained the importance of
a balance between the two. Deists believed that "reality is the creation
of a perfectly benevolent and rational deity—the 'Supreme Architect'—
whose divine rationality and goodness are reflected in his handiwork.
Physical reality, for the deists, conforms to universal, immutable, and
absolute laws of nature set in motion by God." Human beings have
the capacity to understand these laws because they are imbued with
a part of divine reason. As Kerry Walters noted, deists believed that
"in coming to know reality, humans also gain a deeper appreciation of
the Divine Architect's character, since it is through natural law that he
reveals himself. Moreover, the highest form of worship of the Deity is
the exercise of those godlike qualities that he has bestowed on humanity: reason and benevolence."[5]

Thomas Paine was perhaps the most important deist writer of the
eighteenth century. Paine migrated to the colonies in 1774 and was
greatly admired during the 1770s and 1780s for his important pam-
phlet *Common Sense*, as well his "Crisis" essays. He made a case for
independence unlike no other writer of his time, and his writings during
the Revolutionary War helped fortify the colonists at critical junctures.
But his reputation took a turn for the worse after he published *The Age
of Reason*, a small book that nevertheless drew the ire of thousands
of people in the United States and throughout Europe. Paine began
the work by articulating some of his key religious beliefs. "I believe
in one God, and no more," Paine wrote. "And I hope for happiness
beyond this life. I believe in the equality of man, and I believe that religious duties consist in doing justice, loving mercy, and endeavoring to
make our fellow creatures happy." This statement would perhaps be the
least controversial in *The Age of Reason*; however, Paine soon alienated
many readers with his critiques of prevailing religious institutions and
ideas. He and other deists contended that the idea of a special revelation being the foundation for the Christian religion was ludicrous. As
Paine wrote, "every national church or religion has established itself by
pretending some special mission from God, communicated to certain
individuals . . . as if the way to God was not open to every man alike."
While God may be able to make a revelation to one individual, it does
not follow that the revelation should be taken as such by everybody
that person tells. In fact, to everyone aside from the first individual,
the "revelation" is actually hearsay, and disbelief is a valid option. This
statement on Paine's part was especially dangerous, as it undermined

the very foundation of Christianity—namely, a belief in the Bible as a special revelation from God to man.[6]

Strident anticlericalism was also a central component of deism and early American freethought. Just as many writers during the revolutionary period linked political and religious tyranny, so too did Paine. In *Common Sense*, he argued that "monarchy in every instance is the Popery of government." Nearly twenty years later, Paine's views on organized religion had grown even more acrimonious. "The church has set up a system of religion very contradictory to the character of the person whose name it bears," he contended. "It has set up a religion of pomp and of revenue in pretended imitation of a person whose life was humility and poverty." His critique was one common among deist writers of the era, who contended that although Protestant theologians and ministers had called for a return to the simple religion of Jesus since the time of Martin Luther, the efforts to simplify the practice of Christianity had failed. These calls included charges that theological abstractions were common in Sunday sermons and the pure, simple, religion of nature was dismissed as infidelity and idolatry.[7]

Elihu Palmer built on and extended these critiques in his defenses of Paine's *Age of Reason* and other writings during the late eighteenth and early nineteenth centuries. While Paine was the most well-known deist in the early Republic, Palmer was perhaps the most influential. He began his career as a Presbyterian minister in Newtown, Long Island, but was only there a short time before being dismissed for preaching heterodox sermons. In 1791, Palmer joined the Universal Society of Philadelphia, an organization that John Fitch, inventor of the steamboat, founded to promote liberal Christianity in the area. After losing his wife, eyesight, and legal career to yellow fever in 1793, Palmer devoted the rest of his life to preaching the gospel of rational religion. He published two deist newspapers—*Temple of Reason* (1800–1801) and *Prospect* (1803–1805)—that enjoyed a wide readership, and his speeches and organizational work did much to promote deism and freethought in both the North and South.[8]

Palmer's defense of *The Age of Reason* appeared just months after Paine published the book and articulated a hopeful vision for the rise of deism and its place in American society. The publication of Paine's work contributed to Palmer's optimism. According to Palmer, Paine taught the world that any topic is suitable for investigation by rational minds and that no topic is "too sublime to be comprehended by common sense." His latter point represents an important development in early American freethought. While deism had been the preserve of an educated elite prior to the American Revolution, by the mid-1790s, the movement was spreading due, in no small part, to Palmer's organizational efforts. In addition to publishing newspapers, Palmer supported the creation of "temples of reason" and organizations including theophilanthropy societies, two entities in the early republic that helped spread his ideas to the lower and middle classes. For example, in 1796, Palmer founded the Deistical Society in New York City to help spread the democratic and religious principles of the French Revolution, and he later formed the Society of Theophilanthropy in Newburgh, New York, for similar reasons. His grassroots organizing and leadership of the deist movement actually resembled that of evangelical Christians, who were just initiating the Second Great Awakening in the early nineteenth century. Similar to their hopes for a new millennium, Palmer shortly expected "the gradual rise of deism upon the ruins of the Christian system."[9]

Palmer partially realized his optimistic vision of spreading deism in America. While the movement lost some steam after 1810, interest in it resurged during the 1820s. During that decade, celebrations of Thomas Paine's birthday became common among freethinkers, especially in New York City and other urban areas in the North. Artisans who shared overlapping involvement in the burgeoning labor movement and Democratic Party politics generally attended these celebrations. The "free enquiry" movement also grew in scope during the 1820s, producing a new type of conversion narrative to contrast with religious ones: conversions out of Christianity. Free enquirers referred to themselves by many names, including deists, skeptics, moral philanthropists, materialists, and infidels, depending on their metaphysical ideas about God or their appetite for theological dispute. As Eric Schlereth has pointed out, Paine's admirers in this era were often male mechanics who "turned to free enquiry as an alternative to the emerging cultural dominance of evangelical Protestant reform in America's northern towns and cities." Despite the dominance of male artisans in the movement, there was a gendered discourse prevalent at some free enquiry celebrations, with arguments that the movement had the potential to liberate women from the constraints imposed on them by patriarchal Christian norms. For example, a woman, Frances Wright, became one of the foremost religious skeptics of nineteenth-century America. Wright, a Scottish emigrant, helped establish the Hall of Science in New York City. This building hosted weekly debates on freethought and lectures on scientific and moral topics, and it served as the home of the *Free Enquirer*, a paper with a circulation of one thousand issues per week at its height in 1831.[10]

Deism was not nearly as widespread as evangelical religion would come to be, but the movement was nevertheless prominent in American culture and significant in the nation's political and religious life. Drawing some of its principal tenets from the liberal Arminians of mid-eighteenth-century New England, deists posited the existence of a rational world order, created by a benevolent and just god. They rejected Trinitarian theology and usually discounted belief in supernaturalism and divine providence. Jesus was, in their view, only human, and the Bible, while it contained excellent moral precepts, was on the whole inconsistent with the nature of God. Whereas many deists during the revolutionary era accepted the utility of churches, especially for the common people, by the late eighteenth century, deism was characterized by rising anticlericalism and hostility to established churches. This opposition to organized religion fueled their opponents and "helped create a sturdy cultural boundary between acceptable and unacceptable religious expression in a largely Protestant culture." It also represents one of the key components shared between white and black freethinkers in nineteenth-century America.[11]

Slavery and the Problem of Evil

African American freethought arose in the same era as liberal religion and deism and the larger freethought movement—the late eighteenth and early nineteenth centuries. But while the origins of deism and freethought among whites lay in liberal Christianity and Enlightenment philosophy, black freethought grew out of the institution of slavery and the conditions blacks endured within it. One of the key reasons that African Americans in the nineteenth century embraced freethought was an inability to resolve the problem of evil, or the question of how to reconcile the existence of evil in the world with the presence of a benevolent and omnipotent deity. As Epicurus asked more than two thousand years ago, "Is God willing to prevent evil, but not able? Then he is not omnipotent. Is he able, but not willing? Then he is malevolent. Is he both able and willing? Then whence cometh evil? Is he neither able nor willing? Then why call him God?" For many slaves, the problem of evil was intimately related to their daily lives, as a central component of slavery was suffering. This is not to say that there were no moments of joy and happiness in the lives of slaves. A wedding, the birth of a child, time off for the holidays, and reunion with family members—all of these could bring moments of great joy and happiness. But in reading slave narratives, it is impossible to escape the simple fact that slaves' lives were filled with suffering, pain, and loss that were attributed not to life in general but to slavery in particular.[12]

Historians of slavery have long noted that a key feature of the slave experience for women was the constant threat of sexual abuse and exploitation. Kirsten Fischer has argued that "the slave system institutionalized the sexual exploitation of enslaved women by making access to their bodies a prerogative of male slaveholders that the courts consistently ignored."[13] Testimony from former slaves, including Harriet Jacobs, supports this point. Jacobs was born enslaved in Edenton, North Carolina, in 1813. Upon the death of her mistress in 1825, she was left with a new master, Dr. James Norcom, who quickly introduced her to the unsavory elements of the peculiar institution for women. When she was fifteen years old, Norcom "began to whisper foul words in my ear. . . . I tried to treat them with indifference or contempt." But she was unable to do so, as he persisted in his advances. Eventually, Jacobs got into a relationship with a nearby white man, Samuel Sawyer, with whom she had two children. Norcom constantly threatened to sell them if she refused to comply with his advances, and she decided to run away. Jacobs could not get far and had to hide out in her grandmother's attic. Jacob's grandmother was a free woman who also lived in Edenton and was raising Harriet's two children, Joseph and Louisa. It is unclear whether Jacobs knew it going in, but she would remain in that attic for the next seven years, able to see and hear her children but not interact with them. She finally escaped to Philadelphia in 1842, reunited later with Louisa in New York City, and published her autobiography, *Incidents in the Life of a Slave Girl*, in 1861.[14]

Jacobs's narrative is one of dozens, if not hundreds, of slave narratives that discuss in depth the suffering and brutal conditions that drove many slaves to disavow belief in God. She recalled early on, "I once saw a young slave girl dying soon after the birth of a child nearly white. In her agony she cried out, 'O Lord, come and take me!' Her mistress stood by, and mocked at her like an incarnate fiend. 'You suffer, do you?' she exclaimed. 'I am glad of it. You deserve it all, and more too.'" The girl's mother replied that she hoped at least her baby would soon be in heaven. "'Heaven!' retorted the mistress. 'There is no such place for the

like of her and her bastard.' The poor mother turned away, sobbing."
This passage expounds of the suffering and pain of slavery, but it also
references the fact that many masters and mistresses were uncomfortable with their slaves' religious beliefs and mocked them quite often,
which likely drove many to repudiate religion. Jacobs's argument here
also contributed to the growing abolitionist literature linking slavery
with religious skepticism.[15]

In addition to threats of sexual abuse and cruelty toward children
who were the products of liaisons between whites and blacks, nearly all
slaves endured humiliating and dehumanizing forms of physical chas-
tisement from their owners. Austin Steward, an enslaved man in Prince
William County, Virginia, during the early nineteenth century, reflected
in his autobiography on the suffering and evil inherent in a life of bondage. "One pleasant Sabbath morning," he recounted,

> as I was passing the house where she lived, on my way to the
> Presbyterian church, where I was sent to ring the bell as usual,
> I heard the most piteous cries and earnest pleadings issuing
> from the dwelling. To my horror and the astonishment of those
> with me, my poor sister made her appearance, weeping bitterly,
> and followed by her inhuman master, who was polluting the
> air of that clear Sabbath morning, with the most horrid impre-
> cations and threatenings, and at the same time flourishing a
> large raw-hide. Very soon his bottled wrath burst forth, and
> the blows, aimed with all his strength, descended upon the
> unprotected head, shoulders and back of the helpless woman,
> until she was literally cut to pieces. She writhed in his power-
> ful grasp, while shriek after shriek cried away in heart-rending
> moanings; and yet the inhuman demon continued to beat her,
> though her pleading cries had ceased, until obliged to desist
> from the exhaustion of his own strength.[16]

For Steward, it was particularly despicable and hypocritical that this
beating happened on a Sunday morning, when slaves should have had
a day of rest from work and punishment. Another enslaved man named
Henry Bibb wrote of his early life in bondage, "I was brought up in the
Counties of Shelby, Henry, Oldham, and Trimble. Or, more correctly
speaking, in the above counties, I may safely say, I was flogged up; for
where I should have received moral, mental, and religious instruction,
I received stripes without number, the object of which was to degrade

and keep me in subordination. . . . Reader, believe me when I say that
no tongue, nor pen ever has or can express the horrors of American
slavery. Consequently I despair in finding language to express ade-
quately the deep feeling of my soul, as I contemplate the past history
of my life."[17]

Masters also denied slaves access to education and knowledge
of themselves. Dating back to the colonial era, states such as South
Carolina forbade slaves from learning how to read and from congre-
gating in certain areas, a prohibition which often excluded slaves from
being able to attend schools and religious meetings. In the wake of
Nat Turner's 1831 revolt in Southampton County, Virginia, legislatures
passed updated literacy bans throughout the South. Daniel Payne,
future bishop of the African Methodist Episcopal (AME) Church, had
opened a school for enslaved and free black children in 1830 because
he believed God had given him a mission to educate others of his race.
While he was teaching in Charleston, the South Carolina General
Assembly passed a law stipulating that if a free black person taught a
slave to read or write, that free black could receive fifty lashes and a
fine of fifty dollars. The law further stated that free blacks could not
operate a school to educate other free blacks. Payne, one of the most
prominent black Christians of the nineteenth century, noted that after
the assembly passed this law, "I began to question the existence of
God, and to say: 'If he does exist, is he just? If so, why does he suffer
one race to oppress and enslave another, to rob them by unrighteous
enactments of rights, which they hold most dear and sacred?'" Like
Nathaniel Paul, Payne never actually discarded his belief in God, but
his musings nevertheless demonstrate how the institution of slavery
could foster nonbelief. As a free black man, he was able to leave South
Carolina and eventually find a better life for himself, but thousands of
blacks in the state could not.[18]

For Frederick Douglass, the denial of knowledge about himself and
the world was one of the worst aspects of slavery. Douglass was born
enslaved on the Eastern Shore of Maryland, probably in 1817 or 1818.
He escaped around the age of twenty-one and published his famous
Narrative of the Life of Frederick Douglass in 1845. Douglass opened
the work by noting that "I have no accurate knowledge of my age, never
having seen any authentic record containing it. By far the larger part
of the slaves know as little of their age as horses know of theirs, and it
is the wish of most masters within my knowledge to keep their slaves
thus ignorant." He makes it clear that masters keeping knowledge of

slaves' ages to themselves was one of the most dehumanizing aspects of slavery, one that made blacks akin to horses and other beasts, in the eyes of slaveholders. "A want of information concerning my own [age] was a source of unhappiness to me even during childhood," he wrote. When he got a bit older, Douglass went to live in Baltimore, where his new master's wife, Sophia Auld, began to teach him how to read. These lessons were short-lived, as master Hugh Auld caught wind of them and told Sophia that teaching Douglass how to read would spoil him and make him unfit for slavery. To keep men and women enslaved and resigned to their condition, Hugh Auld argued, masters had to keep them ignorant. If not, the slaves might imagine a better future for themselves and learn the means by which to secure that future.[19]

Like Frederick Douglass, Charles Ball was also enslaved in Maryland during the early nineteenth century, and he, too, wrote a narrative that explores in part the lack of education available to slaves. "The cotton planters have always, since I knew any thing of them, been most careful to prevent the slaves from learning to read," he recalled. In Ball's view, this situation hindered slaves' religious development, as many continued to adhere to African beliefs or Islam for want of instruction in Christianity. Harriet Jacobs agreed wholeheartedly, writing that a missionary had "no right to shut out the light of knowledge from his brother." She deplored the fact that so-called heathens were being converted in other regions of the world while slaves were left to their own devices. If America were really to be a Christian country, she implied, slaves must have access to the gospel.[20]

For countless slaves, one of the scariest and most dehumanizing aspects of the institution was the constant threat of sale and separation from their families, a situation that disrupted social life, fragmented slave communities, and caused unfathomable anguish. In regions including New England during the eighteenth century, masters in port cities sometimes had little use for the children of slaves and did not want to provide for their upbringing, leading them to give away slave children. Southern slaves during this period were likewise subject to sale or made to accompany their masters when they moved. Between 1755 and 1782, for example, roughly 20 percent of all slaves in southern Maryland departed the region. And even when slaves stayed in the same area, they might be forced to live on another of their master's plantations or be hired out. The threat of sale for Southern slaves increased markedly during the early nineteenth century, when the abolition of the Atlantic slave trade fostered the growth of an internal slave trade, whereby masters sold approximately one million slaves from the Upper South to the Lower South between 1787 and 1865. Countless slave narratives expound on this fear, including that of Henry Bibb, who lamented, "Deep has been the anguish of my soul when looking over my little family during the silent hours of the night, knowing the great danger of our being sold off at auction the next day and parted forever."[21]

The growth of the internal slave trade was one sign that slavery was not on the road to extinction in the American South as it was in northern states and key areas throughout the Western Hemisphere, including many Latin American countries. Instead, slavery was expanding rapidly in the South and becoming even more important to the economy of the region and of the entire nation. This expansion was greatly facilitated by Thomas Jefferson's Louisiana Purchase of 1803, which led to the addition of nearly one million square miles of territory to the nation, including four future slave states. Jefferson believed this territory would be an "empire of liberty" that would preserve the independence of small farmers, but instead it turned out to be an empire for slavery, spurring the emigration of slaveholders from Virginia, South Carolina, and other coastal slave regions to the new southwest. During the 1810s, the population of states such as Mississippi and Alabama more than doubled, while the number of slaves in the nation increased 30 percent, going from about 1.1 million to 1.5 million in that decade.[22]

Slave Religion

As slavery was growing in the American South, so too was the appeal of evangelical Protestantism throughout the nation. Numbering just a few thousand adherents in the years immediately following the American Revolution, the number of Methodist church members in 1820 had risen to 250,000 and had doubled by 1830. The Baptists also saw tremendous growth, increasing their membership tenfold in the thirty years after the revolution. The Second Great Awakening, as it has come to be known, began with revivals on the Kentucky frontier and soon spread east, leading to the explosion of evangelical denominations and the transformation of sects such as the Congregationalists. Revivalists preached an egalitarian message that all souls were equal before God and that human beings could influence their own spiritual state. Some even preached that human beings could perfect themselves and their society. Whereas many preachers in the eighteenth century had often focused on catechism and religious instruction, revival ministers in the nineteenth century emphasized that their message could be understood by all.[23]

The growth of slavery, the conditions slaves endured—including beatings, starvation, sexual assault, separation from family, lack of adequate medical care, and early death—and new methods and doctrines of evangelical preachers made Protestant Christianity very appealing to some slaves. Many came to believe that the God of Israel was on their side and would one day free them from slavery. Masters had been loath to convert their slaves to Christianity for much of the seventeenth and eighteenth centuries, partially because of racial animosity but also because of the lingering belief that baptism would free their slaves, statutes to the contrary notwithstanding. This situation began to change during and after the American Revolution with the spread of evangelical Protestantism to the South. Whereas the Anglican Communion and the Society for the Propagation of the Gospel had failed to convert slaves, evangelicals were much more successful.

David George formed the first separate black church sometime between 1773 and 1775 in Silver Bluff, South Carolina, an effort that blacks throughout the North and South would duplicate in the years before the Civil War. Although slaves who worshipped in white churches were generally segregated and preached sermons urging obedience, honesty, and industry in the service of their masters, those allowed to worship separately focused on other Christian messages. Chief among these was the story of Exodus, which details the way that God freed his chosen people, the Israelites, from bondage in Egypt. Collapsing sacred and secular time, slaves envisioned themselves as God's new chosen people, whom he would also deliver out of bondage. They likewise blended biblical chronology, with many slaves conflating Jesus and Moses, arguing that turning one's heart over to the former would achieve the same freedom that the latter helped bring about in the Old Testament.[24]

Along with institutional expressions of black Christianity, the religion of slaves was also informal and noninstitutional. Many masters would not allow their slaves to attend church at all, whether whites or blacks ran the service. Events such as the publication of David Walker's *Appeal to the Coloured Citizens of the World* in 1829 and Nat Turner's rebellion in 1831 convinced slaveholders of Christianity's danger to the institution. For example, less than one year after Turner's rebellion,

Virginia passed a law stipulating that "no slave, free Negro or mulatto shall preach, or hold any meeting for religious purposes either day or night." Ironically, the justice of the peace was to whip any offenders with up to thirty-nine lashes. Since slaves could not hear preaching from one of their own color in church, they came up with ways to hear them outside of church. They met in secluded spaces such as woods and ravines (hush harbors), often late at night, to hold their religious meetings out of view of their masters. Here, slaves could sing spirituals, express religious feelings through spontaneous dance and other bodily motions, and listen to sermons proclaiming that they would one day be free. Their religion was a mixture of African cultural traditions and Christianity that allowed some to assert "that their lives were special, their lives had dignity, their lives had meaning beyond the definitions set by slavery."[25]

In addition to Protestantism, slaves practiced Islam and Roman Catholicism throughout the United States. Many had come from Muslim nations in Africa and tried to maintain their faith in the New World. Charles Ball recounted that in the eighteenth and early nineteenth centuries, "I knew several who must have been, from what I have since learned, Mohamedans; though at that time, I had never heard of the religion of Mohamed. There was one man on this plantation, who prayed five times every day, always turning his face to the east, when in the performance of his devotion." Some masters accepted their slaves' practice of Islam, even if they did not respect it, by allowing them to substitute beef for pork in their weekly rations. Many more slaves were likely Roman Catholics. This was especially true of those residing in Louisiana, which the French ruled until 1803, as well as any slaves imported from Spanish or French colonies.[26]

Some historians have argued that Christianity was less prevalent in slave communities than scholars have previously asserted. John C. Willis claims that perhaps no more than 25 percent of slaves in the antebellum period were Christians. This estimate was especially true among young male slaves between the ages of eighteen and thirty. Instead of professing Christianity, they believed in a code of honor that consisted of three primary traits: "refusal to be dishonored, vengeance, and display." Daniel Fountain argues that the opposition of masters to converting their slaves and the types of sermons preached when slaves could go to church precluded most slaves from converting to Christianity. Instead, they adhered to African-derived traditions such as obeah and Santeria in the Caribbean, as well as voodoo and conjure in the United

States. Conjure is a religious system that employs the use of magic for a number of purposes, including divination, healing, self-defense, and protection. A basic assumption of its practitioners was that the world is infused with spiritual powers that could be harnessed by the right individuals. Magic was often an individualistic practice, while religions such as Christianity were usually communal. There is ample evidence for the existence of conjure among slaves, and its practice was blended with Christianity at times, demonstrating the presence of a vast range of religious options available to nineteenth-century African Americans and a fluidity in religious identity that continues to the present day.[27]

Nonbelief in Slave Communities

While many slaves found meaning in religion, whether monotheistic ones such as Christianity or African-derived traditions such as conjure, others rejected religion altogether. Albert Raboteau asserted that the meaning that many slaves found in religion "was not so much an answer to the problem of suffering as the acceptance of the sorrow and joy inherent in the human condition and an affirmation that life in itself was valuable." But others did not believe that a life under slavery was valuable under any conditions and needed an answer to the problem of suffering before they could accept the idea of a god or gods. When this answer did not come, they embraced skepticism and nonbelief as the only logical solutions to the problem of evil.[28]

For decades, historians have used slave narratives to document multiple aspects of the black religious experience, but these narratives also speak to the presence of nonbelief within nineteenth-century slave communities and the way that tying this nonbelief specifically to slavery became a central strategy of black abolitionists. For instance, immediately after describing his sister's brutal whipping on a Sabbath morning in his narrative, Austin Steward asked, "Can any one wonder that I, and other slaves, often doubted the sincerity of every white man's religion? Can it be a matter of astonishment, that slaves often feel that there is no just God for the poor African?" In his account, Steward does not articulate an opposition to slaveholding Christianity alone but rather an embrace of nonbelief among slaves, a mind-set he noted occurred "often." Exactly just how often is unclear; however, nonbelief was likely more prevalent than we have thought because the conditions that fostered it were normal occurrences among slaves.[29] Charles Ball likewise reflected on the irreligiosity present within slave communities. "There is, in general, very little sense of religious obligation, or duty, amongst the slaves on the cotton plantations," he wrote in his autobiography. "And Christianity cannot be, with propriety, called the religion of these people. . . . They have not the slightest religious regard for the Sabbath-day, and their masters make no efforts to impress them with the least respect for this sacred institution."[30]

In this passage, Ball addresses one of the key components of free-thought among slaves—namely, a disregard for the Sabbath that was fostered in part by masters' opposition to converting their slaves. According to Henry Bibb, "the Sabbath is not regarded by a large number of the slaves as a day of rest. They have no schools to go to; no moral or religious instruction at all in many localities where there are hundreds of slaves. Hence they resort to some kind of amusement. Those who make no profession of religion, resort to the woods in large numbers on that day to gamble, fight, get drunk, and break the Sabbath." Masters not only tolerated this behavior, Bibb observed, they actually encouraged it by giving slaves whiskey and urging them to fight and wrestle one another. Peter Randolph made a similar point in his 1855 autobiography *Sketches of Slave Life*. He noted that in some places masters whipped their slaves if they caught them praying and would sooner have slaves dance than practice religion. Randolph observed, "Sometimes, when a slave, on being whipped, calls upon God, he is forbidden to do so, under threat of having his throat cut, or brains blown out." As a result, many slaves rejected religion and observance of the Sabbath, he recalled, and instead spent their Sundays "in playing with marbles, and other games, for each other's food."[31]

William Wells Brown expressed a similar disregard for the sacrality of religion and the Sabbath in his 1847 slave narrative. Brown was born enslaved in Lexington, Kentucky, and then spent much of his early life near St. Louis, Missouri, before running away and becoming a prominent abolitionist, novelist, and historian. For Brown, the Sabbath held little meaning for him and other slaves—not because his master discouraged slave religion but rather because his master seemed hypocritical in his own religious professions. Before his master was converted, slaves were allowed to hunt, fish, and spend their time as they pleased on Sundays. But after his master's conversion, this leniency stopped and slaves had to attend services every Sunday and sometimes during the week. During family worship, Brown recounted, "my master and mistress were great lovers of mint julep, and every morning, a pitcher-full was made, of which they partook freely. . . . I cannot say but I loved the julep as well as any of them, and during prayer was always careful to seat myself close to the table where it stood, so as to help myself when they were all busily engaged in their devotions. By the time prayer was over, I was about as happy as any of them." Brown's honest discussion of his views toward family prayer sessions is unique in that he is one of the few slaves to remark on his own irreligiosity, rather than that of other slaves he observed. For his part, getting drunk was much more pleasurable than listening to his master pray, especially since this master would not hesitate to brutally whip slaves on the Sabbath.[32]

Proslavery religion was another key development that fostered the growth of African American freethought. Religious justifications for slavery were nothing new in the nineteenth century, nor were they unique to the South. Dating back to the early 1700s, Northern ministers such as Cotton Mather had argued that Christianity would actually make slaves more pliable and less likely to resist their bondage. In his 1706 book *The Negro Christianized*, for example, Mather assured masters that "your servants will be the Better servants, for being made Christian Servants." Proslavery religion would become more widespread during the nineteenth century. As Christine Heyrman argues, the spread of evangelical Protestantism to the South after the American Revolution depended on Methodists and Baptists' acceptance and eventual defense of slavery. The only way these sects could spread their appeal beyond women and the lower classes in the South was to stop critiquing slavery and instead accommodate their beliefs to the institution. Thus, it was not uncommon for antebellum Baptist ministers such as Rev. A. T. Holmes of Hayneville, Georgia, to justify slavery on the grounds that it brought Christianity to African Americans, urging masters to "enter the dark cabin of thy servant, and with the lamp of truth in thy hand, light up his darker soul with the knowledge of him, whom to know is life eternal." Thornton Stringfellow, a Baptist minister and planter from Fredericksburg, Virginia, likewise argued that slavery has received "the sanction of the Almighty in the Patriarchal age" and that "its legality was recognized, and its relative duties regulated, by Jesus Christ in his kingdom."[33]

Many Northern churches in the nineteenth century likewise either supported slavery or failed to denounce it. As John R. McKivigan notes, "although some northern churchmen publicly supported antislavery political positions and parties, before the Civil War no major denomination endorsed immediate emancipation." Some observers may think that Northern churches supported abolitionism because of schisms with Southern churches, with the Presbyterians splitting into Northern and Southern factions in 1837 and the Methodists and Baptists following suit in 1844. However, this notion is misleading; Northern Methodists and Baptists allowed thousands of slaveholders in the border states to remain in communion, a situation that drastically undermined their ability to condemn the practice of holding slaves. While abolitionists such as Frederick Douglass and Lydia Maria Child continually tried to enlist the support of Northern churches for the movement, urging them to denounce slavery and cast slaveholders out of communion, most denominations either remained silent or supported gradualist programs for emancipation that included colonization and free soil.[34]

The support for slavery or apathy toward its abolition among Northern and Southern churches fostered the rise of African American freethought. And pointing out the growing examples of nonbelief among slaves likewise helped strengthen American abolitionism. One reason that William Wells Brown never took his master's prayer sessions very seriously was because of slavery's "evangelical bloodhounds, and its religious slaveholders." Indeed, it was thinking about these facets of the institution that kept him going during a runaway attempt during which he and his mother got about 150 miles from St. Louis before their capture. Henry Bibb noted of white preachers that the slaves "with but few exceptions, have no confidence at all in their preaching because they preach a pro-slavery doctrine. They say, 'Servants be obedient to your masters; and he that knoweth his masters will and doeth it not, shall be beaten with many stripes.'" Most slaves believed they would be destined to die in bondage unless they were delivered by some deity, Bibb asserted, but when that does not happen, "they cannot believe or trust in such a religion, as above named." Harriet Jacobs also strongly critiqued the religion of the South in her narrative. After her master joined the Episcopal Church, she thought her life would get easier, "but the worst persecutions I endured from him were after he was a communicant." This theme appears in multiple slave narratives as a principal reason that slaves came to distrust the Christianity of their masters and Southern whites in general. For some, this distrust led to their participation in noninstitutional expressions of Christianity, but for others it caused them to repudiate the religion altogether.[35]

Harriet Jacobs's *Incidents in the Life of a Slave Girl* also speaks to the way that conditions of slavery fostered a lack of religious belief within her family. She recounted a story of going with her grandmother to see her uncle Benjamin, who was put in jail for trying to escape slavery. "We knelt down and took Benjamin's cold hands in ours," she wrote. She continued:

> We did not speak. Sobs were heard, and Benjamin's lips were unsealed; for his mother was weeping on his neck. How vividly does memory bring back that sad night! Mother and son talked together. He had asked her pardon for the suffering he had caused her. She said she had nothing to forgive; she could not blame his desire for freedom. He told her that when he was captured, he broke away, and was about casting himself into the river, when thoughts of *her* came over him, and he desisted. She asked if he did not also think of God. I fancied I saw his face grow fierce in the moonlight. He answered, "No, I did not think of him. When a man is hunted like a wild beast he forgets there is a God, a heaven. He forgets every thing in his struggle to get beyond the reach of the bloodhounds."[36]

For Jacobs's uncle, the dehumanization and commodification inherent in slavery fostered an attitude of nonbelief. While some slaves may have turned to God in prayer and supplication when they found themselves in his situation, being hunted and chased by bloodhounds, he could think only of the people in his life and the pain they would feel were he to take his own life. Solomon Northup had an experience similar to Benjamin's. Northup was born free and kidnapped in Washington, D.C., in 1841. He was quickly sold into slavery in Louisiana, where he would remain in bondage for the next twelve years. He ran away from his master after a fight, and his first response was to pray to God for help, pity, and strength. He stated, "Such supplications, silently and unuttered, ascended from my inmost heart to Heaven." Continuing in this vein, he recalled, "But there was no answering voice—no sweet low tone, coming down from on high, whispering to my soul, 'It is I, be not afraid.'" In one of the toughest challenges he had to face in his life, Northup found he could not count on assistance from the Almighty and would have to rely on himself.[37]

Along with former slaves, travelers to the South likewise noticed and commented on the opposition to Christianity and the presence of nonbelief in slave communities. As early as 1724, Rev. Francis Varnard, the minister at St. George's Parish, South Carolina, recounted hearing a slave remark on the hypocrisy of his Christian mistress cursing at him on the way to church and noted that situations such as those were common impediments to the Christianization of slaves. William Tibbs, minister to St. Paul's Parish in Baltimore County, Maryland, reported that most slaves he encountered refused baptism and religious instruction, while masters in Santee, South Carolina, reported to a missionary there that when a slave becomes a Christian, the other slaves laugh at him. Charles Colcock Jones similarly noted of slaves that "the number of professors of religion, in proportion to the whole, is not large, that can present a correct view of the plan of salvation."[38]

Around the same time that Jones published a book on efforts to convert slaves in the United States, Daniel Payne gave a speech on the occasion of his ordination that demonstrates a growing disbelief in God in slave communities. In this speech, entitled "Slavery Brutalizes Man," he reflected on his journeys throughout the slave South and the impact that the institution had on the culture of the people, including the way it fostered atheism. Many slaves "hear their masters professing Christianity," he recounted. "They see these masters preaching the gospel; they hear these masters praying in their families, and they know that oppression and slavery are inconsistent with the Christian religion; therefore they scoff at religion itself—mock their masters, and distrust both the goodness and justice of God. Yes, I have known them even to question his existence." Payne's speech references two of the main reasons that slaves came to embrace nonbelief. On the one hand, they saw the religion of their masters as hypocritical and came to believe that Christianity did not actually foster morality among its adherents. On the other hand, slaves' situations made them disbelieve the claims of the existence of a just God who cared about them and was looking out for their interests.[39]

A consideration of the audience for slave narratives and travel accounts might at first glance lend doubt to claims about nonbelief in slave communities. After all, these former slaves published their narratives with the explicit purpose of aiding the abolitionist movement and thus may have exaggerated the degree to which slavery fostered irreligiosity. However, the prevalence of the politics of respectability among Northern blacks tells us that irreligion may have been even more prominent among slaves than the autobiographies and travel accounts suggest. Discussing the lack of religion among slaves was likely to elicit support and sympathy from evangelicals and other religious abolitionists. However, being too honest about slaves' rejection of Christianity, adherence to other faiths, or acceptance of no faith at all would have hurt their cause, making whites see blacks as irredeemable heathens. Thus, it is likely that nonbelief was even more prominent in slave communities than the accounts of it by former slaves and travelers to the South suggest.

Freethought among Free Blacks

Freethought was also present among free blacks before and after the Civil War. William Wells Brown developed his distaste for Christianity while enslaved and continued to attack the faith after gaining his freedom in 1834. Brown did not write extensively about his own religious or irreligious views, although his opinions can be gleaned from both his autobiography and his fictional works. As his biographer Ezra Greenspan characterized him, "Brown was as heterodox in his religious as his literary practice. It is far easier to say what he was *not* than what he *was*." For example, Brown was not a Presbyterian because his master Dr. Young had been one. Brown was also not a member of any evangelical church because all of them supported the institution of slavery. According to Greenspan, Brown's disdain for Christianity "did not stop with formal denominations; he also despised missionary and evangelical groups, such as the American Bible Society and the American Tract Society, which refused to disperse their publications among the enslaved community." What is clear about Brown is that his skepticism about Christianity ran deeper than that of most whites and blacks in the antislavery movement.[40]

In 1853, Brown became the first African American to publish a novel, a work that includes extensive critiques of Christianity and organized religion and reinforces the tie between slavery and infidelity. *Clotel or, The President's Daughter* has the feel of an antislavery tract in the opening pages and points out the hypocrisy of Christianity very early in the work. Brown notes that the Shiloh Baptist Association and the Savannah River Association counseled masters to let their slaves remarry even if they had been married on another plantation. The influence of slavery was so strong in the nation that "the ministers of religion, even in the so-called free states, are the mere echoes, instead of the correcters, of public sentiment." The novel revolves around the story of Clotel, a quadroon and the daughter of Thomas Jefferson. It begins with her sale at auction for $1,500, during which the slave trader used her Christianity and moral virtue as selling points. For Brown, this auction spoke to the inherent hypocrisy of American Christianity, as the auction occurred "in a city thronged with churches, whose tall spires look like so many signals pointing to heaven, and whose ministers preach that slavery is a God-ordained institution." Brown's poem at the end of the first chapter argues that the ties between Christianity and American slavery are one of the key reasons that black people have come to reject the faith: "O God! my every heart-string cries, /Dost thou these scenes behold / In this our boasted Christian land, / And must the truth be told? / Blush, Christian! For e'en the dark, / Untutored heathen see /Thy inconsistency; and, lo! / They scorn thy God, and thee!"[41]

Brown's portrayal of religious figures in the book likewise constitutes an attack on Christianity. Greenspan noted that throughout his career, Brown "took special pleasure in mocking the bigoted pieties of religious groups in speech after speech, book after book . . . he typically exposed their hypocrisy to the public by letting them speak through his mediating voice, rather than by subjecting their theology to critical analysis." Such was true of his first work of fiction, where two characters in particular came to represent the problems with proslavery religion. The first of these characters was the Reverend John Peck, who purchased Clotel's mother Currer at the auction. Currer asks Peck to also purchase her daughter Althesa so as not to separate the family, but he refuses. During a conversation with his friend Carlton, Peck reveals his belief that there are no such thing as natural rights because man lost these during the Fall of Adam and Eve. He also asks Carlton "is it not better that Christian men should hold slaves than unbelievers? We know how to value the bread of life, and will not keep it from our slaves." Carlton, who is from Connecticut and who is an infidel, disagrees with Peck and argues in favor of equality between whites and blacks. For Brown, then, Christianity is intimately connected to defenses of slavery in the country, and the first figure in his book that attacks the institution is a nonbeliever.[42]

Brown also uses the character Hontz Snyder to illuminate the many inconsistencies and hypocrisies of American Christianity. Snyder gives a sermon to the slaves on Peck's Natchez plantation that encapsulates many of the reasons why most slaves rejected the Christianity of whites and why some slaves went even further, rejecting the faith altogether. He begins by telling slaves to be happy in their station in life and not to complain about being in bondage. Doing so "will greatly offend Almighty God . . . it is the will of God who hath by his providence made you servants, because, no doubt, he knew that condition would be best for you in this world, and help you better towards heaven if you would but do your duty in it." In Snyder's view, slaves actually have an easier road to heaven than white people do because they do not have the worries and stresses of the world to distract them from salvation. Many slaves might smart at unjust punishments they receive from their masters, but Snyder claims that if they receive a whipping for something they did not do, God probably is punishing them for some infraction they committed in the past. Indeed, slaves should be grateful that God is merciful enough to punish them in this world rather than subjecting them to hellfire in the next world. He concludes by positing that the slaves should serve their masters faithfully "because of their goodness to you. See to what trouble they have been on your account. Your fathers were poor, ignorant, and barbarous creatures in Africa, and the whites fitted out ships at great trouble and expense and brought you from that benighted land to Christian America, where you can sit under your own vine and fig tree and no one molest you or make you afraid." In his mocking portrayal of Christian ministers in *Clotel*, William Wells Brown initiated the vibrant tradition whereby freethinkers used their fictional works to undermine religious adherence.[43]

Frederick Douglass was easily the most well-known black freethinker of the nineteenth century. Scholars such as Scott C. Williamson argue that Douglass grew less religious from 1845 through the 1880s, when his third autobiography was published, progressing from fairly orthodox to liberal theological ideas, yet there are actually atheist themes present in his earliest work. On January 1, 1833, when Douglass was about fifteen years old, he went to live with Edward Covey, a man who had "acquired a very high reputation for breaking young slaves." In *Narrative of the Life of Frederick Douglass*, Douglass subtly compared Covey to both Satan and Jesus. He recounted that Covey "had the faculty of making us feel that he was ever present with us. This he did by surprising us. He seldom approached the spot where we were at work openly, if he could do it secretly. He always aimed at taking us by surprise. Such was his cunning, that we used to call him, among ourselves, 'the snake.'" Douglass's referencing of "the snake" was a clear comparison to Satan, but directly after, he also wrote that Covey's comings and goings "were like a thief in the night." By saying that Covey moved "like a thief in the night," Douglass also conflates him with Jesus, whose Second Coming, according to Peter and Paul, would also be like "a thief in the night," or at an unexpected hour. And this prospect did not inspire much hope in Douglass. If Covey is similar to Jesus, he suggested, then slaves cannot rely on the goodness of God to become free of bondage and instead must rely on themselves.[44]

This theme of cosmic abandonment and self-reliance also appeared in his description of a violent encounter with Covey and the means he used to prevail. After a beating that Douglass received from Covey, he resolved to go to his regular master for relief, which was on a plantation seven miles from Covey's farm. His master, Thomas Auld, sent him back to Covey, a situation that parallels that of the apostle Paul in the New Testament sending back the slave Onesimus to his master. On arriving, Douglass knew he would get another beating, so he hid from Covey and ran into his friend Sandy Jenkins, another slave who was traveling to see his wife. Douglass talked his situation over with Sandy, who said he "must go back to Covey; but that before I went, I must go with him into another part of the woods, where there was a certain *root*, which, if I would take some if it with me, carrying it *always on my right side*, would render it impossible for Mr. Covey, or any other white man, to whip me." Sandy told Douglass that he had been carrying the root for years and had never been whipped by a white man. Douglass took the "root" with him, and Covey actually did not beat him. Douglass attributed this to it being the Sabbath and noted that on Monday morning "the virtue of the *root* was fully tested." The root apparently failed the test, because Covey attacked Douglass anyway. The two fought for hours, with Douglass eventually prevailing. Covey could have had him arrested and possibly even executed, but Douglass believed Covey did not do so because it would have hurt his reputation as a slave breaker. Recalling the battle in 1845, Douglass wrote that it was one of the most significant moments in his life, as it "rekindled the few expiring embers of freedom, and revived within me a sense of my own manhood.[45]

The "root" that Douglass referenced in this situation also symbolized Jesus, and the fact that it did not work, combined with Douglass's resistance to enslavement with physical violence, constitute an early embrace of freethought on his part. Both Old and New Testament writers portray Jesus Christ as a root, and Douglass was certainly familiar with this metaphor. He paraphrases one of them in the *Narrative*, that of Isaiah 53:2, which says of the future Savior that "he grew up before him like a tender shoot, and like a root out of dry ground." When Covey attacked him, Douglass fought back, noting "from whence came the spirit I don't know." Douglass here rejects the example of Christ, and the supposed power of Christ, the root, in helping him navigate the world of slavery. As Zachary McLeod Hutchins argues, "rather than meekly submitting to the prevailing scriptural narratives of crucifixion and reenslavement . . . Douglass figuratively takes up his sword and strikes down Covey, abandoning his faith in a God who could send legions of heavenly defenders to aid weak and helpless slaves, but who chooses not to." Instead, Douglass reclaims his manhood by fighting Covey and offers African Americans "an example of salvation through their own might rather than through faith in a submissive Savior."[46]

Douglass did not gain his freedom immediately after the encounter with Covey but rather when he ran away from his master in 1838. He settled in New Bedford, Massachusetts, after getting married in New York City, and by 1839 he had become a subscriber to William Lloyd Garrison's antislavery newspaper the *Liberator*, a publication that began his long involvement in American abolitionism. As his reading of the *Liberator* suggests, Douglass began his antislavery career as a Garrisonian. William Lloyd Garrison believed deeply that moral suasion—using the power of truth to convert slaveholders and other supporters of the institution—was the best means to attack slavery. As such, he was a pacifist who believed that violence was an unacceptable means of bringing down the institution. Douglass followed Garrison in this belief early in his career, helping to defeat a resolution at an 1843 conference of black leaders, for example, that called for slaves to rebel against their masters. Garrisonians also eschewed participation in electoral politics because they believed the American political system was corrupt, and most were advocates of disunion, thinking that the North should separate completely from the slaveholding South.

In the 1850s, Douglass came to reject the pacifism and nonviolence of the Garrisonians. While he still believed deeply in moral suasion, he also thought that other means might be more effective. These shifts in thinking are not surprising given that a key moment in his own route toward freedom involved the violent encounter with Edward Covey. After the Compromise of 1850, which included a strengthened Fugitive Slave Act, Douglass began to support violent resistance to reenslavement on the part of Northern vigilance committees. And after fighting broke out in "Bleeding Kansas" in the mid-1850s, Douglass supported the efforts of individuals such as John Brown to prevent slavery from gaining a stronghold in the state. While Douglass refused Brown's attempt to enlist him in his raid on Harper's Ferry in the autumn of 1859, Douglass did support the spirit of Brown's mission and had fully come to embrace violence as a just and useful means for ending slavery.[47]

One area in which Douglass stayed true to the philosophy of the Garrisonians was his feminism, which would become a key component of black freethought during the twentieth century, even as white freethinkers often remained aloof from or hostile to the movement for women's equality. In 1840, the American Anti-Slavery Society (AASS) had split into rival factions over two key issues: the participation of abolitionists in electoral politics, and the "woman question," as it was known back then. While Garrisonians supported the participation of women such as Elizabeth Cady Stanton and Lucretia Mott in organizations such as the AASS, conservatives such as Arthur and Lewis Tappan believed that women should work primarily in their own subordinate organizations. Initially, Douglass was troubled by the fact that the "woman question" was causing a split in abolitionist ranks. However, after a discussion with Stanton in which she tried to convince him of the injustice of women's exclusion from politics, he noted that "I could not meet her arguments, except with the shallow plea of 'custom,' 'natural division of duties,' 'indelicacy of women's taking part in politics,' the common talk of 'woman's sphere.' . . . All of which that able woman, who then no less logical than now, brushed away." Stanton was a key figure in both the women's rights and freethought movements of the nineteenth century. Her work and that of Douglass illustrate the degree to which freethought has often intersected with feminism to advocate for a more democratic society.[48]

Douglass's feminism was very much rooted in the nineteenth century. Feminists in this era based their claims for women's equality on perceived biological, physiological, and temperamental distinctions between men and women. Women were portrayed as kindhearted, tender, sympathetic, and virtuous, and as such, their voices were needed in social and political causes. Nineteenth-century feminists such as Douglass went to great pains to argue that equal rights and political participation for women would not disturb or disrupt their work in the home but would in fact advance it. Unlike many feminists today, Douglass and feminist thinkers of his age believed in separate spheres ideology even though their work in the movement helped undermine it. Their feminism was politically radical but socially conservative.

Douglass thought that equal political rights for men and women would come in stages. The first stage, in his estimation, was pushing for women's right to speak in public. During the 1830s, Maria Stewart and the Grimke sisters, among others, had begun to defy social conventions in their speeches before male audiences, and Douglass consistently supported them in the columns of his newspapers and his public speeches. The second step was for women to gain access to higher education, while the third included expanded career prospects. Douglass believed these social and economic changes would lay the foundation for political changes.[49] Douglass was also a proponent of women's suffrage at a time when few male leaders of American abolitionism publicly endorsed this position. He seconded and gave a speech supporting Elizabeth Cady Stanton's resolution demanding women's suffrage at the first women's rights convention in Seneca Falls in July 1848. His support helped the resolution pass by a small margin. For Douglass, suffrage was just another part of the broader women's rights movement because he believed deeply that voting was a natural right of which women should not be deprived.[50]

In the years before the Civil War, Douglass usually put abolitionism before feminism. Even as he spoke in favor of women's suffrage, equal pay for equal work, equality in property ownership, and better education, he still bemoaned the fact that many women started putting their cause ahead of slaves. After the Civil War, the women's rights movement allowed him to redirect his reform energies, but he still argued, for instance, that black men needed the vote more than white women did. "With us, the matter is a question of life and death," he noted. "At least, in fifteen States of the Union. When women, because they are women, are hunted down through . . . New York and New Orleans; when they are dragged from their houses and hung upon lampposts; when their children are torn from their arms, and their brains dashed out upon the pavement; when they are objects of insult and outrage at every turn; when they are in danger of having their homes burnt down over their heads; when their children are not allowed to enter schools; then they will have an urgency to obtain the ballot equal to our own."[51] The issue became moot once the states ratified the Fifteenth Amendment in 1870, and Douglass's speeches and interviews then supported women's suffrage and women's rights for the next quarter century.

Douglass's work on behalf of slaves, free blacks, and women for freedom and equal rights often brought him into conflict with religion. He notes of his religious views in 1855 that they "pass[ed] over the whole scale and circle of belief and unbelief, from faith in the overruling Providence of God, to the blackest atheism." However, from his earliest writings, Douglass was one of the staunchest critics of American Christianity. The focus of his earliest critiques was the religion of the South. He noted in his *Narrative* that religious masters are usually the worst masters:

In August, 1832 my master attended a Methodist camp-meeting held in the Bay-side, Talbot county, and there experienced religion. I indulged a faint hope that his conversion would lead him to emancipate his slaves, and that, if he did not do this, it would, at any rate, make him more kind and humane. I was disappointed in both these respects. It neither made him to be humane to his slaves, nor to emancipate them. If it had any effect on his character, it made him more cruel and hateful in all his ways; for I believe him to have been a much worse man after his conversion than before. Prior to his conversion, he relied upon his own depravity to shield and sustain him in his savage barbarity; but after his conversion, he found religious sanction and support for his slaveholding cruelty.[52]

Both times that he attempted to open a Sabbath school to teach fellow slaves to read the Bible, he recalled, whites broke it up. For Douglass, Christianity in the South was nonexistent. Instead, they practiced a hypocritical religion that sanctioned cruelty and injustice. But the problem was not just Southern churches but Northern ones as well. In his famous 1852 speech "What to the Slave Is the Fourth of July?" he said that "the church of this country is not only indifferent to the wrongs of the slave, it actually takes side with the oppressors. It has made itself the bulwark of American slavery, and the shield of American slavehunters. Many of its most eloquent divines, who stand as the very lights of the church, have shamelessly given the sanction of religion and the Bible to the whole slave system." These "eloquent divines" included ministers such as the Northern Unitarians Ezra Stiles Gannett and Orville Dewey, both of whom preached, for instance, that people should obey man's law before God's and not resist statutes such as the Fugitive Slave Act. By not coming out in favor of abolitionism, ministers throughout the country committed a great sin of omission. "For my part," Douglass thundered, "I would say welcome infidelity! Welcome atheism! Welcome anything! In preference to the gospel, *as preached by those Divines!*" Many Garrisonians were so frustrated with the support organized religion gave to slavery that they advised their followers not to attend church services, but Douglass went even further in saying people should embrace atheism and religious unorthodoxy rather than support ministers who sanction slavery.[53]

Douglass's critique of American Christianity extended beyond white churches and into the post-Civil War era. Of black churches, he felt that most ministers' lack of education was troubling and that blacks would be better served in progressive white churches with a settled, educated minister. He also felt disdain for the emotionalism prevalent in black Christianity. But his biggest critique was that black churches were too otherworldly. He despised any religious creed that said blacks should look to the next life for happiness rather than trying to achieve it now. Along similar lines, Douglass ran into conflict with black ministers in 1870 when, at the final meeting of the American Anti-Slavery Society, he remarked that while many people have thanked God for freeing the slaves, "I like to thank men . . . I want to express my love to God and gratitude to God, by thanking those faithful men and women, who have devoted the great energies of their soul to the welfare of mankind. It is only through such men and such women that I can get a glimpse of God anywhere." The response by black religious leaders was to put forth a statement that "we will not acknowledge any man as a leader of our people who will not thank God for the deliverance and enfranchisement of our race, and will not vote to retain the Bible, the book of God, in our public schools." Douglass, who had also opposed efforts to send the Bible to slaves in the 1840s, replied to the statement "I bow to no priests either of faith or of unfaith. I claim as against all sorts of people, simply perfect freedom of thought."[54]

Douglass expanded on these thoughts in an article that contained at times scathing views of the black church. He ridiculed the fact that AME Bishop Campbell and others had in effect put him on trial for heresy and "dangerous sentiments." Trials for heresy use to be accompanied by torture and death but now all they could do is harm someone's reputation. Nevertheless, if the church still had the power to inflict physical punishment, Douglass had no doubt it would do so. For him, "the condemnations, maledictions, and denunciations of the Church, whether Bethel or St. Peter's, to the outside world, have no more significance than the vulgar curses of the crowd." Douglass refused to acknowledge any special claim to morality by the church, which he argued should focus more on reforming the character of people in this world than worrying about salvation in the next. He ended the piece by noting the charges of heresy by black religious leaders "have no claim to any respect or deference from me or anybody else. Besides destitution of jurisdiction, they are worthless, because *ex parte*, indefinite, illogical, and unfair."[55]

Douglass's irreligious views were shaped in part by his friendship with the feminist and abolitionist Ottilie Assing. Assing, a German reporter, read Douglass's second autobiography *My Bondage and My Freedom* shortly after its publication in 1855. She traveled to Rochester, New York, to interview him and the experience ignited a twenty-six-year-long friendship. Douglass frequently visited Assing's home in Hoboken, New Jersey, and Assing spent many summers with the Douglasses in Rochester and Washington, D.C. She eventually translated his autobiography into German and introduced German readers to the plight of American slaves. Assing had been a follower of the German philosopher Ludwig Feuerbach for years so was excited when she came across an English translation of his book *The Essence of Christianity* in the fall of 1859. In it, Feuerbach argues that God is simply a mental projection or image that human beings have created rather than an independent force outside nature. Men created God, he argues, and then humans came to believe the opposite. Assing and Douglass read Feuerbach together and discussed his ideas at length. In a letter to Feuerbach, she claimed that his book completely changed Douglass's views on religion and that he had become a devout admirer of Feuerbach's work. Assing was likely exaggerating her effect on Douglass because by 1859, he was already a religious liberal and somewhat of a skeptic. As Maria Diedrich points out, however, "Feuerbach's text did not ask Douglass to bend his knees and close his eyes in prayer; it challenged him to continue what he was already doing: stand upright, look unblinkingly at the world, and do what needed to be done. *The Essence of Christianity* was important for providing sound philosophical foundations for a free spirit."[56]

Douglass embraced the goals of the freethought movement during the late nineteenth century and participated in it to an extent. In a speech he delivered on Thanksgiving Day in 1870, Douglass claimed "that he was glad to observe that the old superstitions respecting 'chance,' 'luck,' and 'Providence' were giving way to a more rational and scientific explanation of human success and failure." Four years later, he was invited to speak at the annual convention of the Free Religious Association, an organization founded by Unitarian ministers that was open to people of all faiths or none. It attempted to promote a "religion of humanity" and fought for the separation of church and state. While Douglass was unable to attend the event, his letter declining the offer to speak indicates that he agreed with the Free Religious Association's goals. "Freedom is a word of charming sound," he posited, "not only to the tasked and tortured slaves who toil for an earthly master, but for those who would break the galling chains of darkness and superstition. Regarding the Free Religious movement as one for light, love, and liberty, limited only by reason and human welfare, and opposed to the works of those who convert life and death into enemies of human happiness who people the invisible world with ghastly taskmasters I give it hearty welcome." Douglass went on to become one of two vice presidents of the Free Religious Association in 1889. This position, along with his other writings and speeches, marked him as the preeminent black freethinker of his era.[57]

Along with his endorsement of the Free Religious Association, Frederick Douglass openly embraced the "great agnostic," Robert Ingersoll, during the 1880s. The two met when Douglass introduced him for a speech on the 1875 Civil Rights Act, and after a later encounter with Ingersoll, Douglass remarked that being an infidel was not indicative of one's moral character. Douglass's embrace of Ingersoll is not surprising, given Ingersoll's strongly voiced support of black equality and civil rights. In an 1883 speech on the Supreme Court's overturning of the 1875 Civil Rights Act, for instance, Ingersoll said that "any government that makes a distinction on account of color, is a disgrace to the age in which we live. The idea that a man like Frederick Douglass can be denied entrance to a car, that the doors of a hotel can be shut in his face; that he may be prevented from entering a theatre—the idea that there shall be some ignominious corner into which such a man can be thrown by a decision of the Supreme Court! This idea is simply absurd." Ingersoll was the most prominent white freethinker of his era, and taken together, he and Douglass represent one of the major strands of American freethought; namely, a radical humanism that posits the separation of church and state as the key element in promoting personal freedom and a more democratic society. While both had passed away by 1899, their work and ideas would provide an important foundation for black freethinkers to build on in the early twentieth century.[58]

One black freethinker in the late nineteenth century would be dubbed the "colored Bob Ingersoll" for his work on behalf of the movement. David S. Cincore was an ex-slave and ex-preacher who lived in Philadelphia in the mid-1880s. Cincore attended national freethought conventions and spoke at one of them, noting a desire to become a freethought lecturer so he could "work among my people in the South." Cincore also displayed his familiarity with Ingersoll's work, noting "one of Colonel Ingersoll's pamphlets is more to me than all the Bibles in the world." He likewise claimed that one line from Thomas Paine's *The Age of Reason* "is more than the Ten Commandments. I am an ex-slave, but I did not get my freedom from the church. The great truth that all men are by nature free was never told on Sinai's barren crags, nor by the lonely shores of Galilee." Like Douglass's remarks on God's role (or lack thereof) in the abolition of slavery, Cincore's critiques of Christianity were denounced in the AME Church's organ the *Christian Recorder*, which referred to him as "infidel slime" after a speech he gave to a literary society in Philadelphia.[59]

By 1900, Cincore had returned to the church, but other black free-thinkers arose to take his title as the black Bob Ingersoll. Lord A. Nelson from San Francisco excitedly welcomed Samuel Putnam on a trip out to California and wrote him a letter expressing his support for Putnam's new journal, *Freethought*. "I am strictly secular; an Atheist of the olden type," Nelson claimed in 1888. "'The woods is full' of us," he noted further, probably referring to the rural areas surrounding San Francisco. Another black freethinker of this era was R. S. King, who wrote pieces for the *Truth Seeker*. In one 1904 article, King posited that "there are few, if any, scoundrels in the world who do not believe in the existence of God." And speaking of God's existence, King argued that "no evidence, even to the extent of probability, supports such a conten-tion. The idea of God is born of hope and desire, but neither of these promoters of 'ignorant assurance' furnishes anything in the nature of proof." For King, it was clear that God did not exist and that immorality was often accompanied by religious belief. While King's statement that he was the "only Negro freethought author in the United States" was not exactly true, he was certainly one of the few.[60]

Along with these individuals, at least one group of black freethink-ers was active in the movement in the nation's capital. In March 1901, black freethinkers organized a memorial meeting to commemorate the life of Robert Ingersoll. The two men who took the lead in organizing the event were W. C. Martin, a successful black lawyer, and Dr. Julius Chilcoat, a prominent black physician. Martin stated that Ingersoll "was truly great, and did countless deeds of love and charity. He despised hypocrisy and falsehood. He practiced daily what he preached." One of the white speakers at the meeting, Dr. W. A. Croffut, believed that black freethought was able to flourish in Washington, D.C., because there were many blacks in the city who were independent and wealthy and thus they felt freer to express their religious skepticism. Croffut also believed that "the heartless and cruel assaults which this country has made during the last two years upon the negro populations of the planet, generally backed up in its inhumanity by the Christian church, have also set the colored population to thinking." This meeting was one of many celebrations of Ingersoll's life that freethinkers around the country organized. In tying themselves to Ingersoll, this group of black freethinkers was putting forth the message that they considered themselves equal participants in the movement and were displaying their shared values with white freethinkers.[61]

The second organizer of the memorial, Julius Chilcoat, was also active in other aspects of the freethought movement. Chilcoat, born in Huntsville, Alabama, in 1868, attended Rust University in Holly Springs, Mississippi, and then in 1896 went on to Howard University Medical College. It is unclear just when Chilcoat became a freethinker, but he was active in the movement shortly after finishing medical school at Howard. Along with his organizational work, he was a frequent reader of freethought journals and wrote letters to some of them, including the newly established *Liberal Review*. In one such letter, Chilcoat noted his pleasure that editor Pearl Geer had consolidated the *Torch* and *Freethought Magazine* into one publication, and he also stated his support for Geer's Liberal University, a college first located in Silverton, Oregon, whose education endeavored to remain entirely free of the influence of Christianity or any other religion. "The Liberals have the grandest work in all the world," Chilcoat exclaimed. "Our map is fully made out. We now know what we are driving at; the goal is before us, and it is our duty to do constructive work in the future. And that is why I have an interest in the Liberal University." Chilcoat went on to suggest that a Frederick Douglass Chair be created at the university to honor and spread the principles of the nineteenth century's most prominent black freethinker.[62]

Freethinkers and Race

Some white freethinkers welcomed the greater inclusion of blacks in the broader freethought movement. An embrace of black freethinkers provided an opportunity for some whites to display how much more advanced freethinkers were on racial questions than Christians were, while others seemed genuinely happy to welcome all new members into the freethought fold. But the reactions of white freethinkers to more blacks among their ranks, and to racial issues in general, were not always so positive. The pages of the leading freethought journals of the day demonstrate an ambivalence and even outright hostility to the presence of blacks in the freethought movement and in the country more broadly. For black onlookers to these debates, it was likely difficult to tell exactly where white freethinkers stood on the "Negro Question."

In 1903, a black lawyer named Mr. Carr delivered a speech on this very topic to one of the leading freethought organizations in the country, the Manhattan Liberal Club (MLC). Carr began his oration by giving his views on the mission of the MLC: "I take it that when the Manhattan Liberal Club employs the word 'liberal' it means by that word to indicate that those who congregate here from time to time have minds that are open to reason, and that from the discussions the element of prejudice is eliminated." For Carr, being a freethinker meant that one should judge people on their actual character rather than preconceived notions of an entire race. Carr went on to indict some of the common responses to racial prejudice, placing the onus for eliminating it entirely on the shoulders of whites. He claimed that being honest, law-abiding, hardworking, and educated had not yet helped black people achieve equality. "Is not the real problem that confronts us," he asked, "whether or not the white race of the country is willing to mete out justice to the black race?" He urged black people not to fight for a country that did not give them equal rights and made the case for universal suffrage, arguing that if ignorant white people had the right to vote, the same should be true of black people. Carr ended his speech by stating that "the colored race is beginning to feel that not only are all legal enactments and constitutions a farce and delusion, but that Christian civilization is a farce and a snare."[63]

Following Carr's speech came a discussion that reflects some of the varying perspectives on race from black and white freethinkers. One black attendee, Dr. Roberts, echoed the calls of Carr, saying that African Americans "do not ask for sympathy, but merely justice—what is right." Others dismissed the idea that there was even a race problem in the country. A white man named Mr. Perrin argued that black people in New York are equal before the law and are even employed "in our best institutions," which was likely a reference to Carr's former position as a district attorney. Another white participant named Mr. Boulanger similarly claimed "there is really no race question" and that "agitation will not help this matter. It must work itself out in its own way." Dr. Moncure Conway, one of the most prominent white freethinkers in the South, placed the blame for racism on the backs of poor whites and lamented that "I can see no solution for this negro question at all." Carr finished the discussion by calling the government and its institutions hypocritical, stating that the Supreme Court "has always shown that it has been a negro-hating court. Human rights as advocated by Voltaire, Paine, Ingersoll, and Conway are not considered in relation to the black man."[64]

One response to Carr's speech months later came with a defense of lynching, something that became more frequent among southern white freethinkers in the late nineteenth and early twentieth centuries. J. M. Benjamin took exception to Carr's portrayal of the South, arguing that thousands of schools had recently been built for black people. Benjamin was also displeased with what he believed was a spirit of hostility toward the South in the pages of the *Truth Seeker*. He claimed that he was against lynching as bad policy but immediately went on to defend it when rape was involved, stating that "until you have had the loathsome, hideous horror of such an event laid next to you by personal acquaintance . . . you will risk nothing in being very charitable in judging the Southern, or Northern lynchers." W. L. Dolphyn of Texas also believed the periodical should be more charitable toward lynchers. "Could you stand beside the bleeding form of a six-year-old girl or see the physical wreck of a tottering old lady—victims of the hellish lust of a nigger fiend—you, I think, would want to wipe him out, and do it quick, too," Dolphyn wrote. S. Rittenberg claimed that lynching could actually be an act of mercy toward black people. Because rape was a capital crime in Georgia, "when the mob executes it does no worse than the law would do when it got him, and it saves the poor victim from appearing in public and relating before a jury all the abominable details of the crime of the ravisher."[65]

Other white freethinkers rejected these defenses of lynching, noting that freethinkers should be more moral than Christians. In a response to Rittenberg's article, Charles McBride opined that "it is a mystery to me how any humanitarian can be so heartless as to advocate capital punishment, much less a Freethinker who stands up in public and admits that." According to McBride, the best way to reform black people suffering the ill effects of slavery was to follow the approach of Booker T. Washington and educate greater numbers of African Americans. H. Sandberg likewise registered his protest against lynching, noting that mobs who engaged in the practice furnish "spectacles which shock and horrify the whole civilized world." He also predicted that there could come a return to the practice of killing atheists for their lack of belief because "many Christians fanatics consider that a worse crime than either murder or rape and would punish accordingly." Sandberg, writing from California, believed lynching was wrong because it denied blacks the right to a fair trial. But his last statement shows how he used the subject to ridicule Christians and portray the superior morals of freethinkers. A similar theme appeared in an article that J. W. Mehaffey wrote in 1893. Referring to a spate of lynchings that had recently taken place in the South, Mehaffey asked, "Where was the christian's God when such acts were going on?" While he came out against lynching, it wasn't necessarily a staunch opposition to the practice itself but rather an opportunity to point out the hypocrisy and immorality of Christians.[66]

Mehaffey's opportunistic use of lynching to advance the cause of freethought was replicated in other articles supporting racial equality. That is not to say that these authors were not being genuine in voicing their support for blacks but simply that this support also served a role in freethought's battle against Christianity. Referring to President Theodore Roosevelt's appointment of black people to government offices, the white freethinker Hugh Pentecost posited, "I have not the slightest doubt in the world that President Roosevelt's position is the only decent, manly, true principle he could act on." Threatening the rights of blacks was bad for American democracy, according to Pentecost, and the example of Booker T. Washington demonstrated what black people were capable of were they given a chance to succeed in life. Another white freethinker, Will Andres, protested against the growing segregation of the country, especially in freethought organizations. The constitution of the newly established Assembly of Progress specifically excluded blacks from membership, to which Andres replied that "the black man should be given a chance. That is my doctrine. It should be the doctrine of every American citizen. . . . I like Ingersoll's position as to the negro." While the church might practice segregation, he claimed, freethought organizations had no business doing so. Others expressed excitement that blacks were excelling in new educational opportunities that were opening up in the late nineteenth century. Referring to an oration given at Harvard by black student Clement G. Morgan, an article in the *Boston Investigator* noted that "we rejoice that a colored man was chosen on account of his brains to be the orator of his class at Harvard University, and that the orator honored his class, his college and his race by his oration."[67]

Other white freethinkers were not so charitable toward black people and portrayed them as everything that was wrong with the country and with religion. When asked in 1889 whether there were many black people in the freethought movement, the editor of the *Boston Investigator* claimed he did not know many black freethinkers and that in general, African Americans "are apt to be credulous, and easily imposed upon." Both the editor Eugene Macdonald and multiple writers for the *Truth Seeker* made a similar claim and further argued that black people are naturally immoral. Speaking of black preachers, one writer from Georgia argued that "the fruitful source of so much of this immorality results from the licentious lives of so many of their ministers." Another writer from Boston claimed that "there is a moral sentiment which tolerates the vilest crimes in church members and in preachers, and which upholds the doers of evil." Macdonald agreed with these observations and used them to bolster the moral reputation of freethought. "The lesson learned from the above facts," he wrote, "is that the possession of religion is perfectly compatible with lives of the grossest immorality." Twenty years later, Macdonald's views of black people had grown even harsher, if possible. He posited that many black people were lazy, dishonest, superstitious, and immoral. Because of these factors, he argued, "the negro is unquestionably of an inferior race. . . . He is not and can never be the equal of the white race."[68]

With so many negative views of African Americans, some expressed by leading white freethinkers, it is easy to see why there was a relative scarcity of black freethinkers in the nineteenth century. This scarcity was due in part to indifference and sometimes hostility of whites toward blacks within the freethought movement. Many whites believed blacks were naturally superstitious and it would thus be useless to try to get them into the freethought fold. Also, with the end of slavery in 1865, many slaves who may have embraced nonbelief while in bondage came to believe that perhaps there was indeed a just God looking out for their interests. Independent black churches grew exponentially in the Reconstruction era, and churches continued to be the center of black communities. Those freethinkers who were vocal about their skepticism often ran afoul of religious leaders. Many more likely muted what criticisms of the church they may have had. Nevertheless, black freethinkers of the nineteenth century laid the foundation for the growth of a more organized movement during the twentieth. Harlem Renaissance writers and those involved in radical politics could look back to the examples of Frederick Douglass, David Cincore, the lawyer Carr, and others to see that freethought was a viable option for African Americans and would perhaps be better suited to improving black life than Christianity had been.

The New Negro Renaissance

In the early twentieth century, African American freethought became much more widespread, especially among the literary and artistic figures of the New Negro Renaissance. Whereas Frederick Douglass was the key black freethinker of his era, the 1920s and 1930s would see the presence of atheism, agnosticism, and secular humanism in the writings of figures such as Zora Neale Hurston, Nella Larsen, Langston Hughes, and Claude McKay, among others. Hurston and Larsen's discussion of religious doubt points to the growing importance of freethought among African American women, some of whom came to see the church as an oppressive institution that reinforced patriarchy. While black freethought would remain dominated by men, Hurston and Larsen provided important discussions of irreligion in their writings, works that helped inaugurate the connection between black freethought and black feminism.

Along with the growth of irreligion among women, black freethought evolved in the early twentieth century from the embryonic freethought that characterized the nineteenth century. In the latter era, there is plenty of evidence for the presence of freethought in slave communities and among free blacks such as Frederick Douglass and William Wells Brown. Yet there are only a handful of examples of black people who discuss their own religious skepticism and nonbelief prior to 1900. Most remark on how the conditions of slavery pushed others toward religious doubt and atheism but say little about how slavery affected their own cosmological and theological beliefs. There was also little sense of a coherent freethought movement among blacks and little participation by African Americans in secular organizations such as the National Liberal League. This situation began to change among the writers and artists of the New Negro Renaissance in the 1920s. Authors became much more open about their own lack of religiosity, as well as much more forceful in their critiques of both black and white Christianity. And some of the most prominent black freethinkers of this era also participated in the New Negro Renaissance. This participation meant that they knew one another intimately, partied together, wrote together, ate together, and dated each other. For the first time, African Americans developed a network of secularism that drew from and helped strengthen their already existing literary network. This sense of community became an important space in which black skeptics could formulate and disseminate their critiques of Christianity.

At times, these critiques of Christianity were more forceful than others, indicating the presence of complicated and sometimes inconsistent views of religion and secularism. Just as nineteenth-century freethinkers such as Frederick Douglass moved back and forth between disparate religious views, so too did individuals such as Langston Hughes and Zora Neale Hurston articulate varied positions on religion. As Wallace Best notes of Hughes, his life and artistic production "would always connote a complicated and, at times, fraught relationship with God, with the institution of the church, and with religion more broadly." Hughes may not have been a believer himself but was heavily influenced by Christianity and engaged with religious ideas throughout his career. The same is true of other Harlem Renaissance authors, as Josef Sorrett argues in his recent study of religion and racial aesthetics. While historians and literary scholars have portrayed the New Negro Renaissance as completely secular, Sorrett posits that Christianity remained "a key dimension of the New Negro movement over the long haul," even for those who were personally irreligious.[1]

Black freethinkers of the early twentieth century also helped merge the traditions of black and white freethought prevalent in the 1800s. Most black freethinkers of the nineteenth century were religious skeptics, or atheists, rather than secular humanists. This situation was primarily due to the lack of access slaves had to the ideas of humanism as well their inability to practice humanist beliefs because they were enslaved. On the other hand, white freethinkers of the nineteenth century were by and large deists and humanists, with few espousing atheism, at least not before the Civil War. Many African American freethinkers of the New Negro Renaissance would combine the religious skepticism prevalent among slaves with the humanism prevalent among white freethinkers. They rejected the idea of god or advanced deistic or agnostic positions while also committing themselves to improving the lives of blacks in particular and human beings in general. In doing so, black freethinkers of this period made significant contributions to the history of American freethought.[2]

The Great Migration and the New Negro Renaissance

The New Negro Renaissance in African American life stemmed from the Great Migration of the early twentieth century in which the outbreak of World War I played a critical part. During the war, which lasted from 1914 until 1919, European immigration to the United States declined drastically, going from 1,218,480 immigrants in 1914 to 326,700 in 1915 and dropping even further to 110,618 in 1918. At the same time, 4 million Americans were conscripted for service in the military, the overwhelming majority of whom were white, leading to massive labor shortages, especially in the North. This situation pushed northern manufacturers to look to white women and black southerners to fill their labor needs. During this period, the southern economy was also struggling, making farming difficult for many blacks throughout the region. With the prevalence of sharecropping, a system that kept African Americans in perpetual debt, and the reinvigoration of the Ku Klux Klan in the 1910s, black southerners decided to migrate en masse to northern cities such as Chicago, Cleveland, Detroit, and New York. The Great Migration represented an important shift in black southerners' worldview. Whereas they had previously sought autonomy through land ownership, now they would seek social and economic independence through urban life. From 1916 to 1919, approximately 500,000 black southerners moved to the North, while another million followed suit during the 1920s.[3]

The Great Migration fostered an extraordinary amount of diversity in northern black religious life. One of the principal driving forces of the migration was southern churches. While educators at schools such as Hampton and Tuskegee Institutes advised blacks to stay put, ministers, deacons, and other religious leaders used church buildings to form migration clubs, which provided funds, information, and support to those wanting to move. Sometimes whole congregations moved at once. The growing numbers of southern blacks in northern cities soon caused cultural conflicts, with older settlers trying to inculcate restraint and sobriety in migrants in addition to policing their religious behavior. Nevertheless, a new sacred order arose in northern cities, one that was dominated by women, who comprised more than 70 percent of members in many churches. With a lack of funds to build elaborate church structures, storefront churches became the most common ones created during the Great Migration. Many churches initiated social service programs, generally staffed by women, and cooperated in the promotion of black businesses, especially funeral homes. Worship patterns also changed significantly. Ministers tried to appeal to both the reason and the emotions of their listeners, while gospel music came to replace classical music and Negro spirituals.[4]

While the Great Migration fostered a vibrant religious life among many blacks in the North, the literary and intellectual movement that has come to be known as the Harlem Renaissance or the New Negro Renaissance also paved the way for a more widespread freethought movement. Historian David Levering Lewis notes that the Harlem Renaissance was "a cultural nationalism of the parlor, institutionally encouraged and directed by leaders of the national civil rights establishment for the paramount purpose of improving race relations in a time of extreme national backlash." The national backlash to which Lewis refers took off during the Red Summer of 1919. Black soldiers came home from World War I, where 325,000 had served, with great expectations, but found that they had to fight just as hard, if not harder, for democracy in the United States. During this summer, race riots erupted in twenty-six cities, and seventy-six blacks were lynched, including ten uniformed soldiers. Often, racist mobs would be waiting at train stations to strip the military uniforms off the bodies of African Americans. With the return to a peacetime economy, black workers throughout the country were expelled from labor unions as well. These factors dissuaded many blacks from engaging directly in political radicalism, but they also led to the rise of cultural politics that would play an important role in the black freedom struggle throughout the twentieth century. Charles Johnson, editor of the National Urban League's *Opportunity* magazine, perhaps best epitomized this new attitude, as he believed that "if the road to the ballot box and jobs was blocked . . . the door to Carnegie Hall and New York publishers was ajar. Each book, play, poem, or canvas by an Afro-American would become a weapon against the old racial stereotypes."[5]

The era of the Great Migration was a period of intense transition for the upper Manhattan region. From 1910 to 1920, the number of African Americans in New York City doubled and Harlem began its twenty-year transition into a primarily black neighborhood. In 1920, Harlem was bounded by Lexington Avenue on the east to St. Nicholas

Avenue on the west, a distance of six blocks, and stretched from 125th to 145th streets, a distance of roughly one mile. A decade later, the area had expanded fifteen blocks south and ten blocks north. In addition to its fast-paced growth, during the 1920s Harlem was home to some of the foremost intellectuals and activists in black America, including individuals such as W. E. B. Du Bois, Charles Johnson, James Weldon Johnson, and Marcus Garvey. In addition, Harlem also contained the offices of A. Phillip Randolph and Chandler Owen's *Messenger* magazine, the *Crisis*, and *Opportunity*, three periodicals that would play a vital role in fostering the New Negro Renaissance. Marcus Garvey's United Negro Improvement Association (UNIA) had just begun to take off in 1921. The organization captivated thousands with its philosophy of black economic self-determination, race pride, and anti-imperialism; however, Garvey began to encounter opposition to his plans for American blacks to return to Africa in the early 1920s, especially after he attended a Ku Klux Klan meeting in Atlanta in June 1922. As Jeffrey Ferguson points out, Garvey's demise in 1925 "corresponded with the decline of black political radicalism in the 1920s. This decline would in turn play a decisive role in the rise of the Harlem Renaissance, a cultural movement that preserved some elements of the earlier radicalism even as it made a less direct and dangerous assault on racial injustice."[6]

There were three main phases of the Harlem Renaissance. The first, spanning the period from 1917 to 1923, was dominated by white bohemian writers such as Carl Van Vechten, who also became an important patron of black writers and artists during the 1920s. The second phase spanned 1924 to mid-1926. During this period, civil rights organizations such as the National Urban League (NUL) and the National Association for the Advancement of Colored People (NAACP) became great supporters and patrons of the arts, with poems, short stories, and other works appearing in the NAACP's *Crisis* and the NUL's *Opportunity* magazines. For leaders of these organizations, including W. E. B. Du Bois, artistic and literary accomplishment went hand in hand with advancing civil rights for African Americans. The transition to the third phase of the movement began around mid-1926, when Langston Hughes published his essay "The Negro Artist and the Racial Mountain," which marked the beginning of a rebellion of sorts by artists against established leaders such as Du Bois. Works blacks published from this point until 1934 shifted the focus away from a small, educated group of black leaders and onto the mass of black people and their culture.[7]

The New Negro Renaissance provided fertile ground for the spread of black freethought. After the movement began, Harlem in particular and New York City more broadly became an attractive place for intellectuals and writers of all stripes. This situation, as well as the urbanization and industrialization prevalent throughout the United States in the nineteenth and early twentieth centuries, had significant implications for religious belief. For one, structures fashioned by human hands now towered over nature and God's creation, diminishing their importance in the eyes of many observers. Also, as James Turner points out, when the nation became more urban, "Bible stories, built from the metaphors and folkways of a pastoral and agrarian people, lost their immediate emotional resonance." This is not to say that urbanization necessarily causes secularization. While some people may come to religious skepticism as a result of living in a city, others might try to find community and kinship through participation in religious life. But for many people, including the writers and thinkers of the New Negro Renaissance, urban life helped foster religious skepticism.[8]

The technology prevalent in cities likewise cultivated an analytic-technical bent of mind that Turner argues "favored calculation in factual, impersonal, measurable terms over more amorphous or inward ways of reaching truth. It devalued convictions that eluded demonstration in human experience . . . . in favor of concrete truths explicable and controllable within the boundaries of experience." Some Harlem Renaissance thinkers began to question God and Christianity even before their arrival in New York City, but the conditions they encountered there served to strengthen their nonbelief. David Levering Lewis notes that an occasional minister might have moved in the worlds of the black church and the Harlem Renaissance, "but black evangelism and its cultist manifestations, such as Black Zionism, represented emotional and cultural retrogression in the eyes of the principal actors in the Renaissance." Religion might have had its place in the country, but for some urban dwellers, it was an unsophisticated relic of the past that they were all too happy to discard.[9]

Freethought Conversion Narratives

Narratives detailing conversion to freethought generally take two paths. The first of these notes the importance of education and exposure to atheism, agnosticism, or humanism at a young age. Such is the case with the first two individuals in this section, Alain Locke and Claude McKay. Both encountered either agnosticism or diverse religious ideas in books during their teenage years, and both came to disbelieve the tenets of Christianity and the usefulness of institutional religion as a result. The second type of conversion narrative generally articulates an intense dissatisfaction with Christianity as a result of unpleasant experiences as a youth, including forced religious participation. Michael Lackey refers to these as "Touchstone" narratives and posits four central themes in each—an inability to make the leap of faith, efforts by the congregation to convert the infidel, rejection of the idea of God, and analysis of the damaging effects of religious belief. Langston Hughes and Richard Wright fall into this category, as do later black atheists such as James Forman.[10]

Alain Locke, the man widely heralded as the "father of the Harlem Renaissance," began moving toward freethought at a young age. He attended an Episcopalian church in Philadelphia with his mother but was also introduced early on to the ideas of Felix Adler's Ethical Culture Society. Adler founded this society in 1876 largely as a tool to combat poverty in New York City. Membership was open to anybody, and morality was more important than theology for most members. The society built settlement houses and championed education for the poor. Locke embraced Adler's philosophy early on and would likewise champion education throughout his life. At the age of nineteen, Locke wrote an essay for his school's journal asking, "Is not the school the custodian of the richest and most liable inheritance of man, the combined and formulated achievements of his thought and action?" Just before he started at college, then, Locke was already a believer in two central freethought ideas—namely, that morals do not come from God and that education is more important than participation in institutional religion.[11]

Locke's acceptance of freethought accelerated during his college years. In 1904, he enrolled at Harvard University to study philosophy. That year, Locke began to develop his ideas of the true nature of churches in particular and religion more broadly. He came to believe that churches should not promote specific creeds but rather should promote world unity and the brotherhood of man. "The fallacy is not in adopting creeds, formulas and rituals," he noted of churches, "but in looking upon them as the essential elements without which true religion means nothing." By trying to inculcate strict belief in particular ideas, especially regarding salvation, churches were cutting themselves off from "a universalization of their religion and denying to themselves the right to the name of church." In college, he also joined the Ethical Society, an unaffiliated branch of Adler's Ethical Culture Society. In the fall of 1906, he told his mother that he was "quite a Unitarian by now," and when one friend asked him to become baptized, Locke quipped that "a bath is as much of a compromise with religion as I will make." At twenty-one years old, Locke saw little need for institutional religion or belief in God.[12]

One Harlem Renaissance writer who came to share many of Locke's ideas was Claude McKay. Born in Clarendon, Jamaica, in 1889, the last of eleven children, McKay grew up in a household where his father, Thomas, was a deeply religious man. Thomas served as a deacon in a Baptist church in Clarendon, a position of great respect in the community. However, Claude's brother U. Theo had the most formative intellectual influence on him. At the age of seven, Claude went to live with U. Theo in Montego Bay, and he remained with his brother for seven years. U. Theo was a freethinker and socialist with an impressive library. His freethought perspective was summed up well in a later letter he wrote to Claude: "I believe in independence, especially intellectual independence, which prevents one from accepting theories however respectable traditions may make them. I still stand a free man, where revealed religion is concerned. Try as I may I cannot but regard the teachings of priest and prophet as anything but superstition." U. Theo's agnosticism quickly began to rub off on his younger brother. Claude read Matthew Arnold's *Literature and Dogma*, John William Draper's *History of the Conflict between Religion and Science*, and the works of Herbert Spencer, Baruch Spinoza, Arthur Schopenhauer, Immanuel Kant, and George Berkeley. Claude noted that his brother was very happy when he began to show an interest in agnosticism: "He loosened up and started to tell me about the lives of the great freethinkers of the times such as Thomas Huxley. . . . Now I read the freethinking books with greater interest and thought of life solely from the free thought angle."[13]

Claude soon began to encounter social ostracism and hostility because of his agnosticism, both of which seem to have strengthened his religious skepticism. At the age of fourteen, he moved to Sunny Ville with his parents, and his brother moved there as well, becoming a teacher at a local Roman Catholic school. Claude visited his brother at times and recalled that "the Sisters were attracted to me and gave me pictures which I liked very much for their colour. They made no

religious impression upon me, for I was already a hard little agnostic."
His father, a staunch Calvinist, was angry when he saw the pictures
because he believed his son was becoming a "Romish heathen." U. Theo
assured Thomas that Claude was not becoming a Catholic or Protestant heathen but was "safely in the ranks of the agnostics." Shortly
after Claude and U. Theo came to Sunny Ville, there was a large revival
in his neighborhood and the pressure was on for both brothers to convert to Christianity. When Claude refused to do so, he recounted, "the
villagers now looked at me strangely as one who was among them but
not really of them, chiefly because I did not believe in their gods." Not
only did he not convert to Christianity, but he began to convince other
young boys to embrace agnosticism as he had. Presbyterian minister
Reverend C. A. Wilson of Jamaica argued that during this time, irreligion flourished in certain areas because of denominational rivalries
and the inefficiency of the church. Even among those who went to
church, Wilson noted, probably one-third were not actually believers.
McKay and others had some success in spreading agnosticism, as the
records of the Rationalist Press Association, one of the leading freethought organizations in the world, show an increase in membership
on the island during the early 1910s.[14]

Along with Alain Locke and Claude McKay, one of the principal
figures of the New Negro Renaissance to embrace freethought was
Langston Hughes. Hughes was born in Joplin, Missouri, in 1902 but
spent most of his childhood in Lawrence, Kansas. With his father and
mother separated and the latter traveling often to find work, Hughes
went to live with his grandmother early on, in addition to spending
stretches of time at the home of two relatives, Mary and James Reed. It
was while living with Auntie and Uncle Reed, as Hughes called them,
that he first developed not only a fascination with black religion but
also a distaste for church and an eventual rejection of belief in Jesus.
Auntie Reed ran the Sunday school at Saint Luke's Methodist Episcopal Church in Lawrence, and while Langston was living with her,
she demanded he attend the school every week. He was not a fan of
this requirement and noted that he came to loathe church after Auntie Reed made him stay inside on a beautiful spring day and memorize
Bible verses while other kids played. However, even as he grew to dis-
like aspects of church, Hughes became intensely fascinated by the
drama of black religion. Auntie Reed was a Methodist, but she still
attended services at the black Warren Street Baptist Church, where
townspeople and others would gather for singing, poetry recitations,

essay readings, and other cultural events. These activities would appeal to Hughes later in life, but as a teenager he was extremely interested in the fiery sermons, ecstatic worship style, and influence of the Holy Spirit on the congregation's members. His interest in black religion would not necessarily push him to accept the church's beliefs, but it did alert him to the power of language and artistic sensibilities residing in black culture, a realization that would have a powerful impact on his career as a poet and artist.[15]

After attending a revival service at the age of thirteen, Hughes came to disbelieve in God, although he never openly avowed this disbelief. Following an entire day in church, there was a special meeting for children in the evening, at which Hughes was placed on the mourner's bench with other kids who had not yet accepted Jesus. The mourner's, or anxious, bench, a technique Charles Grandison Finney developed in his revivals throughout the North during the 1830s, provided a place whereby attendees could pray, meditate, and explore the state of their souls under the watchful eyes of other revival participants. This was one part of Finney's "new measures" intended to bring the excitement and success of frontier camp meetings to urban America. These measures would prove wildly successful for Finney and continued to influence revivalism well into the twentieth century.[16]

Before his experience on the mourner's bench, Hughes was a Trinitarian who believed that God used the Holy Spirit and Jesus to reconcile sinners to himself. "My aunt told me that when you were saved you saw a light," he noted. "And something happened to you inside. And Jesus came into your life! And God was with you from then on! She said you could see and hear and feel Jesus in your soul. I believed her. I had heard a great many old people say the same thing and it seemed to me they ought to know. So I sat there calmly in the hot, crowded church, waiting for Jesus to come to me." The preacher called the children to come to Jesus, while the men and women of the church prayed over all of them. Some went, some just sat there on the mourner's bench. Through it all, Hughes "kept waiting to *see* Jesus." Finally, there were just two children left on the bench who had yet to be saved, Hughes and a friend named Wesley. With the temperature in the church being extremely high, Wesley could no longer take it and whispered to Hughes, "'God damn! I'm tired o' sitting here. Let's get up and be saved.'" Wesley did just that and was "saved," after which Hughes "was left all alone on the mourner's bench. My aunt came and knelt at my knees and cried, while prayers and songs swirled all around me in the little church. The whole congregation prayed for me alone, in a mighty wail of moans and voices. And I kept waiting serenely for Jesus, waiting, waiting—but he didn't come. I wanted to see him, but nothing happened to me. Nothing!"[17]

Hughes eventually started to feel bad that he was holding things up. It was getting late and the entire congregation had been there for hours praying over him and the other children. "I began to wonder what God thought about Wesley, who certainly hadn't seen Jesus either," he recalled. "God had not struck Wesley dead for taking his name in vain or for lying in the temple. So I decided that maybe to save further trouble, I'd better lie, too, and say that Jesus had come, and get up and be saved." Just as Wesley did, Hughes stood up and lied to the congregation, claiming that Jesus had come to him and he had been saved. Everyone was proud of him, especially his Auntie Reed, but he was not proud of himself, and he cried for one of the last times in his life that night. While his aunt woke up and thought he was crying out of joy at having seen the Holy Ghost and accepting Jesus into his life, Hughes noted that "I was really crying because I couldn't bear to tell her that I had lied, that I had deceived everybody in the church, that I hadn't seen Jesus, and that now I didn't believe there was a Jesus any more, since he didn't come to help me."[18]

There are a number of key ideas and moments in Hughes's recollection of how he came to disbelieve in God. First among these is the way that he describes his friend Wesley's eventual "conversion." While the congregation rejoices that Wesley finally decided to accept Jesus as his lord and savior, and Wesley likely also rejoiced that he no longer had to sit on the mourner's bench, Hughes knows the sordid truth behind this conversion; namely, that it was one of expedience and that it actually began with an expression of blasphemy. By recalling Wesley's attempt to propitiate the church members through a feigned conversion, Hughes implicitly raises the questions: How widespread is this practice? How many individuals do we believe are Christian who only converted because of community pressure? Hughes does not take a direct jab at African American religiosity. However, he does suggest that atheism, agnosticism, or other forms of freethought might be more widespread than most people have imagined.

The primary reason Hughes gave for his own inability to believe is also telling. He indicated a sincere desire to believe in Jesus, yet simply could not bring himself to take the Kierkegaardian leap of faith. By saying he could not see Jesus, and thus could not believe in him,

Hughes suggests that his idea of reality is bounded by sensory perception and the analytic-technical bent of mind that James Turner notes became increasingly common in American society during the Industrial Revolution. If the pastor and others in the church could not physically demonstrate that Jesus existed, then Hughes had no reason to believe in him, despite the fact that he wanted very much to believe in a savior. Also, Hughes's time on the mourner's bench was a period fraught with anxiety, despite its short duration. The fact that he seemingly received no assistance from Jesus in this time of trouble simply further confirmed for him the futility of religious belief.[19]

Hughes's development as a freethinker continued during his high school years. For a brief period in the late 1910s, he sold the *Appeal to Reason*, the official organ of the Socialist Party and the top-selling socialist weekly in the country, for an older gentleman in Lawrence "who said his paper was trying to make a better world." The *Appeal to Reason* was first published by Julius A. Wayland, and then later by Emanuel Haldeman-Julius, who bought the paper in 1919. Haldeman-Julius was one of the most prominent publishers in the country at the time, especially with the publication of his "Little Blue Books." These books were 3½-by-5-inch texts reprinting classical philosophical works, as well as biographies, histories, and other educational materials. Many of the works were aimed partially at undermining religious restrictions in the nation. The editor of another paper in Lawrence advised Hughes to stop selling the *Appeal to Reason* "because it was a radical sheet and would get colored folks in trouble." This editor, whom Hughes does not name, noted that Hughes had to make a choice between the two papers, so Hughes reluctantly decided to give up the socialist paper. Nevertheless, the newspaper likely had an effect on his intellectual development in a number of ways. Hughes would continue to see religion in a negative light, at least for himself personally, and he would also later become a staunch believer in socialism, an economic philosophy that attracted a number of black freethinkers in this era.[20]

At one point during his high school years, Hughes chose Auntie Reed's church as the location where he would defy his mother, who was never very present in his life as a young man. He recalled that when he was around fifteen years old, there was a children's day program at Saint Luke's Methodist Episcopal Church where he was scheduled to do a poetry reading. He recounted that he "deliberately and with malice aforethought, forgot a poem I knew very well, having been forced against my will to learn it." He climbed the stairs and got up on the platform in the church, said a few lines of the poem, "and then stood there—much to the embarrassment of my mother, who had come all the way from Kansas City to hear me recite. My aunt tried to prompt me, but I pretended I couldn't hear a word. Finally I came down to my seat in dead silence—and I never had to recite a poem in church again." The location of Hughes's defiance against his mother is symbolic of his rejection of Christianity. He is quick to point out, in multiple passages in this brief story, that all this occurred in church, and he seems to take pleasure in the fact that he never had to recite poetry in church again.[21]

A couple years later, in 1919, Hughes's father, James Hughes, came to Lawrence and took him to Mexico for the summer, an experience that is noteworthy because Hughes later provides insight into his father's lack of religious belief. When Langston arrived in Mexico, he soon met three female friends of his father who always seemed to be around. "Their only worry about my father concerned his soul," he recounted. "He was not a Catholic and never went to mass. The first thing they gave me as a present was a little amulet of the Virgin Guadalupe. But my father laughed when we got back to the hotel and said he hoped I did not believe in this foolishness. He said greasers and niggers would never get anywhere because they were too religious, always praying." James Hughes's nonchalant attitude toward Roman Catholicism and religion in general may well have strengthened Langston's already present sense of religious doubt. But James's views also provide insight into one of the key reasons for the rise of black freethought in this era—namely, a belief that the social and economic position of blacks in the United States was partly a result of African American Christianity and its perceived otherworldliness. This argument is one that black freethinkers emphasized throughout the twentieth century.[22]

One of Hughes's good friends before they had a falling out over a play was Zora Neale Hurston, who was also a freethinker. Hurston was born in 1891. After living in Notasulga, Alabama, for a couple years after her birth, Hurston's family relocated to Eatonville, Florida, a prosperous black town. Her father was a minister at the Missionary Baptist Church in Eatonville, so she had much exposure to religion and religious education during her youth. Despite this upbringing, she became skeptical of the central tenets of Christianity at a young age. Some of her questions revolved around human frailty and weaknesses as well as God's omnipotence and omniscience. "I wanted to know," she recounted in her 1942 autobiography *Dust Tracks on a Road*, "why didn't God make grown babies instead of those measly little things that messed up didies and cried all the time? What was the sense in making babies with no teeth? He knew that they had to have teeth, didn't He?" She also wondered why "if Christ, God's son, hated to die, and God hated for Him to die and have everybody grieving over it ever since, why did He have to do it? Why did people die anyway?"[23]

Hurston felt guilty about her skepticism and feared rejection by her community for doubting the tenets of Christianity. "When I was asked if I loved God," she noted, "I always said yes because I knew that was the thing I was supposed to say. It was a guilty secret with me for a long time." She wondered whether or not her friends actually meant it when they said they loved God with all their heart and soul, and she feared their reactions when they found out she hadn't figured out how to do so, thinking they might not play with her anymore. Hurston recognized the irony of a preacher's daughter questioning religion but simply could not help herself. "As early as I can remember," she recalled, "I was questing and seeking."[24]

In addition to her questions regarding God's power and omniscience, Hurston moved closer to freethought because those who claimed to be God's people seemed too similar to everybody else. She thought that attending love feasts and participating in other religious rituals should have been enough to alleviate her doubts, yet they only raised more suspicion. When people were baptized, converted, or otherwise heavily involved in the church, Hurston believed "they should have looked and acted differently from other people after experiences like that. But these people looked and acted like everybody else—or so it seemed to me." What is the use of religion, she wondered, if it does not actually make someone a better person? Implicit in this question is once again skepticism regarding God's omnipotence. If God is so powerful and conversion is supposed to make you a new person, why do converts seemingly act the same as those who had not experienced the "New Birth"? Hurston also attacks one of the chief arguments for God's existence: the moral argument. This line of reasoning states that there are common moral principles throughout the world, and given the variations in cultures and environments, this morality must come from God. Critics of this argument such as Hurston are quick to point out that while there are indeed common moral principles in the world, there are also common moral failings that produce unimaginable suffering, a situation that casts doubt on God as the author of morality. And if morality exists independent of God, then human beings do not need him in order to be good people.[25]

Hurston's path toward freethought continued in college. As a preacher's daughter, Hurston had to attend church regularly and, like Langston Hughes, she came to love the excitement of testimonials, revivals, and other facets of the conversion process. Speaking of these elements of religion, she recalled, "I know now that I liked that part because it was high drama. I liked the baptisms in the lake too, and the funerals for the same reason. But of the inner thing, I was right where I was when I first began to seek answers." Hurston was able to put her questions aside for a while, but the doubts would begin again when she began to study history and philosophy at Barnard College in New York City during the mid-1920s. When Hurston read history, she learned that Christianity was not always spread through revivals and good preaching, as it often was in Eatonville, but rather through the sword. In short order, she embraced Ludwig Feuerbach's claim in his 1841 book *The Essence of Christianity* that our ideas of God are merely reflections of our own hopes and desires. "People need religion because the great masses fear life and its consequences," she wrote. "Its responsibilities weigh heavy. Feeling a weakness in the face of great forces, men seek an alliance with an omnipotence to bolster up their feelings of weakness, even though the omnipotence they rely upon is a creature of their own minds. It gives them a feeling of security." Hurston started to see God not as an independent force outside of nature, as he is traditionally depicted, but rather a mental projection that helps human beings deals with the realities of life, an "opiate of the masses," to use Karl Marx's oft-quoted formulation.[26]

Hurston's studies in philosophy at Barnard also served to reinforce her criticisms of orthodox Christianity. It is unclear whether she read Friedrich Nietzsche while there, but she came to accept one of his key ideas regarding Christianity: that it is a religion of the weak. "Strong, self-determining men are notorious for their lack of reverence," she asserted. "Constantine, having converted millions to Christianity by the sword, himself refused the consolation of Christ until his last hour. Some say not even then." Her argument here is similar to one that Nietzsche articulated in a number of his works, including *Thus Spake Zarathustra* (1883), *The Genealogy of Morals* (1887), and *Beyond Good and Evil* (1886). In this latter work, Nietzsche argued that "from the start, the Christian faith is a sacrifice: a sacrifice of all freedom, all pride, all self-confidence of the spirit." According to historian Will Durant, Nietzsche hoped in these works "to destroy the old morality, and prepare the way for the morality of the superman," or the individual who relied on strength, pride, and the sword, rather than Christian meekness, humility, and peace. While Hurston was likely not trying to construct a new ethical system, she nevertheless accepted the idea that religion is unnecessary for those strong enough to face the challenges of life. "I do not expect God to single me out and grant me advantages over my fellow men. Prayer is for those who need it. Prayer seems to me a cry of weakness, and an attempt to avoid, by trickery, the rules of the game as laid down. I do not choose to admit weakness. I accept the challenge of responsibility."[27]

Like Hurston and Langston Hughes, Richard Wright became a religious skeptic at a young age. The former two both retained a great amount of respect for black religious traditions, even if they did not believe in them personally, but Wright often expressed horror and revulsion at orthodox Protestantism, so much so that his discussion of his path toward religious skepticism is one of the central themes of his 1945 autobiography *Black Boy*. The text would be updated in 1977 to include *American Hunger*, the unused portion of the original manuscript detailing his life after he moved to the North, but freethought nevertheless remains a key part of the book. While Wright published his most well-known works after the New Negro Renaissance had ended, he moved to Chicago during the Great Migration and began his literary career during the tail end of the movement, making his connection to freethought similar to those of other writers in this era.

In a situation repeated often in African American folklore, Wright suggests that a greedy preacher was an important early factor that turned him away from Christianity. After his father deserted the family, his mother became somewhat devout, taking him to Sunday school and church more often. One night she invited the preacher over to dinner, and young Richard immediately resented him because the preacher seemed too similar to his father. Nonetheless, Richard was excited because there was a big platter of fried chicken on the table, a rare delicacy in this time of extreme poverty for his family. But if Wright thought he was going to have his fair share of chicken that night, he was sorely mistaken. His mother told him to eat his soup first, and while he was doing so, the preacher began to pick out the choice pieces from the platter. As piece after piece was eaten, Wright was unable to finish his soup and he "grew hot with anger. The preacher was laughing and joking and the grownups were hanging on his words. My growing hate of the preacher finally became more important than God or religion and I could no longer contain myself. I leaped up from the table, knowing that I should be ashamed of what I was doing, but unable to stop, and screamed, running blindly from the room. 'That preacher's going to eat *all* the chicken!' I bawled. The preacher tossed his head back and roared with laughter." Wright specifically chose to include this event in his autobiography for a reason. The preacher's seeming greediness in this instance represents the way that religion reinforces economic hierarchies in modern America. His family was incredibly poor and really could not afford to throw a dinner party for the preacher, but they nevertheless sacrificed their own needs to gratify his desires. And to top it all off, instead of recognizing their financial situation and taking pity on children who were often deprived of decent sustenance, the preacher took advantage of the situation and even laughingly mocked Richard when he complained.[28]

Wright became further disillusioned with religion when he went to live with his grandmother at the age of seven. His grandmother had taken in a boarder named Ella, a local schoolteacher, and one day while she was reading on the porch, Richard asked what the book was about. Ella began to tell him the story of *Bluebeard and His Seven Wives*, and as she did so, "the tale made the world around me be, throb, live. As she spoke, reality changed, the look of things altered, and the world became peopled with magical presences. My sense of life deepened and the feel of things was different, somehow." This was one of the most exciting experiences of his young life, one that sparked his imagination and opened up limitless possibilities for him. However, his grandmother soon found out and said to Ella, "'You stop that, you evil gal! . . . I want none of that Devil stuff in my house!'" Richard replied that he liked the story, but his grandmother said he would burn in hell if he listened to stories, and she wanted none of that in her house. He was dejected, of course, and slowly but surely began to equate religion with anger, hostility, and unreasonableness.[29]

Richard and his brother moved back in with their mother for a short time, but after she fell ill, the two were split up and he returned to his grandmother's house in Jackson, Mississippi. While he preferred living with her to living with his uncle in nearby Greenwood, his grandmother's ardent faith, as well as that of his Aunt Addie, would become an even greater source of consternation throughout his teenage years. Wright noted that she was a Seventh-Day Adventist and that he was "compelled to make a pretense of worshipping her God, which was her exaction for my keep." It is significant that Wright specifies it was "her God" he had to worship and not just God, as this perception situates him along the same lines as Hurston, who we have seen believed God was not an independent force outside of nature but rather a mental projection that human beings create. The theology at his grandmother's church was primarily fire and brimstone, with the elders and the pastor expounding on "images of vast lakes of eternal fire" and "the moon turning to blood." In listening to these sermons, Wright "was pulled toward emotional belief, but as soon as I went out of the church and saw the bright sunshine and felt the throbbing life of the people in the streets I knew that none of it was true and that nothing would happen."[30]

Wright often clashed with both his grandmother and Aunt Addie over his lack of religiosity. As a minor and a grandchild, an "uninvited dependent," he says that his position in the house was a tenuous one. His biographer notes that while his grandmother considered Richard "a stray sheep for her to present to God, she treated him as an evil presence that might contaminate the household." Granny often told him that God's wrath might come down on the entire household because of his stubborn refusal to convert, and she even argued that his mother's long illness was a punishment from God resulting from his faithlessness. In response, Wright "became skilled in ignoring these cosmic threats and developed a callousness toward all metaphysical preachments." While he could ignore his grandmother's cosmic threats, it was a bit harder to ignore Aunt Addie's physical threats. She proposed that Richard attend the local religious school rather than the secular one, to which Granny agreed, and then Aunt Addie ended up teaching at the school. This development resulted in an intense antagonism between the two, partly because Aunt Addie was determined to assert her authority and show the class she was not playing favorites, but also because Richard was a close relative who would neither join her church nor adopt her Christian faith. Their disagreements resulted in her employing corporal punishment on him in the classroom and at home on multiple occasions.[31]

Wright's experiences with the students at school served to further convince him that religion was simply not useful and indeed could be somewhat harmful. He considered the kids at the religious school a "docile lot" and very different from the type of children who attended secular schools. "These boys and girls were will-less, their speech flat, their gestures vague, their personalities devoid of anger, hope, laughter, enthusiasm, passion, or despair," he wrote.[32] His description here contrasts sharply with traditional depictions of black folk culture, which

Hurston's anthropological writings show to be replete with joviality, laughter, anger, rivalry, sadness, and numerous other traits common to all people. Rather than an actual picture of what these students were truly like, his description likely reflects his own biases of the way that extreme religiosity affects people's character.

Along with these behavioral traits, Wright felt that the ethics of the Christian students were lacking when compared with the code of the streets. One day Aunt Addie accused him of throwing walnuts on the floor when it was actually a boy next to him who had done so. He denied doing it but was unsure whether he wanted to say who did. "My street gang code was making it hard for me," he said. "I had never informed upon a boy in the public school, and I was waiting for the boy in front of me to come to my aid, lying, making up excuses, anything. In the past I had taken punishment that was not mine to protect the solidarity of the gang, and I had seen other boys do the same. But the religious boy, God helping him, did not speak." Wright expected that in a highly religious setting, with students ostensibly committed to truth and fairness, one would have admitted the misdeed to save him from punishment, but that never happened. Along similar lines, Wright believed that Christianity should have made for a more stable home life. Instead, "there were more violent quarrels in our deeply religious home than in the home of a gangster, a burglar, or a prostitute." He would hint at this fact to his grandmother from time to time, all to no avail. Ultimately, Wright came to realize that wherever he encountered religion in his life, he "found strife, the attempt of one individual or group to rule another in the name of God. The naked will to power seemed always to walk in the wake of a hymn."[33]

It is no surprise that Wright was forced to participate in religious rituals against his will, events that served to turn him further away from Christianity rather than drawing him toward the faith. His grandmother made him pray in the morning and night, during breakfast and dinner, followed by each family member reading a Bible verse after meals. In addition to both Sunday and weekday services, Wright occasionally had to attend all-night prayer sessions because his grandmother was the oldest church member and had to show that she was in control of the spiritual fate of her household. During the passionate prayers at these sessions, Wright would sit squirming on the bench, "listening indifferently to the theme of cosmic annihilation" and glancing at his grandmother to see when it was acceptable for him to go to sleep. He recalled that a number of the religious symbols were appealing to his sensibilities but that "full emotional and intellectual belief never came." This lack of belief was largely, in his view, because he was not fully exposed to the church until his teenage years. He asserted that had he consistently attended church from a young age, things might have been different, but as it stood, he "felt that I had in me a sense of living as deep as that which the church was trying to give me, and in the end I remained basically unaffected." While many people at the time, and now, would argue that atheists and those with no faith communities have trouble finding purpose in life, Wright argued that even as a young child, he realized he did not need religion in order to enjoy a full and meaningful life.[34]

It wasn't long before the pressure on Richard to convert began to intensify. When he was thirteen, there was a revival coming up at his grandmother's church, and the family was more anxious than ever for his conversion because he was transferring to the local public school. He soon noticed that "the entire family became kind and forgiving," but he suspected the motives behind their behavioral change; these suspicions drove him even further away from religion. Even boys who had avoided him at the religious school called on him to try to soften him up for conversion. One in particular came and asked him if he believed in and loved God. Wright was not quite sure and replied that if there was a God, he likely did not care what human beings thought about him. "Embedded in me was a notion of the suffering in life," he said, "but none of it seemed like the consequences of original sin to me; I simply could not feel weak and lost in a cosmic manner. Before I had been made to go to church, I had given God's existence a sort of tacit assent, but after having seen His creatures serve Him first hand, I had had my doubts." If he did have any faith, it was one "welded to the common realities of life" and "anchored in the sensations of my body and in what my mind could grasp." Like both Hurston and Hughes, Wright simply could not believe in things that he could not see and refused to worry about an afterlife or a deity that nobody could even prove existed.[35]

A more intense pressure to convert to Christianity came when Richard's mother recovered a bit from her stroke and began to attend the local black Methodist church. He went to Sunday school with her to meet his classmates, a situation he enjoyed at times but one that also made him feel like an outsider. He recounted that he "longed to be among them, yet when with them I looked at them as if I were a million miles away. I had been kept out of their world too long ever to be able to become a real part of it." After a few months, he consented to go to a revival at the church, yielding to pressure from his classmates. His experience there would closely parallel that of Hughes and other black writers, so much so that literary scholar Qiana Whitted refers to it as the trope of the mourner's bench. The congregation sang and prayed over all the boys who were not saved, and this tactic worked for some.[36] However, when others remained, the preacher turned up the pressure, asking the mothers of the reluctant boys to come to the front of the church and implore their sons to accept Jesus. "My mother grabbed my hands and I felt hot tears scalding my fingers. I tried to stifle my disgust." His mother pleaded with him to accompany her to the altar and signal his willingness to be baptized, which in effect changed the rules of the game. Now, if he did not convert, he was not just saying that he did not believe in God or did not think he needed to be saved. He was saying that he did not love his mother, which was incredibly taboo in that small, tight-knit black community. In the end, he decided to bow to community pressure even though he "had not felt anything except sullen anger and a crushing sense of shame." He confessed this to his mother, who told him that he would grow into feeling God's love over time. On the day of his baptism, he wanted to back out but said nothing and went through with the ritual. Even after becoming a member of the church, religion continued to bore him, as it did the other boys in Sunday school. Eventually, "the boldest of us confessed that the entire thing was a fraud and we played hooky from church." Like Hughes's discussion of his friend Wesley's "conversion," Wright alluded to the fact that religious skepticism is more prevalent among blacks than most people think. Even those who seem to be good Christians may have been faking their belief at the time of their conversion and beyond. As one friend of Wright's said to him, what they believed was not very important. "The main thing is to be a member of the church," he asserted.[37]

Central Critiques of Christianity

Alain Locke's 1925 book *The New Negro*, widely hailed as a central text of the Harlem Renaissance, articulates Locke's secular vision for African American freedom. For Locke, it would be the production of black artists and writers, rather than black ministers and church folk, who could usher in a period of racial equality. Locke knew that black religion would not disappear, nor did he necessarily desire it to do so. But he ardently believed that cultural production could make a better argument against racism than religion could. By the mid-1920s, many black people still believed in religion and platitudes about freedom "but not in blind trust that they alone will solve his life-problem." For Locke, one of the major gains for African Americans during the decade was "the releasing of our talented group from the arid fields of controversy and debate to the productive fields of creative expression. The especially cultural recognition they win should in turn prove key to that revaluation of the Negro which must precede or accompany any considerable betterment of race relationships." For racism to end, whites must come to see blacks on a level of equality. Religion has not produced that, but art might be able to, according to Locke.[38]

Along with his role as an intellectual midwife to Harlem Renaissance artists, Locke was a philosopher who argued throughout his career that cultural pluralism, a secular ideology, should be the basis for democracy. After completing his undergraduate degree at Harvard, Locke studied at Oxford University on a Rhodes scholarship. He taught English and philosophy at Howard University in 1912 before returning to Harvard to complete his doctorate in philosophy in 1918. At both Harvard and Oxford, Locke became interested in pragmatism, which posits that knowledge comes from experience and that the truth of an idea is relative to its time and place. Out of pragmatism came Locke's belief in cultural pluralism, a belief that he spent the better part of three decades trying to spread. Cultural pluralism was a forerunner to multiculturalism and, according to Christopher Buck, "provides a philosophical foundation for unity in diversity by extending the idea of democracy beyond individuals and individual rights to the equal recognition of cultural, racial, and other group rights."[39]

For different cultural and racial groups to achieve equal recognition, Locke argued that religious creeds and frameworks must be deemphasized in favor of commonalities between disparate peoples. Speaking about intense nationalism in the early 1940s, Locke argued "the fundamentalist lineage of 'hundred per-centism,' for all its ancient and sacrosanct derivation, is only too obvious. It is a heritage and carryover from religious dogmatism and extends its blind sectarian loyalties to the secular order." Ostensibly secular creeds such as patriotism and nationalism often derive their practice of requiring blind loyalty from religious sects, and both are harmful to world unity, Locke contended. As he noted later in the same speech, "democratic liberalism, limited . . . by its close affiliation with doctrinal religious and philosophical traditions, modeled its rationale of democracy too closely to authoritarian patterns, and made a creed of democratic principles." Still evincing the influence of pragmatism, Locke believed that the truth of an idea was shown through its utility and that contemporary democratic theory had failed to promote world peace or unity, partially because democracy was similar in form to religious loyalty.[40]

Rather than promoting peace and harmony, Locke believed that Christianity and other institutionalized religions have caused irreparable harm throughout the world. During a television segment in 1942 on the question of whether there could be a spiritual basis for world unity, Locke developed this critique of Christianity. The president of Howard University, Mordecai Johnson, spoke just before Locke and argued that a reverence for human life was embedded in Christian and Hebrew theology. Locke disagreed, arguing that "one of the troubles of today's world tragedy is the fact that this same religion, of which Dr. Johnson has spoken with his grand idealism, has, when institutionalized, been linked with politics and the flag and empire, with the official church and sectarianism." Among the major factors Locke saw as standing in the way of world unity were selfishness, nationalism, racism, cultural allegiances, and tribalisms, all of which could be tied to religion in one way or another. World unity and peace could thus only come about by destroying the traditions and practices that have led to wars throughout human history, Locke argued: "Self-righteous creeds and religions expounding monopolies on ways of life and salvation are poor seedbeds for world unity and world order. In fact, they are its eventual doom."[41]

Locke's secular ideology of pluralism influenced his decision to join the Baha'i faith in 1918. Baha'i originated in mid-nineteenth-century Persia under the leadership of a man named Bahá'u'lláha and spread to the United States, Europe, and other parts of the world in the early twentieth century. Core principles of the faith included the following: people should investigate truth for themselves and put aside their prejudices to do so; science and reason must be compatible with religion; religion should lead to love and unity, and if it does not, it is not true religion; extreme wealth and extreme poverty must be done away with for true religion to flourish; and the human race should unite. This latter point was especially appealing to Locke, who first heard about Baha'i while attending the First Universal Races Congress, organized by Felix Adler, in 1911. Locke joined the Baha'i congregation in Washington, D.C., in 1918 and remained a member for nearly thirty years.[42]

The appeal of the Baha'i faith for Locke was that it reinforced his secular ideology of cultural pluralism and gave him an outlet to express his spirituality. While the founder and many members of the Baha'i faith were monotheists, Locke did not subscribe to this aspect of their theology. Instead, he felt that the Baha'i insistence on unity and world peace could be the foundation for a new democratic order. He knew that many people, especially African Americans, would not accept Baha'i teachings if they knew the source; thus, Locke secularized the faith's religious principles into his own philosophical outlook. "Translated into more secular terms," he argued, "a greater practical range will be opened up for the application and final vindication of the Bahá'í principles. Only the narrowly orthodox will feel any loss of spirituality in this, and the truly religious-minded person will see in it a positive multiplication of spiritual power." Just as the Baha'i taught, Locke argued that religion should promote love, so any Baha'i should be happy having him translate their ideas into secular terms that other people could accept.[43]

In contrast to Alain Locke, Langston Hughes's main critiques of Christianity show up in his poetry. In the fall of 1921 and with financial assistance from his father, Hughes enrolled in Columbia University and found himself living in Harlem during the early years of the New Negro Renaissance. Hughes had begun writing poems even before his move to the mecca of black America. In fact, Hughes wrote one of his most famous poems, "The Negro Speaks of Rivers," while on the train from Cleveland to Mexico in the summer of 1920. Some of his earliest poems, including this latter one, were published in the NAACP's *Crisis* and helped bring his work to the attention of some of the key figures of the Harlem Renaissance, including Du Bois and Locke, whose 1925 compilation *The New Negro* featured some of Hughes's writing. Indeed, Hughes "was Locke's ideal author: urbane, steeped in the tradition of black folk literature, and portraying its contours with a sense of their universal value," according to Leonard Harris. Like other black writers of the period, Hughes was deeply concerned with questions of identity, black culture, heritage, and American politics.[44]

Hughes also addressed religious themes such as the problem of evil and the nature and existence of God in a number of works published in the 1920s and 1930s. Perhaps the first such work was his poem "Song for a Dark Girl," which appeared in his 1927 book *Fine Clothes to the Jew* but was first published in *Crisis* five years earlier:

Way Down South in Dixie
(Break the heart of me)
They hung my young black lover
To a cross roads tree.

Way Down South in Dixie
(Break the heart of me)
I asked the white Lord Jesus
What was the use of prayer

The subject of this poem was racial lynching, a practice that was becoming increasingly common during the 1920s. The victims of lynching were usually men, but here Hughes highlights the plight of black women whose loved ones fall victim to racial violence. He does so by mimicking the call-and-response pattern of African American religious music with the repetition of the refrain "break the heart of me." Much of his poetry, and that of other New Negro writers, drew heavily from Negro spirituals and the blues, but here Hughes uses black musical traditions to critique belief in "the white Lord Jesus" that is seemingly incapable of preventing the wanton destruction and mutilation of black bodies in the American South. Just as he himself had futilely tried to pray to Jesus a decade earlier, he notes that millions of African Americans engaged in the same practice with the same results. His critique of African American religion in this poem also displays his political consciousness and growing belief in secular humanism. If Jesus cannot protect black people, then black people must take action to protect themselves.[45]

Hughes expounded on the theme of divine powerlessness in a number of other works, including his poems "Litany" and "Who But the Lord." In the first of these, he advises his reader to "gather up / In the arms of your pity . . . Gather up / In the arms of your love" the sick, the tired, and those who are viewed as the scum of Harlem because these are people "who expect / No love from above." Shifting the scenery away from the South and to the plight of the urban North, where hundreds of thousands of black southerners found themselves in the 1920s, Hughes draws attention to the limited economic opportunities, poor housing, inadequate healthcare, and other social problems black people faced and posits that his readers must take pity on and show love to these people because God is not going to do so.[46]

Hughes highlights another persistent problem facing African Americans throughout the country in "Who But the Lord?"—namely, the problem of police brutality.

> Now, I do not understand
> Why God don't protect a man
> From police brutality.
> Being poor and black,
> I've no weapon to strike back
> So who but the Lord
> Can protect me?

Hughes makes the connection between many blacks' class and racial identities, noting that victims of police violence often have no recourse because they are both "poor and black." With no one to stop police violence against blacks here on earth, they naturally look to heaven for divine assistance but are once again let down, either because God doesn't exist or because God is white and does not care about black people. Hughes and many other Harlem Renaissance writers are often unclear on just which claim they believe. Qiana Whitted argues that much of their literary production was concerned not so much with positing a definitive answer to the question of God's existence but rather with "illustrating an angst-ridden process that is both critical and creative." Either way, the result is often the same for black writers such as Hughes, who posit that African Americans should stop looking to the church and to God to solve their problems and instead find their own creative solutions to address the persistence of white racism.[47]

One of Hughes's most well-known and irreverent poems was his 1932 piece "Goodbye, Christ," a poem that reiterates the main themes of his earlier work but in much stronger and more forceful language. Hughes wrote the poem while he and twenty-one other blacks were on a trip to Russia working on a film exploring American race relations. Otto Huiswood, one of the foremost black communists in the United States, published the poem in the European magazine *Negro Worker*, which led to Hughes being bitterly attacked by black clergymen throughout the United States. Like some of his earlier pieces, Hughes is ambivalent about the existence of Jesus Christ but is clear that even if he does exist, human beings do not need him:

Listen, Christ,
You did alright in your day, I reckon—
But that day's gone now.
They ghosted you up a swell story, too,
Called it Bible—
But it's dead now,
The popes and the preachers've
Made too much money from it.
They've sold you to too many . . .

Goodbye,
Christ Jesus Lord God Jehova,
Beat it on away from here now.
Make way for a new guy with no religion at all—
A real guy named
Marx Communist Lenin Peasant Stalin Worker ME—

Hughes's central reason for rejecting human beings' need for a god in "Goodbye Christ" is the monetary value that people have placed on religious belief and the prosperity that it has brought to religious and political leaders throughout human history, especially at the expense of the working classes. Instead of black people benefitting from religion, Hughes argues that a secular ideology such as communism is much better suited to addressing the needs of individuals here on earth, largely because communism has been articulated and spread by "a real guy"—for example, Karl Marx, Vladimir Ilyich Lenin, Joseph Stalin, and others whose existence is not in doubt.[48]

Hughes's views in the poem are influenced in part by his association with the "big black Saint Becton / Of the Consecrated Dime." He notes that in the early 1930s, George Becton facilitated some of the most amazing revivals Harlem had ever witnessed. Becton was born in April 1890 to Matthew and Lucy Becton and grew up in Clarksville, Texas, where he came to be known as the "boy clergyman." As a teenager, he moved to Wilberforce, Ohio, to attend Payne Theological Seminary, where he earned a Bachelor of Divinity degree in 1910. He preached at the Zion Baptist Church in nearby Xenia, Ohio, for twelve years before moving in 1925 to Harlem, where he became a pastor at the Salem Methodist Episcopal Church at 129th Street and Seventh Avenue. F. A. Cullen, father of Harlem Renaissance poet Countee Cullen, headed this congregation, and it was here that Becton became one of the most popular preachers in Harlem. Becton would saunter onto the stage of the church attired in a fine pearl-gray suit, white silk gloves, and a top hat, and would be followed by "twelve disciples," all the while being welcomed by the music of a jazz band consisting of anywhere from seven to fifteen players. He referred to his show as the "World's Gospel Feast Party," with the primary component of it all being the "consecrated dime."[49]

While most Harlemites loved George Becton, shown by the fact that a small riot broke out at his funeral in 1933, Langston Hughes could not stand this early proponent of the prosperity gospel. "Dr. Becton was a charlatan if there ever was one," he claims. But Becton put on a great show and was able to fill up a large church. One of Hughes's main critiques was Becton's seeming duplicitousness in bilking money out of his congregation: "Dr. Becton had an envelope system, called 'The Consecrated Dime—A Dime a Day for God.' And every Sunday he would give out his envelopes. And every Sunday he would collect hundreds of them from the past week, each with seventy cents therein, from the poor working men and women who made up the bulk of his congregation. Every package of dimes was consecrated to God—but given to the Reverend Dr. Becton." For Hughes, this practice seemed unconscionable, especially given the fact that it took place during the height of the Great Depression, a time when poor blacks in Harlem could not, in his view, afford to give away seventy cents a week.[50]

One day the good reverend invited Hughes to his home to talk a little business, a discussion that certainly did not raise Hughes's estimation of Becton and, by extension, other ministers who employed similar methods. Becton revealed to him that he had been a student of behavioral psychology and knew how to keep his audience enthralled and giving more money. As Hughes recounted, Becton also noted that "he knew the effects of music and rhythm on the human emotions . . . and he knew how to handle them. Now, he was looking for someone who was clever with the written word to do with the people through the printed page what he could do with them in person. During his talk with me, never once did he mention God. In the quiet of his study, he talked business, God being, no doubt, for public consumption."[51]

Hughes declined Becton's job offer, despite his interest in finding out whether or not Becton actually believed his own professions of religion. This experience was yet another in a long line of events that would turn Hughes away from Christianity and toward a form of secular humanism that posited the ineffectiveness of divine assistance in forwarding racial and economic justice in the United States. This is not to say that Hughes articulated a strong atheism, nor to say that he tried to completely separate himself from African American religious traditions. He would use religious language in his work for decades and continued to attend religious services throughout his life. But his professions of Christ and God's weakness in a number of works certainly undermined one of the key attributes of God's character, according to orthodox followers, that of omnipotence. His doubts about Jesus and about Christian ministers suggest that he was an agnostic at least and certainly one of the foremost freethinkers of his era. And as literary scholar Michael Lackey argues, Hughes's political critique of religion, when taken in tandem with those of other black secular writers, would provide one of the most "compelling arguments for turning our backs on God, religion, and theological 'thinking.'"[52]

Zora Neale Hurston also never articulated an atheist position, but her ideas about God and prayer show her to be a deist. Most deists believed that while there may be a god, this deity is not a providential force in human life but rather one that created the world and let it run according to the natural laws that Enlightenment science discovered. "As for me," Hurston wrote, "I do not pretend to read God's mind. If He has a plan of the universe worked out to the smallest detail, it would be folly for me to presume to get down on my knees and attempt to revise it. . . . So I do not pray. I accept the means at my disposal for working out my destiny." The "if" is important in that last sentence because Hurston strongly questions whether or not there could be some type of benevolent and loving plan for the world, given the extent of human suffering. At the same time, we can see a bit of ambivalence regarding the omnipotence of God in her thinking. Whereas earlier she had questioned God's ability to prevent moral and natural evil, here she speculates that if God does exist, he is so powerful and all-knowing that human prayer is not likely to have any effect on his plans for the world. This ambivalence should not cast doubt on her overall cosmology, however, as either line of thinking effectively places the fate of humankind upon the shoulders of humankind, showing her to be a secular humanist.[53]

Hurston also reveals herself to be a materialist, another reason why she cannot accept orthodox ideas about God. "The stuff of my being is matter," she contended. "Ever changing, ever moving, but never lost; so what need of denominations and creeds to deny myself the comfort of all my fellow men?" She did not think there is an afterlife in the Christian sense of the soul departing to another realm, but she did still feel that the matter of which she was composed had been present before her birth and will "still exist in substance when the sun has lost its fire, and disintegrated into infinity." As a materialist, however, Hurston clearly still had feelings of transcendence akin to spirituality. She may not have believed in a spiritual realm, but she did believe there was a deeper meaning and interconnectedness to all life on earth that human beings could perceive and appreciate through their physical bodies. "Somebody else may have my rapturous glance at the archangels," she stated. "The springing of the yellow line of morning out of the misty deep dawn, is glory enough for me." In this sense, nature itself represents the sacred for Hurston, just as it has for freethinkers dating back to eighteenth-century deists and many nineteenth-century transcendentalists. As Ralph Waldo Emerson stated in his 1836 work *Nature*, "the noblest ministry of nature is to stand as the apparition of God. It is the great organ through which the universal spirit speaks to the individual, and strives to lead the individual back to it." This reverence for and appreciation of nature present in the writings of Emerson and Hurston would be and remains a central characteristic of humanism in the United States.[54]

Hurston believed in a rudimentary form of materialism from a young age, although her ideas about this philosophical approach undoubtedly became more refined as she read the works of philosophers and scientists in college. As a child, Hurston could not "understand the passionate declarations of love for a being that nobody could see. Your family, your puppy and the new bull-calf, yes. But a spirit away off who found fault with everybody all the time, that was more than I could fathom." Her declaration here is similar to Hughes's experience as a teenager waiting to see a physical manifestation of Jesus but being disappointed. It may be the case that when writing her autobiography in 1942, she was reading her present materialism back into the past, but she nevertheless articulates an important stream of black freethought—that is, a championing of the superiority of sensory perception over spiritual faith. If nobody can prove that God exists in the physical realm, then people have no responsibility to organize their lives around religious creeds.[55]

Hurston retained great respect for religious traditions and religious people even though she personally did not share many of their beliefs. While she believed that organized creeds "are collections of words around a wish," she also said that she "would not, by word or deed attempt to deprive another of the consolation it affords. It is simply not for me." Her deeds, in fact, likely served to make certain religious beliefs more popular among African Americans and better known to the broader American public. In 1932, she produced a show replete with black spirituals, *The Great Day*, at the John Golden Theatre on Broadway. Her first novel, *Jonah's Gourd Vine*, published in 1934, featured a black preacher modeled after her father as the central character. And part 1 of her anthropological work *Mules and Men*, published in 1935, included an extensive discussion of African American folklore, prayers, and sermons, while part 2 explored the practices of hoodoo in New Orleans in great depth. Indeed, as Cheryl Wall notes, Hurston believed that hoodoo, "metaphysically decentered and clerically nonhierarchical . . . offered some women a more expansive vision of themselves than did Christianity. Within hoodoo, women were the spiritual equals of men. They had like authority to speak and act." Hoodoo became a means by which African Americans could exert themselves and control their interior lives, according to Hurston.[56]

Feminism and Freethought

Nella Larsen, another well-known Harlem Renaissance writer, included secular themes in her writing, although her explorations of freethought appeared in her fictional work. While Larsen published just two books in her career (plus a number of shorter pieces), her literary acclaim nevertheless "helped establish the novel as a creative form for New Negro writers, and her success . . . focused attention on women as literary artists in a cultural movement of highly visible men, most of whom initially wrote poetry or short fiction," according to her biographer. Larsen was born in 1891 and spent most of her youth in Chicago before leaving in 1907 to attend Fisk University in Nashville, Tennessee. After graduating, she moved to New York City to train as a nurse, went to Alabama to work at Tuskegee Institute for a year, and then in 1916 returned to New York City, where she married a physicist named Elmer Samuel Imes. She soon began writing and published her first essay in the *Brownies' Book* in 1920. After quitting her job as a nurse and taking a position as a library assistant at the 135th Street branch of the New York Public Library, now the Schomburg Center for Research in Black Culture, her career as a writer gathered momentum. In March 1928, she published her first book, *Quicksand*, a novel that was unique in a number of ways, not the least of which is its treatment of religion and sexuality.[57]

The central character in the novel is a twenty-two-year-old woman named Helga Crane, and the story begins with her articulating her dissatisfaction with Naxos, a fictional school that was a composite of Fisk and Tuskegee universities. From the novel's onset, Helga Crane feels out of place, primarily because of religion. While in her room and hoping to get a few minutes to rest and change clothes, instead "hundreds of students and teachers had been herded into the sun-baked chapel to listen to the banal, patronizing, and even the insulting remarks of one of the renowned white preachers of the state." The preacher discussed at length how Naxos Negroes were better than other blacks because they knew to stay in their place. He also said that he greatly admired blacks for their progress but urged them to know when and where to stop pushing for more. "And then he had spoken of contentment, embellishing his words with scriptural quotations and pointing out to them that it was their duty to be satisfied in the estate to which they had been called, hewers of wood and drawers of water. And then he had prayed." From the first three pages of the work, Larsen portrays Christianity as a stifling religion, one that whites skillfully employ to retard racial progress and African Americans use to inhibit the expression of black culture. A little while later, she talks to the school's dean of women, a character likely representative of Margaret Murray Washington, wife of Booker T. Washington, who tells Helga that black women should never wear bright colors such as green, red, or yellow, but instead should wear brown, navy blue, and black. Helga could not understand this, thinking that bright colors were exactly what darker women should be wearing. "These people yapped loudly of race, race consciousness, of race pride," she pronounced. "And yet suppressed its delightful manifestations, love of color, joy of rhythmic motion, naïve, spontaneous laughter." Again, for Helga, the respectability that went hand in hand with black Christianity was not helping African Americans but rather stifling their individuality and repressing their beautiful culture. Because of this situation, Helga felt that Naxos was no longer a school or even a community. Instead, "it had grown into a machine. It was now a show place in the black belt, exemplification of the white man's magnanimity. . . . Life had died out of it."[58]

Helga soon leaves to return to her hometown of Chicago, where she grows to distrust black Christianity even more. She spends weeks in Chicago looking for work, all to no avail. Her education seemingly hurts her prospects, as most jobs available for black women are for domestics, and employers do not want to hire a former teacher. So, Helga turns to the church, as many southern migrants did during the Great Migration, to help her find employment. As Larsen describes this turn of events, "Helga Crane was not religious. She took nothing on trust. Nevertheless, on Sundays she attended the very fashionable, very high services in the Negro Episcopal church on Michigan Avenue. She hoped that some good Christian would speak to her, invite her to return, or inquire kindly if she was a stranger in the city. None did, and she became bitter, distrusting religion more than ever." Once again, Helga feels betrayed by black Christians. It is not just her inability to find a job that vexes her, but rather the lack of acceptance she felt within the community.[59]

Helga soon travels to Harlem, where she stays for a few months. She is unhappy there, especially with what she sees to be the pretentious black middle class copying the mannerisms of middle-class whites, and she travels to Denmark to stay with family. She lives there for two years before coming back to Harlem, where she is spurned by the former principal of Naxos, after which she accidentally stumbles into a storefront church, an experience that would profoundly shape the course of her life. The church group begins to pray for her, both members and the minister, calling her a Jezebel and hoping for her salvation. Larsen captures Helga's reaction thus: "Helga Crane was amused, angry, disdainful, as she sat there, listening to the preacher praying for her soul. But though she was contemptuous, she was being too well entertained to leave. And it was, at least, warm and dry." So, Helga stays and listens to the passionate prayers to God for her salvation, accompanied by intense shouting and groaning of the church members. "Particularly she was interested in the writhings and weepings of the feminine portion which seemed to predominate," Larsen relates. "Little by little the performance took on an almost Bacchic vehemence. Behind her, before her, beside her, frenzied women gesticulated, screamed, wept, and tottered to the praying of the preacher." Larsen's portrayal of the church service contains a not-so-subtle critique of African American religious practices. Black churchwomen are portrayed as "frenzied" and out of control. Elsewhere, she refers to the service as a "weird orgy" and notes that the congregation seems possessed by madness. Helga is enthralled, however, "possessed by the same madness" and eventually accepts Jesus and becomes saved.[60]

The next day, Helga makes a rash decision to marry the revival preacher from the night before, a man from Alabama named the Rev. Mr. Pleasant Green. She does so partially because the conversion experience was the only nonmaterial thing she felt she had ever had in her life, even though she was already starting to feel the ecstasy and spiritual release from the previous day slipping away. The two move to Alabama, where Helga quickly adapts to life as a preacher's wife, starting a sewing circle, attempting to help other women, and having children in quick succession. In one twenty-month period she has three children, a set of twin boys and a girl, and after having a fourth child she becomes incredibly sick and is confined to bed for weeks. Larsen writes that during Helga's sickness she "had learned what passion and credulity could do to one. In her was born angry bitterness and enormous disgust. The cruel, unrelieved suffering had beaten down her protective wall of artificial faith in the infinite wisdom, in the mercy, of God. For had she not called in her agony on Him? And He had not heard. Why? Because, she knew, He wasn't there. Didn't exist." Here we see a similar theme that Hughes mentions in his autobiography: the inability or unwillingness of God to respond to the problems of human beings. Larsen likewise picks up on another theme Hughes would mention: the idea that perhaps if there was a God, this deity only cared about white people. "With the obscuring curtain of religion rent," Larsen writes of Helga, "she was able to look about her and see with shocked eyes this thing she had done to herself. She couldn't, she thought ironically, even blame God for it, now that she knew he didn't exist. No. No more than she could pray to him for the death of her husband, the Reverend Mr. Pleasant Green. The white man's God. And his great love for all people regardless of race! What idiotic nonsense she had allowed herself to believe. How could she, how could anyone, have been so deluded. How could ten million black folk credit it when daily before their eyes was enacted its contradiction?" Like Hughes's father, Larsen equates religion with backwardness and argues that blacks would be better off without the church.[61]

Helga soon comes to realize that in marrying Green, a choice that symbolized her conversion to Christianity, she had ruined her life. This decision "made it impossible ever again to do the things she wanted, have the things that she loved, mingle with the people she liked. She had, to put it as brutally as anyone could, been a fool. The damnedest kind of fool." However, even after this realization, she almost wishes that religion had not failed her. Even though she now realizes it was an illusion, it is "better, far better, than this terrible reality. Religion had, after all, its uses. It blunted the perceptions. Robbed life of its crudest truths. Especially it had its uses for the poor—and the blacks." Larsen's

critique of religion here is a common one among black freethinkers—
namely, that faith in God is useful for the weak and downtrodden but
unnecessary for those with the strength to navigate life's challenges.
She further reinforces her earlier argument that Christianity is an
appropriation of white culture and something meant to keep blacks in
a subordinate place in America's racial hierarchy.[62]

Larsen's *Quicksand* contained probably the most extensive exploration of religious skepticism in African American literature before 1930.
This fact alone does not mark Larsen as a freethinker in her own right,
but contemporary evidence points to her lack of religious belief. A
short biography of Larsen published in the New York *Amsterdam News*
said that she was "a modern woman, for she smokes, does not believe
in religion, churches and the like." Further, in a letter to her literary
patron Carl Van Vechten, she noted that she was no fan of the black
church and that the Imes family she married into was "tiresome" and
"ultra religious." Like her character Helga Crane, Larsen's experiences
at both Fisk and Tuskegee universities turned her away from religion,
as the various missionary endeavors she was forced to participate in
seemed to exaggerate "the negative stereotypes of the needy, backward,
and downtrodden race," according to her biographer Thadious Davis.[63]

Contemporary reviewers quickly recognized the affinities between
Helga Crane and Nella Larsen. For some, these similarities were positive. E. Merril Root wrote that "the book, in so far as it is Miss Larsen
herself, is excellent. She has, in so far as she has simply bared a modern
soul, race-divided and disillusioned by our current misophosy, done us
a service." For others, the affinities between fiction and real life were
nothing to be praised. Davis notes that many blacks were offended
by "the portrait of the unwashed minister and his primitive Alabama
congregation. Religious African Americans saw it as an affront to the
church." And the Imes family, which had been prominent in the black
church and Alabama missionary work for decades, took the work as a
personal insult. For them, the fact that she could write such negative
portrayals of their family heritage was a shameful betrayal.[64]

Larsen's *Quicksand* is a key text in the history of black freethought
because it intimately ties gender inequality and sexual oppression to
religion. In the text, heterosexual marriage is not celebrated but rather
decried as a symbol of oppression and serves "as the focal point of at
times biting critiques of bourgeois black society and so-called middle-
class black values," argues Ann duCille. Cheryl Wall supports this
point, noting that the novel "exposes the sham that is middle-class

security, especially for women whose dependence is morally debilitat-
ing." Furthermore, Larsen shows that patriarchy is not the preserve
of white men alone but rather something that black men employ to
oppress black women. Lastly, Larsen recasts the bedrock of the black
community, the black family, as something that serves to constrain
black women and keep them from achieving their dreams. While African American literature to that point had celebrated child-rearing and
the creation of a stable family life, Larsen challenges this depiction and
forces us to consider the ways in which traditional family values serve
to disrupt rather than strengthen community. This work is thus one of
the first black feminist novels and helped inaugurate the intimate ties
between feminism and African American freethought.[65]

Zora Neale Hurston would continue the work that Larsen began in
tying together religion, sexuality, and gender in powerful critiques of
American patriarchy. In her literary explorations of female empowerment, Hurston demonstrates a close tie between black freethought and
black feminism. In *Mules and Men*, for example, Hurston recounts that
while sitting on a porch in Eatonville within hearing distance of a Baptist church service, she and a number of people engaged in a theological
debate about the power and strength of the black church. At one point
during the debate, a woman named Mathilda argued that women have
the power to take advantage of men and went on to explain the origins
of this power. At the beginning of time, Mathilda noted, man went to
God and asked for more strength to control women, which God gave to
him. The woman then went to God and asked for an equal amount of
strength and God refused, saying that he could not take back what he
already gave and that giving her more strength would be equivalent to
taking it away from man. "De woman was so mad she wheeled around
and went on off. She went straight to de devil and told him what had
happened. He said, 'Don't be discouraged, woman, You listen to me and
you'll come out mo' than conqueror.'" Hurston's purposeful selection
and inclusion of this story in her book is significant because it argues
that under Christianity, women will never be equal to men, and that if
they want equality, they must reject God and turn to his ultimate rival,
the devil. Hurston notes later in the book that for rural blacks, "the
devil is not the terror that he is in European folk-lore. He is a powerful
trickster who often competes successfully with God. There is a strong
suspicion that the devil is an extension of the story-makers." In turning
to the devil for strength, then, women are actually relying on human
cunning and ingenuity rather than that of a Supreme Being.[66]

In a later discussion of the jook, Hurston further posits the connection between female empowerment and a rejection of traditional religious mores. The jook served as a dance hall, a place to shoot craps and engage in other games of chance, and an all-around pleasure house. While in the jook, one of the central characters of *Mules and Men*, a woman named Big Sweet, turns and asks a man named Texas who is singing too loudly, "Did somebody hit yuh tuh start yuh? 'Cause if dey did Ah'm goin' ter hit yuh to stop yuh." As Hurston continues her description of the encounter, "Texas and Big Sweet did what is locally known as 'eye-balling' each other. His eyes fell lower. Her knife was already open, so he strolled off." The fact that Big Sweet was carrying a knife, gambling with the men, and unafraid of engaging them in physical combat displays the transformative potential of the jook. As Cheryl Wall points out, for Hurston, "the ethics of the jook . . . give women far more personal freedom and power than the women on the store front porch enjoy. Free of the constraints of ladyhood, the bonds of traditional marriage, and the authority of the church, women improvise new identities for themselves." Historian Tera Hunter supports this viewpoint, noting of jook joints and dance halls that they served "as a respite from the deadening sensation of long hours of poorly compensated labor—critical to the task of claiming one's life as one's own." While the respectable black elite spurned such places, they were important spaces for working-class men and women to blow off some steam, assert their individuality, and even engage in some irreverence. Such pursuits, Hurston argues, were even more important in helping women assert their equality and challenge the patriarchal culture in which they resided.[67]

Hurston would continue her challenge to traditional gender roles in her most well-known work, the 1937 novel *Their Eyes Were Watching God*, a text that further demonstrates the connection between freethought and feminism. The central character in this story, Janie Crawford, marries two men in quick succession and at a young age. Logan Killicks is a prosperous farmer whom Janie's grandmother insists she marry after Janie was caught kissing a boy over the fence. This marriage is a loveless one, and after meeting Jody (Joe) Starks, Janie runs off with him to Eatonville, Florida, where he becomes the new town's first mayor. There is a lot of promise in the relationship at first, but Joe suppresses Janie's individuality, mocks her physical appearance, and never provides the true love Janie had anticipated. When Jody is on his deathbed more than twenty years later, Janie finally has a serious talk with him about her feelings, telling him "you ain't de Jody ah run off down de road wid. You'se whut's left after he died. Ah run off tuh keep house wid you in a wonderful way. But you wasn't satisfied wid me de way Ah was. Naw! Mah own mind had tuh be squeezed and crowded out tuh make room for yours in me." Here Hurston offers a powerful indictment of traditional marriage. Even though Jody cared for her material and physical needs, something her grandmother intensely desired, he did not help her cultivate her mind or her individuality. It is not until she meets a much younger man, Tea Cake, at age forty, that Janie is able to find real love and happiness.[68]

Their Eyes Were Watching God is one of the most important feminist novels in the African American literary canon. The work strongly critiques institutional marriage and, by extension, the religion which supports that institution. Not only does Janie become happier after the death of her second husband, she also gains her financial and physical independence. The work is not necessarily critical of marital relationships in and of themselves but rather "of the power imbalances—the relations of dominance and submission—such interactions inspire in a patriarchal society," according to duCille. While the novel and the entire corpus of her works would be virtually forgotten for thirty years after publishing her autobiography in 1943, Hurston's rediscovery in the 1970s would have profound significance on writers such as Alice Walker, who would become a prominent black freethinker in her own right.[69]

Among the reasons Hurston fell into obscurity during the late 1930s and early 1940s were negative reviews of her work by fellow black freethinkers, reviews that reflected a changing literary culture and the end of the New Negro Renaissance. Yoshinobu Hakutani notes that after 1940, "quaintness and idealized folksiness disappeared from African American literature," two traits which reviewers decried in Hurston's work. Among these reviewers were Alain Locke, who wrote of Hurston's work in *Opportunity* in 1938 that "progressive southern fiction has already banished the legend of these entertaining pseudo-primitives whom the reading public still loves to laugh with, weep over and envy. Having gotten rid of condescension, let us now get over oversimplification!" Richard Wright critiqued *Their Eyes Were Watching God* along similar lines, arguing that Hurston had no desire to write serious fiction and that the novel "is not addressed to the Negro, but to a white audience whose chauvinistic tastes she knows how to satisfy. She exploits the phase of Negro life which is 'quaint.'"[70]

In addition to his lengthy exposition of his path toward religious skepticism in his autobiography, Richard Wright also explored the foundations and significance of black atheism in his novels. Wright moved north in 1927, living first in Memphis before heading to Chicago, where he would reside for about a decade. He then moved to Harlem, where he published his best-known novel, *Native Son*, in 1940. *Native Son* revolves around a young black Chicagoan named Bigger Thomas who murders two women, one the white daughter of his employer and the other his girlfriend with whom he was going to flee town. Bigger had felt that dealing with whites would be problematic, and much of the story is his attempt to rebel at the seemingly deterministic social and economic structures of 1930s America. Wright posits that Bigger was a composite of many rebellious black people he had met in his life. In answer to those who asked why Bigger revolted against American society the way he did, Wright responded that there were two psychological factors behind his attitude: "First, through some quirk of circumstance, he had become estranged from the religion and folk culture of his race. Second, he was trying to react to and answer the call of the dominant civilization whose glitter came to him through the newspapers, magazines, radios, movies." For Wright, then, rejecting Christianity went hand in hand with rejecting African American culture more broadly, and this process occurred almost by accident. Here he could have been describing himself, as his own experiences with religion were likely not out of the ordinary, but because of the way he was brought up and the fact that he did not go to church early in his life, he ended up rejecting the traditions to which most blacks adhered.[71]

Richard Wright and other black writers' nonbelief represents a key development in the history of black freethought. Whereas earlier black freethinkers might arguably have been opposed primarily to white Christianity, freethinkers of the period between the two world wars made it clear that they did not believe in the white or black man's God. The same social, political, and economic conditions that undergirded African American religious belief also propelled others into religious skepticism and nonbelief. For some, the reasons were largely personal, as family strife and negative experiences with religion at a young age pushed thinkers such as Wright and Langston Hughes into rejecting religion. For others, such as Nella Larsen, religion was equated with the bourgeois respectability of the black middle class, a respectability that seemed to take its cues from white Americans. For blacks to truly be free, including men and women, religion and its support for the patriarchal traditions of American culture needed to be overwhelmingly reformed or done away with altogether.

The political function that the concept of God served likewise turned African American writers and intellectuals away from religion. Religion seemed to support the racist system of Jim Crow and was seemingly not useful in alleviating the economic and social conditions of blacks in the United States and the broader African diaspora. With the onset of the Great Depression, ministers and churches should have turned their attention to bolstering the economic position of blacks in the nation, yet many ministers seemed to care only about their own personal finances. As Hughes asked, why should poor parishioners give a dime of their hard-earned money to the church each day when they could barely afford to feed and clothe their families? Rather than trust in a god who cannot be seen, African Americans would be better off placing their trust in each other and working together for the betterment of all mankind. This view became especially prominent among those black secularists who embraced socialism and communism during the 1920s and 1930s.

Socialism and Communism

On July 28, 1919, Harry Haywood stepped off a train in Chicago during the middle of one of the bloodiest race riots in American history. With more than three dozen people killed and hundreds more injured, this riot was the worst of the twenty-six that occurred during that Red Summer. Haywood had just been mustered out of the army three months before and was working as a waiter on the Michigan Central railroad traveling between Chicago and Detroit. On coming home and witnessing the turmoil, Haywood realized then "that I had been fighting the wrong war. The Germans weren't the enemy—the enemy was right here at home." While the brutality and death toll of the Red Summer led many blacks to eschew overt political radicalism and turn instead to literary production, it led others to reject what were seen as bourgeois institutions such as the National Association for the Advancement of Colored People (NAACP) in favor of the Socialist and Communist political parties. Haywood would dedicate nearly seven decades of his life after this incident to combating racism and economic inequality. Within a decade of 1919, he had emerged as one of the leading African American communists in the nation, helping to develop the "Black Belt" thesis of the Communist International (Comintern) organization and working tirelessly to make the Communist Party more appealing to blacks in both the urban North and rural South.[1]

Harry Haywood has long been recognized as a black radical for his political thought, but he should likewise be recognized as such for his religious skepticism. Indeed, the two can hardly be separated. Haywood's atheism paved the way to his embrace of communism, a political philosophy grounded in a theory of historical materialism. And among black radical thinkers between the world wars, Haywood was not alone in tying atheism, agnosticism, and secular humanism with socialism and communism. Many of the key African American theorists

81

and activists in the Socialist and Communist parties, including Hubert Harrison, A. Phillip Randolph, Richard Wright, and Louise Thompson Patterson, were also atheists or agnostics. For these secular thinkers, the internationalism and anticolonialism of Marxist thought intersected nicely with their secular humanism. Seeing the church as a tool of white capitalist oppression, black freethinkers of the interwar period embraced overtly secular political parties that became increasingly hostile to traditional religious ideas and institutions. Religious skepticism and Marxist theory thus dialectically reinforced and strengthened each other among black political activists of this era.

Whereas the New Negro Renaissance brought disparate secular thinkers together in a literary movement, radical leftist politics became the glue that held them together. Black socialists and communists created publications such as the *Crusader* and the *Messenger* that served as both radical political publications and freethought journals. New institutions such as the African Blood Brotherhood, the Harlem Unitarian Church, and the American Negro Labor Congress likewise brought together black freethinkers under common political and cultural agendas. Participation in radical politics helped inaugurate a tradition of organized black secularism, a tradition that would gain strength over the course of the twentieth century.

Marxism and Freethought

Freethought and Marxism have so closely intersected because they arose out of similar social and economic conditions in Europe and the United States. We have seen in chapter 2 how increasing urbanization and industrialization influenced the rise of black freethought among writers in Harlem and Chicago. These same conditions initially gave rise to variants of socialism and communism in the early 1800s and fueled the massive spread of both in the 1900s. The growth of the factory system quickly outpaced that of the rural economy in nineteenth-century Europe, leading to a collapse of older social norms and to momentous political shifts. Liberal thinkers celebrated the rise of individualism that seemed to accompany that of capitalism, but early socialist thinkers sought a return to the communalism of early modern European society. Instead of celebrating the rise of the middle class, socialists called for the abolition of distinct classes and a radical equality between all citizens. Immigration to the United States as well as the rise of manufacturing and the concomitant growth of cities would start to bring socialism into the country slowly during the early 1800s but much more rapidly after the Civil War. Bringing together immigrant communities, rural farmers, and urban workers, the first major socialist party in the United States was formed in 1901.[2]

Leading socialist and communist thinkers in Europe and the United States have been intensely critical of and hostile toward Christianity, but not all socialists and communists were religious skeptics. For example, many nineteenth-century French socialists believed that communism represented the highest ideals of Christianity and that Jesus had been the first communist. When Karl Marx, Moses Hess, and Arnold Ruge led a delegation of progressive German intellectuals to Paris (where socialism had been invented) in the fall of 1843, they found that the people with whom they would make common cause were quite wary of their atheism. So Marxism certainly has complicated ties with religion, but they are ones that have been characterized more by hostility than respect. Friedrich Engels dismissed religion based on his belief that "all statements, including religious ones, are ultimately reducible to statements about the movement of matter." Marx deplored religion on both functional and metaphysical grounds. He believed that religion was a tool that capitalists used to control the proletariat, and he accepted Ludwig Feuerbach's argument that human beings have created God rather than the other way around.[3]

Some of the chief Marxist theorists of the twentieth century also saw little use for religion and undermined the church at every opportunity. In his 1905 essay "Socialism and Religion," Vladimir Ilyich Lenin tied capitalist exploitation to religious dogma and called for the complete separation of church and state. For Lenin, "religion is one of the forms of spiritual oppression which everywhere weighs down heavily upon the masses of the people, over burdened by their perpetual work for others, by want and isolation." Capitalism makes the exploited masses turn to religion and ideas of an afterlife as an escape from their lives, while religion supports the capitalist system by counseling patience and submissiveness in the face of worldly suffering, Lenin contended. He thus called for religion to be a completely private affair and posited that "religion must be of no concern to the state, and religious societies must have no connection with governmental authority."[4]

Joseph Stalin was very much in line with Lenin's views on religion. He had abandoned his own religious faith at the age of thirteen and in the mid-1920s began a campaign to purge the influence of Orthodox clergy in Russian society. Additionally, during the 1920s, the Comintern made it clear that atheism and religious skepticism were the default positions for communists. After a controversy over religion in Sweden, for example, the Comintern passed a resolution stating in part, "Communists demand that every citizen shall be free to acknowledge any religion he chooses or no religion, that is to be an atheist, which normally every conscious communist is." The Comintern followed up this demand with the directive that the Communist Party was to implant in all members "the clear-cut and homogenous world outlook of Marxism, of which atheism is an essential part." The message to American Communist Party members in the early twentieth century, then, was that religion and communism were incompatible and in order to be an adherent of the latter, one must reject the former. This is the context in which African American intellectuals and political activists began to engage with Marxism.[5]

Some African American socialists and many more communists were actually able to reconcile their political ideology with Christianity. Reverdy C. Ransom, an African Methodist Episcopal (AME) minister who was influenced by the increasingly dire economic straits of urban blacks and the social gospel prevalent during the early 1900s, created his own variant of socialism that aimed to transform the black social gospel movement. Believing that capitalism had led to an individualism run amok, Ransom admired the radical egalitarianism of socialist thought and felt it was best suited to African American life. Ransom was one of few black religious leaders, along with George Washington Woodbey, to openly espouse socialism. However, when communism later spread into the rural South, it greatly appealed to many black Christians. The black church was on the periphery of black radical politics during the 1920s and 1930s, but, as Robin D. G. Kelley notes, "a radical interpretation of Christianity continued to thrive outside of the organized church," and this radical religion drew many blacks to the Communist Party.[6]

Hubert Harrison

Like Woodbey and Ransom, Hubert Harrison felt that socialism presented the best opportunity for blacks to achieve political and economic equality in the United States. Unlike these two men, however, Harrison was an agnostic who did not think socialism was compatible

with Christianity. Harrison was born in St. Croix in 1883 and emigrated to Harlem in 1900. By the following year, he had left orthodox
and institutional Christianity for good, although the process had been
a gradual one that came after he read Thomas Paine, Voltaire, and
Jean-Jacques Rousseau, among others. As is typical among black freethinkers, Harrison's rejection of religion was not an easy one. He notes
of his "conversion" that he was "not one of those who did not care: I
suffered. Oh, how my poor wounded soul cried out in agony!" After
putting aside the authority of the Bible and belief in God, Harrison
wrote in a letter, "I now had a new belief—Agnosticism. I said belief:
what I did mean was philosophy-of-life, point-of-observation, attitude-
towards-things." Agnosticism for him was not simply a lack of belief in
God but a philosophical bent of mind that stressed reason, curiosity,
and humility. Harrison thus claimed he was "not a dogmatic *dis*believer
nor a bumptious and narrow infidel. I am not at all of Col. [Robert]
Ingersoll's school" but rather aligned more closely with Thomas Huxley,
the person who coined the term *agnosticism*.[7]

Hubert Harrison's publications indicate that he was serious about
being an active contributor to the American freethought movement
and that he believed that freethought went hand in hand with socialism. At a Thomas Paine commemoration dinner that freethought
leaders hosted, Harrison gave a speech on Paine that was later published in the *Truth Seeker*. Here he argued that "it is this dual aspect
of Paine—militant unbelief and democratic dissent—that is most truly
representative of him in the thought of our time." For Harrison in
1911, democratic dissent would have fit most easily with the Socialist
Party, as the Republicans represented imperialism and monied interests, while the Democrats seemed to be the party of white supremacy.
Paine's great contribution to freethought, in Harrison's view, was that
he "popularized the arguments against Christianity and brought them
down to the level of the democracy." The ideas and reach of the freethought movement would not have succeeded without Paine's unique
contribution because the masses would be unlikely to read the philosophical works of freethinkers such as David Hume.[8]

Harrison saw himself as an intellectual descendant of Paine who
could use similar methods to help bring freethought to greater numbers
of African Americans. "It should seem that Negroes, of all Americans
would be found in the Freethought fold," he proclaimed, "since they
have suffered more than any other class of Americans from the dubious blessings of Christianity." These dubious blessing included biblical

justifications for slavery, especially the Curse of Canaan, as well as churches' support of the institution. Even in the early 1900s, according to Harrison, "the church among the Negroes today exerts a more powerful influence than anything else in the sphere of ideas. Nietzsche's contention that the ethics of Christianity are the slave's ethics would seem to be justified." Harrison's position here on the function of Christianity is similar to Zora Neale Hurston's later claim that only weak individuals need religion. Throughout his time in New York City, Harrison heard countless black speakers applaud the fact that blacks never rose up in vengeance against their masters during the Civil War. While this nonviolence may have seemed positive to many listeners, for Harrison it reflected passivity and an act of forbearance possible only because slaves' spirits had been crushed by the institution "and to accomplish this, Christianity . . . was the most effective instrument."[9]

Harrison further supported his appeal to blacks by arguing that religion and religious institutions first created the color line. This point was the primary reason why black scholars still tried to advance equality by compiling statistics related to black progress, in Harrison's opinion. These types of appeals, he noted, were rooted in an eighteenth-century epistemology, and he contended that the time had come to adopt new methods for bringing about political equality. These new methods would require new leaders. Harrison decried the overwhelming focus on technical education by Booker T. Washington and his supporters and argued that a broader liberal education would serve blacks better. This broader education would come from new leaders but was also dependent on systemic change in American society. "I am inclined to believe that freedom of thought must come from freedom of circumstance," Harrison wrote; to achieve true higher education, blacks must have greater economic prospects and political rights.[10]

Harrison began his efforts to bring blacks into the Socialist Party in 1911. To do so, he had to appeal to African Americans as well as the leaders of the Socialist Party. In speaking to blacks, he noted that socialism by itself would not immediately remove racism because the ignorance behind racial animosity would likely remain. But he did argue that socialism "will remove racial injustice and lighten the black man's burden. I do expect that it will take the white man off the black man's back and leave him free for the first time to make of himself as much or as little as he chooses." Harrison's argument to Socialist Party leaders was a pragmatic one aimed at broadening the tent of the party. Historically, he claimed, socialism's goal had been the unification of the working class, and the party was not one for white men or black men only, at least in theory. If the party ever hoped to overthrow capitalism, in this country or worldwide, it had to embrace workers of all races.[11]

Harrison remained committed to socialism and labor organizing for blacks but departed from the central focus on class when it was clear that the Socialist Party and major labor unions in the United States were doing the same. He was especially critical of the American Federation of Labor (AFL) and its leader Samuel Gompers, who consistently rejected the idea of one big union for all workers. The AFL's base was in construction trade unions and railroad brotherhoods, and leaders of the organization allowed racist and segregated unions to thrive. In 1905, Gompers stated, "We are not going to let the [white] standard of living be destroyed by Negroes, Chinamen, Japs or any others." The Socialist Party likewise remained indifferent to the needs of black workers. As Sally Miller notes, the party's allowing African Americans to join was incredibly egalitarian for the period, but Eugene Debs and other members of the party leadership consistently refused any special consideration or policies for black socialists. In response, Harrison came to put the needs of black workers above those of workers in general. After a 1917 race riot in East St. Louis, Harrison explained that he understood the condition of the working man and wanted to see them triumph over capitalists. At the same time, however, his "first duty, here as everywhere, is to the Negro race. . . . Since the A. F. of L. chooses to put Race before Class, let us return the compliment." Blacks should continue to form unions such as the Railway Men's Benevolent Association or the Colored Employees of America, Harrison urged, arguing that only when they had achieved a level of equality might they be able to merge with larger and more established ones such as the AFL.[12]

Harrison's ideals and activities are characteristic of the main tenets of African American Marxist freethinkers. In Harrison's view, religion and global capitalism were together largely responsible for imperialism in Africa and among other darker peoples. "The Nineteenth Christian Century," he began in one of his most well-known essays, "saw the international expansion of capitalism . . . and its establishment by force and fraud over the lands of the colored races." Local developments within the United States could not be divorced from events across the Atlantic. The East St. Louis riot, in which 244 buildings were destroyed, causing $373,000 in property damage, was a prime example. In Harrison's mind, this event "was simply the climax of a long series of butcheries perpetrated on defenseless Negroes which has made the murder rate of Christian America higher than that of heathen Africa and of every other civilized land." Imperialist wars were the "natural and inevitable effect of the capitalist system, of what (for want of a worse name) we call 'Christendom.'" Capitalism and Christianity, then, were twin systems of oppression that activists must combat simultaneously if they were to achieve their goals of elevating the working class and ending white supremacy.[13]

Like the "great agnostic" Robert Ingersoll, Hubert Harrison advanced the cause of freethought primarily through the lecture circuit. Unlike Ingersoll's, Harrison's lectures took place largely on soapboxes in New York City. But despite the fact that fewer people heard Harrison, he was still widely regarded as one of the most learned and effective speakers of his time, even without the benefit of a formal education. Richard B. Moore first heard Harrison speak in Madison Square Park and noted "his ability to make complex subjects clear and simple, and the power of his logic and presentation gained him a hearing in some very difficult situations." In describing Harrison's presence on the soapbox, Moore recalled, "Harrison was not prepossessing but quite impressive. His sparse hair covered his head lightly and his high forehead seemed to make his head taller and add to his stature. His keen black eyes could almost transfix an opponent; when they opened slightly and his lips pulled up somewhat, then a withering blast was on its way." Others referred to Harrison as the "Black Socrates," for both the power of his intellect and his ability to elucidate complex subjects in an engaging manner for his audience. Claude McKay wrote that Harrison "lectured on free-thought, socialism, and racialism, and sold books. He spoke precisely and clearly, with fine intelligence and masses of facts. He was very black, compact of figure, and his head resembled an African replica of Socrates." Even though Harrison often derided the NAACP as the "National Association for the Advancement of Certain People," William Pickens, an officer of that organization, wrote of Harrison, "It is not possible that Socrates could have outdone Hubert Harrison in making the most commonplace subject interesting. Here is a plain black man who can speak more easily, effectively and interestingly on a greater variety of subjects than any other man we have ever met, even in any of the great universities." Harrison's lectures clearly had a wide impact and were the key part of why he came to be known as the "father of Harlem radicalism."[14]

Along with his soapbox lecturing in Harlem, Hubert Harrison launched the Liberty League of Negro-Americans in 1917 to achieve some of his political goals. First on the agenda was breaking away from older leaders such as W. E. B. Du Bois, none of whom were invited to the organizing meeting on June 12 at Harlem's Bethel AME Church. Harrison stated that the main goal of the league was "nothing less than the demand that the Negroes of the United States be given a chance to enthuse over democracy for themselves in America before they are expected to enthuse over democracy in Europe." A chief demand of Harrison and league organizers was national legislation against lynching, and Harrison urged southern blacks to organize themselves for self-defense. As he would write in the league's Declaration of Principles, "if the national government should refuse to take any steps to protect its Negro people from murderous mob-violence, then we should call upon our people to defend themselves against murder with the weapons of murder." Harrison also continued to speak to global black oppression with the creation of the Liberty League and its newspaper, the *Voice*. He noted that the league would stand with other organizations around the world trying to fight against colonialism and imperialism. "With the 250 millions of our brethren in Africa we feel a special sympathy, and we will work for the ultimate realization of democracy in Africa," he stated. So even as he moved away from organized Socialist Party political activity, Harrison remained true to one of its core principles in the 1910s, that of anti-imperialism.[15]

A. Philip Randolph and the *Messenger*

One of Harrison's most important protégés was A. Philip Randolph, who quickly emerged as a key African American freethinker and socialist in his own right. Randolph was born in Crescent City, Florida, in 1889, the same year the state legislature passed a poll tax and election restrictions that made it difficult for blacks to vote. When he was two years old, his family moved to Jacksonville as part of a migration of blacks to southern cities in search of economic opportunity. Twenty years later, Randolph would follow the thousands of blacks in his generation to New York and other northern cities. Shortly after his arrival in Harlem in the spring of 1911, Randolph tried to become an actor and, failing at that, moved around from job to job. He took classes in history, public speaking, philosophy, economics, and political science at the City College of New York between 1912 and 1917. While there, a leftist philosophy professor named J. Salwyn Shapiro introduced him

to Marx's writings and those of other socialists. It was during this time
that he also became a follower of fellow Harlemite Hubert Harrison.
Randolph joined the Socialist Party in 1916 and began to lecture at its
Rand School on black history and political economy.[16]

From an early age, Randolph rejected the main theological tenets of
his religious upbringing in the AME Church, and this rejection continued into his political career in New York City. Randolph started having
doubts about religion while living in Jacksonville. He attended Baptist
and Methodist churches after moving to Harlem, yet he nevertheless
"had only the most secular use for churches, mainly as platforms for his
political opinions." This approach was not so different from his mentor
Hubert Harrison, who formed the Liberty League in an AME church in
Harlem. Even as they rejected the theological and cosmological ideas
of black churches, freethinkers continued to need their resources to
achieve political ends. So, while a select few black secularists may have
seen no use for churches, Randolph was not among their number. He
recognized the power of black churches and the cohesiveness they
offered to black communities. But in his view, there was not likely to
be "any great emancipation of the Negro or anybody else because of
religious beliefs."[17]

Randolph would instead use the press to advance his secular political ideals. After meeting Chandler Owen, whom Randolph noted was
even more religiously radical than he was, the two started the *Messenger* magazine with the important support of Randolph's wife, Lucille,
who was a successful hairdresser in Harlem. They launched the paper
in November 1917 and noted in that first issue that "our aim is to
appeal to reason, to lift our pens above the cringing demagogy of the
times, and above the cheap peanut politics of the old reactionary Negro
leaders." The paper would not appeal to African American patriotism
but rather to justice for blacks. They would not advocate loyalty to the
U.S. government when that government was not loyal to black people.
And above all, Randolph and Owen made it clear that "prayer is not
one of our remedies. . . . We consider prayer as nothing more than a
fervent wish; consequently the merit and worth of prayer depend upon
what the fervent wish is. Still we never forget that all wishes, desires,
hopes—must be realized thru the adoption of sound methods. This
requires scientific education." Building on this last point, Randolph
and Owen billed their publication as "the only magazine of scientific
radicalism in the world published by Negroes."[18]

The contents of the *Messenger* indicate that the editors were serious about challenging traditional religious ideas and advancing their cause of "scientific radicalism" among blacks. From its first issue, the magazine provided a forum for individuals to critique Christianity's role in African American culture as well as the role that religion played in justifying the racist oppression of blacks. The editors published two poems by Walter Everette Hawkins in that inaugural issue. The first of these, entitled "Too Much Religion," posited,

> There is too much time for doctrine;
> Too much talk of church and creeds
> Far too little time for duty,
> And to heal some heart that bleeds
> Too much Sunday Church religion,
> Too many stale and bookish prayers;
> Too many souls are getting ragged,
> Watching what their neighbor wears.
>
> There is too much talk of heaven,
> Too much talk of golden streets,
> When one can't be sympathetic,
> When a needy neighbor meets;
> Too much talk about riches
> You expect to get "up there,"
> When one will not do his duty
> As a decent Christian here.[19]

For Hawkins, there were a number of facets to religious observance that were troubling. He criticized the tendency of people to wear their "Sunday best" while seemingly neglecting the disparate social and economic problems prevalent within American society. And he further disparaged what he saw to be the hypocritical practice of employing religious language without exhibiting religious behaviors of caring for one's neighbor, a common complaint of black freethinkers. His next piece, "Here and Hereafter," highlighted another common theme in black freethought literature—namely, the idea that hell is not the destination for sinners but rather the current ontological state of African Americans: "And it's mighty poor religion / That won't keep a man from fear; / For the next place must be Heaven, / Since 'tis Hell I'm having here."[20]

The following year, Randolph and Owen published "The Mob Victim" by an anonymous author that began,

> And it was in a Christian land,
> With freedom's towers on every hand,
> Where shafts to civic pride arise
> To lift America to the skies,
> And it was on a Sabbath day,
> While men and women went to pray.
> I passed the crowd in humble mode
> In going to my meek abode.
> From out the crowd arose a cry,
> And epithets began to fly;
> And thus like hounds they took my track—
> My only crime—my face was black.
> And so this Christian mob did turn
> From prayer to rob, to rack and burn.
> A victim helplessly I fell
> To tortures truly kin to hell.[21]

Like Langston Hughes's "Song for a Dark Girl," this piece sharply critiques the practice of lynching and ties it to American Christianity. In giving space to works such as these, Randolph and Owen turned their magazine into a publication that significantly contributed to the freethought movement at a time when it was under sharp attacks from fundamentalists dismayed at the growing influence of secularism in America.

Along with criticizing religion, Randolph and Owen used the *Messenger* to advocate for another central issue of American freethought—women's rights. As we have seen with their commitment to socialism, freethinkers of the twentieth century, black and white, were no longer content to simply be against the church. Freethought instead complemented other political commitments and ideologies, including feminism. Rachel Scharfman notes that feminist freethinkers "demanded fundamental changes in the gender order of society. Freethought's impact on their feminist ideologies is clear in their arguments positing male supremacy, capitalism, and religion as the unholiest of trinities, united to perpetuate women's subordination." Feminism gained in popularity during the 1910s and included demands for birth control, sexual liberation, increased access to education, and expanded political and economic rights. The *Messenger* was especially supportive of these latter two goals. Along with its sharp critique of religion, the first issue of the magazine contained an editorial arguing strongly for women's suffrage. Women pay taxes, consume, and produce goods just like men, Randolph and Owen argued, and should thus also have the right to vote: "The sentimental and puritanical objections advanced by squeamish moralists won't stand. Sex is no bar to women's participating in the industrial world and it should be none to her participating in the political world." In referencing the "puritanical objections" to women voting, the editors implicitly tied female subjugation to American Christianity. Giving the right to vote to women was not just a feminist issue but also a racial one. It would give more political power to blacks in general, and thus black men had a special obligation to support female suffrage.[22]

The *Messenger* quickly gained a reputation as the most radical paper in the United States for its espousal of socialism, feminism, freethought, and opposition to American involvement in World War I. While W. E. B. Du Bois welcomed the U.S. entry into the war in 1917 (the same year as the Russian Revolution) largely because he felt it might inaugurate a socialist revolution, Randolph and Owen argued, as did Hubert Harrison, that the war was a capitalist, imperialist one designed to keep Africans, Asians, and other darker races in check. Du Bois had also argued that a German victory would sound the death knell for blacks' hopes of gaining political rights, but Owen retorted that black people's participation in conflicts such as the American Revolution had not helped their political or economic fortunes thus far and was unlikely to do so in the future. The *Messenger* did not come to the attention of authorities until the third issue came out in the summer of 1918, just as Randolph and Owen were on a speaking tour of the Midwest. That issue contained an editorial calling for the confiscation of all corporate war profits as a disincentive for continuing the war. The two were arrested in Cleveland under the Espionage Act but were released because the paternalistic judge did not believe they had written the articles attributed to them. Efforts against the magazine intensified during the Red Summer of 1919, with the U.S. Post Office raising the price for mailing and Chandler Owen being conscripted for military duty. Attorney General A. Mitchell Palmer noted that the paper was black America's most dangerous publication.[23]

From 1916 until the mid-1920s, Randolph was active in Socialist Party politics, and he soon surpassed Harrison as the most important black socialist of the early twentieth century. His and Owen's newspaper, along with his lectures at the Rand School, helped expand the reach of the party in New York City. During the mayoral election of 1917, for example, 25 percent of blacks who voted cast their ballot for the Socialist Party candidate, Morris Hillquit. While Hillquit received more than 100,000 votes, he did lose the election. The sizable support he received from black voters, however, must have given hope to Owen and Randolph. Just three years later, Randolph ran for New York secretary of state on the Socialist Party ticket and garnered 17 percent of the black vote. In 1920, Randolph and Owen also founded the Friends of Negro Freedom, an all-black organization aimed at promoting civil rights and organizing black workers, either in interracial unions if possible or independent black ones if not.[24]

Randolph's adherence to socialism and emphasis on the class struggle led him to oppose the largest black political group of the time, Marcus Garvey's Universal Negro Improvement Association (UNIA). Garvey and the UNIA emphasized race pride, Pan-Africanism, and black nationalism. Marcus and his wife, Amy, had established the UNIA in Jamaica in 1914 and set up the first branch in the United States in 1917. A central component of the UNIA's black nationalism was a Back-to-Africa movement, which would be funded in part by developing global black capitalism and economic independence. Randolph took issue with Garvey's lack of class critique and with his black nationalism. Manning Marable notes that for Randolph, "race and ethnicity played no role in the 'scientific evolution' of class contradictions; class was an economic category without cultural or social forms." Randolph thus began to see any variant of black nationalism as a hindrance to working class unity. The Friends of Negro Freedom that he and Owen had organized began to undermine the UNIA, and the pages of the *Messenger* were filled with every misstep of the organization. And much of the antireligious rhetoric contained in the paper was aimed at Garveyism, which had a significant Zionist component.[25]

The African Blood Brotherhood and Caribbean Radicalism

While A. Philip Randolph was busy denouncing Marcus Garvey at every chance he got during the early 1920s, he came under attack himself from other radical black leaders who were beginning to denounce the Socialist Party in favor of communism. After the Russian Revolution and the end of World War I, the Socialist Party split, and members of its radical left wing, including Otto Huiswood, founded two separate parties in 1919—the Communist Labor Party and the Communist Party of America. They merged in 1922 into the Workers Party of America and changed their name to the Communist Party, USA (CPUSA) in 1929. Huiswood, who was from Suriname, became the first black member of the party and would remain a central figure in it for decades. He was joined by other West Indian activists, including Claude McKay and Cyril Briggs. Briggs was born in Nevis and emigrated to New York City in 1905. He began writing for the New York *Amsterdam News* in 1912, and for the next seven years he consistently emphasized race pride, self-determination, and black nationalism in his work. To advance these goals, Briggs formed the African Blood Brotherhood (ABB) with Huiswood, Richard B. Moore, W. A. Domingo, and others in 1919 to bring together his anticapitalist, anticolonialist, and nationalist political agenda.[26]

During the early 1920s, Briggs and the ABB worked to advance the goals of communism while also sharply critiquing religion's role in justifying the social order. In doing so, Briggs and other black communists were inaugurating a new tradition of black political thought. They argued strongly against assimilation and instead called for socialist transformation. They also pushed the leadership of black politics away from the middle class and toward the working class. And instead of pursuing alliances with bourgeois whites, they now sought alliances with the white working class. The organ of the ABB, the *Crusader*, also served to undermine traditional religious ideas and demonstrates the continuing ties between Marxism and freethought. Briggs first encountered freethought as a teenager in St. Kitts. He was working in the library of a Baptist minister there when he first read some of the writings of Robert Ingersoll. Like Randolph's *Messenger*, Briggs's *Crusader* contained a number of articles criticizing Christianity and arguing that black advancement would be better achieved with Marxism than with religion. One editorial claimed that "it has long been evident that the Christian religion was being prostituted by the white man to his own selfish and *racial* ends." Rather than promoting the brotherhood of man, Briggs wrote, Christianity "was being pushed upon non-Christian races because of its value as 'a pacific creed' that would help in the maintenance of white political control over those races." Here Briggs makes the same connection as Harrison, Randolph, and countless other Marxists of this era—namely, that religion and capitalism were employed to great effect by imperialists and colonizers. In a later piece, Briggs argued that salvation for blacks would not come from on high but rather from earthly efforts. The surest way to promote this salvation, he claimed, was "to combine the two most likely and feasible positions, viz: salvation for all Negroes through the establishment of a strong, stable, independent Negro state in Africa or elsewhere; and salvation for all Negroes (as well as other oppressed peoples) through the establishment of a Universal Socialist Co-operative Commonwealth." Briggs here placed himself among a new generation of black intellectuals calling for secular rather than religious solutions to blacks' ills.[27]

Richard B. Moore was another key leader of the ABB who embraced both freethought and Marxism. Moore spent his formative years in Barbados and emigrated to New York in July 1909. He was raised in an intensely devout household and quickly sought out religious fellowship upon emigrating to the United States. On Eighth Avenue in Manhattan he found the Christian Missionary Alliance, a sect that appeared similar to the evangelical Christian Mission he had been a part of in Bridgetown. However, he was quickly disappointed because the congregation segregated blacks in the gallery. This disappointment, combined with racism he experienced at the Fifty-Seventh Street YMCA, where he was turned away from a typing class because he was black, led him to question religion. Seeking answers to the problems of racism led him away from the church and toward the street corner, where in listening to orators such as Harrison, he began to pick up his radical political ideology. Moore befriended Huiswood and had joined the Communists by the mid-1920s. Moore notes of this decision, "I was becoming more and more militant . . . and I was looking for a more militant means of action against this system. Finally I was impelled to join the Communist Party because I considered that to be the most militant in acting against the conditions which were quite distressing."[28]

Moore became a staunch atheist during the 1920s and spoke frequently on atheism and communism throughout New York City. One such venue was the Harlem Unitarian Church that Rev. Egbert Ethelred Brown led. Brown had attended the Meadville Theological School from 1910–1912 and was ordained in the Unitarian church in Meadville, Pennsylvania, before returning home to Jamaica and establishing liberal churches in Montego Bay and Kingston. He moved to New York City to establish the Harlem Unitarian Church in 1920. Instead of traditional services found in AME or Baptist congregations, the Harlem Unitarian Church often held forums on both religious and political topics, including freethought, "Jesus and Marx," and "The Church and the Negro Problem." Brown believed that Unitarianism was "the religion of the future—the religion with an emancipatory message which all peoples of every race may understand and accept."[29]

Brown and most, if not all, of his parishioners thought that religion should be reasonable and should speak to the concerns of this world. For them, distinctions between the sacred and the secular were artificial, and it did not matter as much what people believed as what they did. Brown often posited that "religion is not confined within any walls or within any book." Indeed, for Brown, scientists, researchers, and doctors should be considered holy men and ministers just as he himself was because they labor tirelessly to discover nature's secrets. Brown also argued that men and women should not be forced to lay aside their reason to be Christians. He claimed that the Bible is merely "a collection of documents, according to the judgment of men arbitrarily selected from a number of floating documents and put in a volume." Since this was the case, he argued, then the Bible was not infallible. Unlike most of the freethinkers of his era, Brown was not an atheist or an agnostic, although he was a socialist. But his conception of God was expansive enough to allow him to welcome atheists and people of all faiths into his church. As he asked in one sermon, "What of labels? Were we Mahomedans or Buddhists or Jews or Atheists all would be well if we lived the life of sacrificing service."[30]

Moore spoke often at Brown's church, as he considered it the ideal place to highlight the historic role that Christianity had played in the oppression of black people. When a visiting minister came to the church to discuss how he had been saved, Moore responded with a talk on how he had lost his faith in God. He soon came under criticism from communists who felt he should have no connection with a church at all, even a liberal one. Moore noted of his involvement with the congregation, "I was proud because of the Communist, atheist propaganda which I had conducted" and debates he took part in where "I had taken the negative of such propositions as Resolved that Christianity Can Solve the Race Problem, holding Communism to be the solution, exposing the role of religion as 'the opium of the people' and the Church as a force of capitalist-imperialist oppression."[31]

As the examples of Harrison, Briggs, and Moore suggest, Caribbean immigrants were leading secular thinkers and were among the most radical political voices in New York City. During the 1910s, 45,000 Caribbean blacks emigrated to the United States, and a total of

102,000 settled in the country between 1901 and 1924, when a restrictive immigration law limited the number of migrants from the region. By 1930, Afro-Caribbeans comprised approximately 25 percent of Harlem's population. Some of the same factors that drove southern blacks to northern cities spurred Caribbean emigration. Droughts, inadequate harvests, plant diseases, and falling sugar prices combined to devastate local economies and make many Afro-Caribbeans seek economic opportunity in the United States. Joyce Moore Turner and W. Burghardt Turner note that for many of these immigrants, "the land of opportunity had failed to live up to their expectations. Not only were they barred from decent jobs, in some cases denied access to education, forced to live in particular neighborhoods, and insulted by white clerics and their congregations, but they read daily of lynchings and other brutalities heaped upon blacks in the United States." While there was certainly racial prejudice in the Caribbean, it seemed to be of a very different nature than that in the United States, a much subtler type of racism that was more strongly tied to class distinctions. Jamaican immigrant and freethinker Claude McKay wrote in 1918 that moving to New York "was the first time I had ever come face to face with such manifest, implacable hatred of my race, and my feelings were indescribable. . . . I had heard of prejudice in America but never dreamed of it being so intensely bitter."[32]

A number of factors contributed to Caribbean religious and political radicalism even before emigration to the United States. First, some migrants had been members of trade unions and nationalist organizations back home, and these memberships gave them significant political and organizational experience. McKay, for example, was already a freethinker and a socialist before he left Jamaica in 1912, while Garvey started the UNIA two years before his arrival in New York. Second, many migrants had served in the British West Indies Regiment during World War I and experienced racism from British soldiers; these experiences also radicalized them before they migrated to the United States. Third, as Winston James argues, travel also played a key role in migrants' radicalization, as those who were able (or forced) to do so "developed an internationalist, pan-Africanist perspective through interacting with black people from different countries and through observing the common oppressed condition of black humanity around the world." Fourth, Caribbean migrants were less religious and less attached to the Christian church than their African American counterparts were. Some had been forced to attend church in the Caribbean and were happy to be free of this constraint when they arrived in the United States, while others became disenchanted with the racism they encountered from American Christians.[33]

The Growing Appeal of Communism to Blacks

The combination of Marxism with black nationalism that was so prevalent among these radical Caribbean emigrants marked a turning point in the Communist Party's appeal to African Americans. The communists were initially little different from socialists in their treatment of race, subsuming racial issues under class and arguing that the communist revolution would alleviate racial tensions. Around 1924, the Comintern started to shift its position and recognize the importance of racism to blacks and the need to address it if blacks were going to get on board with their economic message. The Comintern supported the creation of the American Negro Labor Congress in 1925, which endeavored to purge racism from labor unions, replace the black bourgeoisie with the working class, and centralize black labor. In 1928, the Communist Party made another tremendous stride in its efforts to recruit blacks by adopting the "Black Belt" thesis. At the Sixth Comintern Congress held in Moscow that year, Harry Haywood pushed for a new party line toward African Americans—namely, that southern blacks represented a nation within a nation, a separate culture and distinct people whose self-determination communists should promote at every opportunity. This position appealed to potential Black communists for two primary reasons. First, it departed sharply from traditional approaches that had barely considered blacks as workers, let alone part of the class struggle. And second, positioning black politics within global struggles for self-determination gave a revolutionary character to their strivings.[34]

Haywood's formulation of the Black Belt thesis situated him as one of the leading African American intellectuals in the party, and, like numerous other black Marxists, he combined his political radicalism with secular humanism. Haywood's parents were members of the AME church in South Omaha, Nebraska. Born there in 1898, Haywood began to seriously question his faith at the age of twelve, when the furor over Halley's Comet swept the community. For many people around him, the excitement drove them to greater displays of religiosity. Prophets and messiahs were preaching the end of the world in churches and on street corners, while hardened sinners realized the error of their ways and repented. When the comet passed by the earth and the end times failed to materialize, Haywood thought to himself, "It's not true . . . the fire and brimstone, the leering devils, the angry vengeful God. None of it is true." During his childhood, his family had dutifully attended church every Sunday, and the dominant emotion he recalled from these experiences was fear at his preacher's fire-and-brimstone sermons and of the violence depicted in the Bible. But after Halley's Comet, "it was as if a great weight had been lifted from my mind. It was the end of my religion, although I still thought that there was most likely a supreme being." If God did exist, Haywood thought, he was likely nothing like the God of the Bible. A few years later, Haywood recalled, "at the age of fourteen or fifteen, I read some of the lectures of Robert G. Ingersoll and became an agnostic, doubting the existence of a God. From there, I later moved to positive atheism." Haywood's comment regarding the influence of Ingersoll marks an important development in black freethought. Prior to the twentieth century, much of black atheism had developed in response to slavery and independent of the freethought movement among whites. Both Haywood and Hubert Harrison's account of their acceptance of agnosticism and atheism note the importance of white freethinkers such as Thomas Paine and Robert Ingersoll for their religious development, and the same was true of other black Marxist freethinkers of the era.[35]

His return to Chicago after serving in the army played a key role in Harry Haywood's early embrace of political radicalism. During the 1910s, the number of blacks in northern industry increased from 551,825 to 901,131, yet only 15 percent of these workers held skilled or semiskilled positions in 1920. Haywood referred to Chicago in the early 1920s as "an ideal place and time for the education of a Black radical." With the influx of migrants from the South, approximately 250,000 between 1910 and 1935, Chicago had one of the biggest concentrations of workers in the nation and was also a central location in the nation's industrial commerce. Initially, Haywood tried to go the traditional route by getting married and living a stable middle-class lifestyle. He took a job and married a woman named Hazel in 1920. The marriage broke up that same year, partially because of her aspirations to be somebody important in the world while he just wanted to be free. "Hazel slavishly accepted white middle class values," he recalled. "I, on the other hand, was looking around for a way trying to figure out how to maladjust." He was disenchanted with middle-class values and aspirations, and he rejected the status quo and "determined to do something about it—to make my rebellion count."[36]

Haywood's rejection of religion was also closely tied to his move toward communism in the 1920s. Around the time of his divorce, he was trying to figure out the root cause of racism and of blacks' position in the world. "Religion as an explanation for the riddles of the universe I had rejected long before. I knew that our predicament was not the result of some divine disposition and therefore must be changed by man. How? Well, that was the question to be explored." He had little knowledge of the natural or social sciences, having gleaned only tidbits from reading the works of Robert Ingersoll, where he first learned about Charles Darwin's theory of evolution. So Haywood sat down to read Darwin, who showed that human beings had evolved from other life forms and had not been created instantaneously. "Here at last was a scientific refutation of religious dogma," Haywood proclaimed. "I had at last found a basis for my atheism." But his search for answers could not stop at proving his atheism. Haywood then began to ponder the ties between Darwin's theory and the Social Darwinists and could not understand how the former could be used to support the latter. His older brother Otto cleared him up on this point, noting that Darwin's theory could not be transferred to human relations. Otto then told him that if he wanted to figure out the laws of human society, he should "quit reading those bourgeois authors and start reading Marx and Engels."[37]

Haywood began to do just that and soon developed his critique of capitalism and plan for advancing the interests of the working class. It started while working for the post office in Chicago in 1921. He organized a discussion group for about a dozen of his coworkers that met every Sunday to examine the race problem. This group in effect became an alternative to church for Haywood and his colleagues. An important topic of discussion was the Garvey movement and its prospects for alleviating racism. Haywood and his group had no qualms with the cultural nationalism of Marcus Garvey—his focus on race pride, dignity, and self-determination. They rejected his calls for a return to Africa, however, "as fantastic, unreal and a dangerous diversion which could only lead to desertion of the struggle for our rights in the USA." Just as Frederick Douglass had argued against the colonization movement nearly eighty years prior, Haywood declared that blacks had spilled their sweat and blood in building this country and were entitled to reap the benefits. Perhaps even more important than Garvey's back-to-Africa movement in his eyes was Garvey's attitude toward race. "We could not go along with Garvey's idea about inherent racial antagonisms between Black and White," Haywood noted. This idea was a concession to racists throughout the country and did not accord with his personal experience. By pondering the tenets of Garveyism and observing the attacks on white labor during the Palmer raids in 1920, "the racial fog lifted and the face and location of the enemy was outlined. I began to see that the main beneficiaries of Black subjugation also profited from the social oppression of poor whites, native and foreign-born." What was needed to address this was not a form of black nationalism that urged separation between the races but rather one that postulated equality between them. Haywood would join the African Blood Brotherhood in 1922, partly because the ABB was hostile to Garvey's program, and he followed up this action by joining the Workers' Party in 1925.[38]

Just two years after Haywood officially became a member of this Communist Party (which would be renamed the CPUSA two years hence), Richard Wright arrived in Chicago and in short order followed in Haywood's footsteps, combining his atheism with Marxist theory and eventually joining the party. Wright was initially skeptical of the communists he encountered in Chicago's Washington Park, partly because many of them "were deliberately careless in their personal appearance." Many black people in the city agreed with their agenda, he noted, but they would not join because of the shabby appearance of those blacks who were already members. In a harbinger of battles to come, Wright also deplored the seeming fanaticism and anti-intellectualism of the communists he encountered. But after attending a meeting of the Chicago John Reed Club, the literary arm of the CPUSA, Wright began to change his mind. Reading communist literature showed him that there was an organized and concerted search for truth regarding the lives of oppressed peoples. He decided to join the CPUSA and believed that his unique contribution could be as a proletarian writer who could explain the symbolism and ideas of the party to the black masses. Wright put great importance on this responsibility and committed himself to illuminating working-class lives and consciousness.[39]

Wright attempted to provide this illumination through his reflections on the craft of writing itself. In his 1937 essay "Blueprint for Negro Writing," Wright called for a more authentic form of African American literature that better spoke to the black condition and culture. Too much of black cultural production, in his view, took its cues from white Christian America. "Even today," he argued, "there are millions of American Negroes whose only sense of a whole universe, whose only relation to society and man, and whose only guide to personal dignity comes through the archaic morphology of Christian salvation." Instead, black writers should draw from the tradition of the folktales, blues, and spirituals through which "the Negro achieved his most indigenous and complete expression." The question for Wright, then, was whether "Negro writing be for the Negro masses, moulding the lives and consciousness of those masses toward new goals, or shall it continue begging the question of the Negroes' humanity?"[40]

In his most famous novel, Wright sought to answer this question and pave a new direction for both African American literature and American communism. *Native Son* attempted to show a more authentic and historically accurate image of the proletariat that was so central to Marxist thought. Whereas many if not most blacks found some way to deal with racism, whether through religion, alcohol, music, or education, Wright's protagonist Bigger Thomas is one who revolted against the racially proscriptive mores of twentieth-century American society. "Why did Bigger revolt?" Wright asks in his essay on the birth of Bigger Thomas. It was because he had abandoned the religious and folk culture of other blacks and because he was trying to adapt, unsuccessfully, to capitalist modernity. Unless working-class blacks were understood on their own terms, Wright argued, they would not be able to play their part in the coming proletarian revolution.[41]

Soon after publishing *Native Son*, Wright became disenchanted with Marxism and abandoned it for Sartrean existentialism. Wright initially felt welcomed at Communist Party meetings, especially because he did not experience racial discrimination there. After one meeting of black communists, however, he was laughed at after giving a report and could not find out why. He later discovered that the members thought he was too intellectual and "talks like a book." Wright's manner of speech labeled him as bourgeois, and he began to encounter other unsavory aspects of the party, including thought policing from members who told him he should not read bourgeois books because they would confuse him. Wright quickly discovered to his chagrin Fraser Ottanelli's point that "joining and remaining within the CPUSA was an all encompassing experience, one that demanded a total commitment." Had he not begun to experience discrimination from other black communists, Wright might have been willing to make that commitment, but such was not the case and he ended up leaving the party. Despite this break with the CPUSA, and despite his later acceptance of existentialism,

Wright still saw value in Marxism. Cedric Robinson states "as an *ideology*" Wright understood that Marxism "had never transcended its origins. It remained an ideology *for* the working classes rather than an ideology *of* the working classes. However, as a *method* of social analysis he found it compelling." This method continued to include a rejection of religion, which Wright still believed to be a central component in black suffering. His participation in the Communist Party had actually been a substitute of sorts for religion, but by the early 1940s, he had come to believe that communism was "the God that failed."[42]

Black Women, Communism, and Freethought

Even as Wright eventually came to find the CPUSA lacking, the party retained its appeal for many other black freethinkers, including some black women. Black women were attracted to the Communist Party for a number of reasons. Despite the implementation of Franklin D. Roosevelt's New Deal, African American women continued to suffer from high levels of unemployment, poverty, and poor living conditions. Relief agencies, especially those in the South, often discriminated against blacks. Many black women came to see the CPUSA as the most effective organization working toward black liberation and one that could also promote gender equality. The party gave women leadership opportunities, and many women held local and national offices in the CPUSA and its affiliate organizations, including the League of Struggle for Negro Rights (LSNR) and the International Labor Defense (ILD). Women also participated in party activities such as selling the *Daily Worker*, attending international conferences as representatives, working as soapbox orators, and even running for office on the Communist Party ticket. Moreover, women appreciated the relief efforts of the party's organizations. Both the LSNR and the ILD helped black women with housing evictions, food relief, and hunger strikes. And the ILD played a central role in defending the "Scottsboro Boys," a group of nine black teenagers accused of raping two white women in Alabama, partially by facilitating the activism of their mothers. The Communist Party thus showed itself to be much more receptive to the needs of women than the Socialist Party had been earlier in the twentieth century.[43]

By participating in the Communist Party, black women also challenged prevailing ideas of womanhood, proper behavior, and respectability. Just

as Nella Larsen and Zora Neale Hurston used their novels to undermine patriarchy and sexism, as well as critique bourgeois respectability,
black female communists such as Audley Moore, Williana Burroughs,
Grace P. Campbell, Louise Thompson Patterson, and Elizabeth Hendrickson employed confrontational strategies that undermined notions
of female respectability. Hendrickson had been one of the first black
women to join the party during the 1920s and worked as a soapbox orator alongside Hubert Harrison at the corner of 135th Street and Lenox
Avenue. Speaking in the streets allowed women such as Hendrickson
to develop politically and intellectually, master thinking quickly on their
feet, and say whatever was on their mind in whatever way they wished.
Audley Moore noted that street orators were necessary for radical politics because "none of the churches would let [us] in with our kind of
talk." Her observation suggests the extent to which black churches in
this era shied away from radical politics, which was the very reason that
many started to abandon the church in favor of communism.[44]

Grace P. Campbell was the first black woman to join the Communist
Party (known as the Workers' Party at the time she joined). Campbell
had been active in the Socialist Party during the late 1910s, and in 1920
ran on the party ticket for the New York State Assembly to represent
Harlem's Nineteenth District. At that time, Campbell was a relative
newcomer to radical politics. She had moved to Harlem in 1908 and
had a career as a social worker and community activist. During the
early 1910s, she was firmly ensconced in the black middle class, both
financially and ideologically, espousing bourgeois respectability. A number of factors contributed to her increasing radicalization throughout
the decade. Her position as a social worker and prison officer put her
in contact with some of the city's poorest and most vulnerable black
women, which made her attuned to the interconnections between racism, gender oppression, and poverty. Sexism on the part of male leaders
in the community likewise drove her to more radical political positions.
Campbell was dismissed from the board of the Committee on Urban
Conditions in 1913 because she refused to defer to its male leaders.
Over the years, Campbell developed friendships with some of Harlem's most radical male leaders, including Hubert Harrison, Richard B.
Moore, A. Philip Randolph, and Cyril Briggs. Indeed, she was a key figure in the African Blood Brotherhood from its inception, serving on the
organization's executive board.[45]

Along with Helen Holman and Elizabeth Hendrickson, Grace Campbell was one of the most gifted female street corner and soapbox orators

in Harlem. This made her an effective advocate for both the ABB and the communists. Hermina Dumont Huiswood noted decades later that Campbell "never wavered in her conviction and without proselyting . . . guided many towards political clarity." Five years after Campbell became a member of the Workers' Party, Dumont Huiswood followed suit. The two became friends and allies in the struggle to advance the causes of workers and black women. Their brand of communism differed markedly from that of their white and black male colleagues because they articulated a "triple oppression" paradigm that combined a focus on race, class, and gender. In doing so, they prefigured the black feminism of the 1970s by nearly half a century and made significant contributions to Marxist theory.[46]

Campbell and Dumont Huiswood's work with the Harlem Tenant's League exemplifies their brand of feminism and influence on the Communist Party's tactics in the community. Leaders of the organization, created in 1929, included Richard B. Moore (president), Hendrickson (vice president), Campbell (secretary), and Dumont Huiswood. The organization included many individuals active in the Communist Party who aimed to help the community survive by various means, including blocking the wrongful eviction of tenants, organizing rent strikes, and ensuring that landlords maintained healthy living conditions. Campbell and others organized hundreds of women in the community to advocate for better living conditions before and during the Great Depression. In doing so, they challenged "Marxist-Leninist notions that the shop floor constituted the key site for producing class consciousness and for initiating transformative change," according to Erik McDuffie. Black women, and not white workingmen, Campbell argued, were actually the vanguard of the inevitable communist revolution.[47]

Like her black male counterparts in the Communist Party, Campbell was a religious skeptic and freethinker. She was reared in a staunch Catholic family but became an atheist as an adult. It is likely the case that Campbell's friendships with some of the leading black freethinkers in Harlem informed this transition. She was also close with white female communists and freethinkers such as Elizabeth Gurley Flynn, who was known as one of New York City's most radical women for her espousal of freethought and socialism. Working closely and socializing with these individuals on an almost daily basis undoubtedly informed Campbell's skeptical views. But Campbell likely had a radicalizing effect on the religious and political views of those around her. Her acceptance of freethought demonstrates her digression from the politics and respectability of groups such as Garveyite and church women of the time and places her squarely within the orthodox communist position on religion.[48]

Grace Campbell has not received her due in history as one of the key political organizers in both the ABB and the Workers' Party, but she was recognized as such during her time. Indeed, the Bureau of Investigation surveilled her for years, which is one of the main reasons we know about her activities, as she left behind no writings. Speaking of her work for the ABB, a 1923 report by the bureau described Campbell as "one of the prime movers in the organization." Meetings of the Supreme Council often took place in her home at 206 West 133rd Street. She handled much of the ABB's correspondence, and meetings never took place when she was ill or otherwise unable to make it, although they were still held in the absence of the ABB founder Cyril Briggs. Winston James notes that "although she often spoke in public, her forte was organizing. Making sure halls were booked, dues collected, comrades delegated to particular tasks."[49]

Like Campbell, Louise Thompson Patterson also challenged middle-class respectability through her participation in the Communist Party and her religious skepticism. Patterson, born Louise Thompson in 1901, grew up on the West Coast in mostly white towns such as Walla Walla, Washington, and Bend, Oregon. She had little exposure to black churches, and while in Bend she attempted to enter a Sunday School class in the local church "but they would not admit me into their 'house of God.'" Her mother was not traditionally religious, Patterson recalled. "I never knew her to read the Bible, but she followed many of its precepts." After graduating from the University of California at Berkeley in 1923, Thompson could not find a teaching job in the Bay Area and thus took a position at the Agricultural, Mechanical and Normal School in Pine Bluff, Arkansas. Her lack of religiosity soon got her into trouble in this small southern community. The first Sunday she was there, Thompson ate breakfast and then began to head back to her room. "When I entered the hall, I looked up and saw all the women teachers dressed in their Sunday finery ready to go to church." The women naturally asked her if she would be joining them. "'No,' I replied. And you know they didn't like that and said so. 'I can't help that,' I responded, 'I don't have to go to church. I didn't sign a contract to go to church.'" The principal Mr. Malone soon heard of this incident and responded by making her superintendent of the Sunday school. This only angered Thompson even further because she "didn't understand what I might learn about black culture and history by attending church." Even if she could be made to understand, her attitude toward religion was nevertheless a functional one, and she made it clear she saw little value in church services. This viewpoint reappeared later when her good friend Langston Hughes sent her a postcard from Mexico and wrote, "I tried hard to find a card that didn't have a church on it." Instead, he sent her one with palm trees.[50]

After a brief stint at Hampton Institute, Thompson moved to New York City and quickly became involved with the Communist Party. In the summer of 1927, she first met William Patterson, who introduced her to many of the tenets of Marxism (and whom she would marry in 1940). Thompson had leftist leanings before her first pilgrimage to the Soviet Union in June 1932, after which she returned to the United States as a committed revolutionary. Traveling to the Soviet Union helped Thompson and other black female Communists "come to think critically about gender, race, and class in a global context," according to Erik McDuffie. More specifically, Thompson observed the greater freedom that women had in that country, including the ability to get abortions and to do work that would be considered the domain of men in the United States. She also witnessed an acceptance of African Americans to an extent that was unheard of at home. This trip and subsequent ones fostered her commitment to leftist politics, which went hand in hand with her religious skepticism.[51]

Thompson, Campbell, and other black women communists were comfortable with what Christine Stansell labels "sexual modernism." Advocates of sexual modernism redefined sexual roles and rejected Victorian sensibilities by championing birth control, rejecting domesticity, and supporting women's economic independence. Campbell was close to the bisexual Jamaican writer Claude McKay and had ties with white radicals and bohemians throughout New York City. Thompson was briefly married to Wallace Thurman, a homosexual who edited the journal *Fire* and authored the novel *The Blacker the Berry*, among other works. They wed in 1928, but the marriage ended quickly, not necessarily because Thurman was a homosexual but rather because "he would never admit that he was a homosexual," and he also engaged in multiple drunken escapades. Thompson's and Campbell's openness to alternative lifestyles marked a sharp departure from the worldview and ideologies of black clubwomen or those active in church circles.[52]

Soon after returning from the Soviet Union, Thompson became the head of the ILD as it was working to free the Scottsboro Boys. In this role, she worked with fellow black communist freethinker Richard B. Moore to galvanize public opinion about the case. While the NAACP preferred to employ strictly legal methods of defense, the ILD and the Communist Party believed that political tactics such as mass organization and community pressure were critical to the defense. Thompson helped raise funds for the defense and get publicity for the case. She organized the "Free the Scottsboro Boys March" to Washington, D.C., on May 8, 1933. This event drew five thousand people and received national media attention, as it was the first significant march for racial equality and presaged future efforts, including one by fellow freethinker A. Phillip Randolph in the 1940s. After her work on the Scottsboro Boys case, Thompson became assistant director for the National Committee for the Defense of Political Prisoners as well as the secretary for the International Workers Order, a fraternal association that served as a social and cultural outlet for blacks in the CPUSA.[53]

A number of individuals tried to discourage Thompson from this active involvement with the Communist Party. Thompson noted that "practically everybody I knew—Walter White, Mary McLeod Bethune, W. E. B. Du Bois . . . has asked me not to work closely with the Communist party." They feared she was throwing away her life, but Thompson simply could not stomach the values and approaches of traditional civil rights organizations. While working for the National Urban League in New York, for example, her main task had been to write reports about urban poverty. This was a necessary start, but for Thompson, it did not go nearly far enough, and only the communists were taking direct action to address racial, gender, and class inequality. The fact that the party members were unlikely to push religion on her was likely a bonus.[54]

W. E. B. Du Bois

While he had counseled Louise Thompson to avoid openly affiliating with the Communist Party in the early 1930s, W. E. B. Du Bois would emerge the following decade as a leading black communist and freethinker in his own right. During the first two decades of his life, Du Bois had more or less adhered to the traditional Calvinist beliefs of the First Congregational Church he had attended in Great Barrington, Massachusetts. This rigorous Calvinism posited the sinful nature of man, literal interpretation of Scripture, salvation through faith in Christ alone, and hell for all unredeemed sinners. For young Willie, as he was known until his Harvard days, church was an opportunity to show off his knowledge of Greek and expound on the scriptures during Sunday school. Even though he would abandon many of the theological beliefs of Calvinism, his ethical beliefs would remain informed by his religious upbringing throughout his life. In 1885, Du Bois moved to Nashville, Tennessee, to attend Fisk University, where he first began to seriously question the existence of God, the central tenets of Christianity, and the role of the church in black political and cultural life.[55]

Du Bois joined the Congregational church at Fisk during his first year and even taught Sunday school but stopped doing so after he was disciplined for planning a dance and because of disgust with a book that all students were required to read. With regard to the dance, Du Bois was brought up on charges by an older student named Pop Miller and was astonished because he had grown up in a very religious environment but had nevertheless danced all his life. Du Bois notes that in this dispute with Miller, "the teachers intervened and tried to reconcile matters in a way which for years made me resentful and led to my eventual refusal to join a religious organization." Given that Du Bois did not drink, steal, lie, or engage in premarital sex, he came to see these strictures on dancing as excessive and a waste of the church's time. Additionally, Du Bois posited that at Fisk "a very definite attempt was made to see that we did not lose or question our Christian orthodoxy" by making all students read George Frederick Wright's *The Logic of Christian Evidences*. Wright was a geologist, an amateur historian, and, at the time Du Bois was at Fisk, a professor of New Testament language and literature at Oberlin Theological Seminary. While the administrators at Fisk certainly hoped Wright's text would bolster students' religious beliefs, for Du Bois it had the opposite effect. He claimed that the book "affronted my logic" and "was to my mind, then and since, a cheap piece of special pleading." These two situations set Du Bois on "an intellectual journey that would end, after a very short time, in serene agnosticism," according to David Levering Lewis.[56]

It was after Fisk that Du Bois finally abandoned his faith in God and replaced it with a faith in himself and in the black race that bordered on the religious. He received his Bachelor of Arts degree in philosophy from Harvard University in 1890 and two years later set sail for Germany, where he was to study abroad as part of the work for his Harvard doctorate. He later wrote that "in Germany I became a freethinker," and after his return in 1894, he took a position at Wilberforce University, a Methodist school, where he refused to lead students in prayer and to attend the annual revivals of religion. Du Bois related that "it took a great deal of explaining to the board of bishops why a professor at Wilberforce should not be able at all times and sundry to address God in extemporaneous prayer." The only thing that saved him from getting fired, in his view, was his tireless work ethic. Referring to his later work ethic on behalf of the race, Du Bois noted, "therein lay whatever salvation I have achieved." So, by the age of thirty, Du Bois was already an agnostic and a humanist. His authority to lead the race, in his view, came from his education and his work ethic, and this work would become the defining feature of his life. While he did not have faith in God to solve African Americans' problems on earth, he did have faith in science honed during nearly a decade of higher education.[57]

Du Bois began to put this faith in science into practice during his next position, a visiting instructorship at the University of Pennsylvania. Whereas his doctorate from Harvard had been in history, while studying in Germany he developed a lifelong love of and devotion to sociology. British sociologists such as Herbert Spencer had spent much of their careers in system building and constructing ideal theories, but Du Bois's professors at the University of Berlin attempted to modernize social science by making it useful and practical, attempts that would have profound implications for the course of his future work. By the time he moved to Philadelphia in 1896, he noted that his "vision was becoming clearer. The Negro problem was in my mind a matter of systematic investigation and intelligent understanding. The world was thinking wrong about race, because it did not know. The ultimate evil was stupidity. The cure for it was knowledge based on scientific investigation." He spent the next year interviewing five thousand black people in Philadelphia for what would become *The Philadelphia Negro*, his first major attempt at applying logic and science to the race problem. While his position at the University of Pennsylvania was a temporary one, his work there laid the foundation for the numerous sociological studies he would conduct as a faculty member at Atlanta University for nearly fifteen years.[58]

Du Bois left Atlanta University in 1910 to work for the NAACP and immediately hatched the idea for the *Crisis* magazine, a periodical that would soon become his "agnostic pulpit," according to Brian L. Johnson. Du Bois conceived of the publication as one that would report on news around the world relevant to blacks, review important works of literature, publish articles related to race relations, and advocate for democratic rights for blacks. The magazine was in part an expression of Du Bois's notion of the "Talented Tenth," an idea that posited that a small, educated group of black leaders bore the responsibility for improving the plight of all blacks in the country. His conception of the Talented Tenth was a secular one that argued that morality, culture, refinement, and education were prerequisites for this leadership class. With a few exceptions, including figures such as Alexander Crummell, Du Bois thought these qualities were lacking from the black church and most of its ministers. He would thus use the magazine "for disseminating a newfangled version of reform for the African American community that would not be grounded in unknowable dogma but in knowable scientific study," akin to what he had undertaken in Philadelphia and Atlanta for the previous fifteen years.[59]

Just two years after launching the *Crisis*, Du Bois published what was probably the harshest criticism of the black church by an African American leader during the early twentieth century. His 1912 article "The Negro Church" admitted that the institution had some utility in teaching morals, promoting stable family life, and developing business acumen within the black community. But for Du Bois, black churches in the country were lacking in significant ways. First, there were too few good and learned men leading the church. "The paths and the higher places are choked with pretentious, ill-trained men," he claimed. "And in far too many cases with men dishonest and otherwise immoral. Such men make the walk of upright and business like candidates for power extremely difficult. They put an undue premium upon finesse and personal influence." His criticism here echoed that of another early black humanist, Frederick Douglass, who, we have seen, registered his dismay at black ministers' lack of education as early as the 1850s. Nearly thirty years after he had been disciplined for dancing at Fisk, Du Bois was disheartened to see that black churches were "still inveighing against dancing and theatergoing, still blaming educated people for objecting to silly and empty sermons, boasting and noise." Perhaps most problematic of all was the constant building of new and elaborate churches when black people all over the country were still without homes and schools. Unlike late-twentieth-century black humanists, Du Bois did not suggest doing away with churches altogether (even if he desired that) because that sentiment would not have gotten him far with the mass of African Americans. Instead, he called for reform of the black church along liberal lines. To fix its current predicament,

Du Bois asserted, the black church should elect honest and upright leaders, weed out the ministry, have positive educational and social uplift programs, and exert every effort to make the institution a place where black men and women can work together for the good of the race "regardless of their belief or disbelief in unimportant dogmas and ancient and outworn creeds."[60]

Du Bois did not reserve his animus for black churches alone, as he also used the *Crisis* to inveigh against American Christianity more broadly. One year after his editorial on the black church, he published "The Church and the Negro," wherein he noted that from the colonial era, Christian churches "aided and abetted the Negro slave trade; the church was the bulwark of American slavery; and the church today is the strongest seat of racial and color prejudice." Frederick Douglass had made a similar point (using similar language) in his famous speech "What to the Slave Is the Fourth of July?" wherein he argued that "the church of this country is not only indifferent to the wrongs of the slave, it actually takes side with the oppressors. It had made itself the bulwark of American slavery, and the shield of American slavehunters." According to Du Bois, if 100 of the most morally pure and upright African American citizens in the country attempted to join a white church, 999 out of every 1,000 ministers would do all they could to keep blacks out, including lying, and they would defend such lies as in line with Christ's teachings.[61]

Du Bois developed these arguments further in a 1929 *Crisis* essay entitled "The Color Line and the Church," which he began by contending that "the American Church of Christ is Jim Crowed from top to bottom. No other institution in America is built as thoroughly or more absolutely on the color line." The central crisis faced by American Christians was whether or not churches wanted to continue to proclaim their divine origin and foundation in supernatural power or "whether the church must acknowledge itself to be a human organization largely composed of the rich and respectable, desirous of better things and groping for social uplift but restrained by inherited prejudice, economic privilege, and social fear." In Du Bois's view, it was clear that the church was choosing the latter alternative, and this choice marked it "as a deliberate hypocrite and systematic liar." Christians might claim to "love thy neighbor" as themselves, he wrote, but their treatment of blacks belied this principle. Additionally, Du Bois argued, the church had opposed every great social reform movement in American history, including the rise of democracy, the labor movement, abolitionism, women's rights, and the spread of science. Given this situation, Du Bois implied, the nation would likely be much better off without religious dogma and religious institutions.[62]

In addition to his own critiques of religion in the pages of the *Crisis*, Du Bois used the magazine to offer space for the writings of other freethinkers. Franz Boas, for example, mentor to the black freethinker Zora Neale Hurston, was one contributor to the magazine, as was his colleague at Columbia University John Dewey. Dewey's presence in the pages of the *Crisis* was notable because he was one of the leading humanist thinkers of his day and one who "completely discards all supernatural forces and entities and regards mind as an instrument of survival and adaptation developed in the long process of evolution," according to Corliss Lamont. Livingston Farrand, the irreligious anthropologist at Columbia University, also contributed to the magazine, as did Clarence Darrow, the famous lawyer from the 1926 Scopes trial. Darrow's 1931 article for the *Crisis* actually drew the ire of black newspapers around the country because they were angry at both his and Du Bois's critique of the church and its ministers.[63]

In more than twenty years of editing the *Crisis*, W. E. B. Du Bois clearly demonstrated his humanist bona fides. He used the magazine to articulate some of the harshest critiques by a black leader of both African American and American Christianity, arguing that the former was too focused on the superficial and the latter was inexorably racist. He embraced Darwinian evolution and invited some of its main proponents to write for the magazine. Additionally, he promoted the literary and artistic work of a new generation of black freethinkers, including individuals such as Langston Hughes and Zora Neale Hurston. Du Bois resigned his post in 1933 to return to Atlanta University, a move that represented a significant transition for both his career and his personal intellectual development.

Du Bois's embrace of freethought early in his career almost certainly informed his growing acceptance of communism from the 1930s to the end of his life. He was first exposed to socialism while a student in Germany and even attended meetings of the Socialist Democratic Party, although his status as a student prevented him from engaging in any organizing activities among workers. Before Woodrow Wilson's election in 1912, he had briefly joined the Socialist Party but abandoned it for the Democrats, as he believed Wilson's progressive agenda would be beneficial to African Americans. For the next two decades, Du Bois would be ambivalent toward socialists and communists. He supported the U.S.

entry into World War I in 1917, for example, because he believed that it might inaugurate a socialist revolution that would undermine the twin influences of capitalism and racism in the world. But in a 1921 *Crisis* editorial, he rejected the Bolshevik revolution because he thought change would best occur not through revolution but through reason, proper education, and human sympathy. Four years later, he started to change his tune a bit, supporting the socialist A. Phillip Randolph and the Brotherhood of Sleeping Car Porters in their fight against the Pullman Railroad Corporation while keeping an open mind toward Soviet economic proposals. But when the communists emerged as the chief activists in the fight to save the Scottsboro Boys from the death penalty in the early 1930s, Du Bois was troubled and argued that the NAACP alone would be better suited to the task. His growing acceptance of Marxism as an ideology remained colored by the continual racism of the white working class and unions, as there were 2.5 million blacks employed in nonagricultural work in 1928, yet only 66,000 were allowed in white unions such as the AFL.[64]

Just as it did for Louise Thompson, traveling to the Soviet Union for a second time in the mid-1930s helped solidify Du Bois's growing belief in communism as the solution to racism in the United States. He had first gone to Russia in 1926 and observed that at that time the nation "was handicapped by 90 percent illiteracy among her peasants, and nearly as much among her working classes; by a religion led by a largely immoral priesthood, dealing in superstition and deception, and rich with the loot of groveling followers." When he returned a decade later, and nearly twenty years after the onset of the Russian Revolution, things had changed drastically. "This was no longer a people struggling for survival," he recalled. "It was a nation sure of itself. . . . The golden domes of churches were not so numerous and tall office buildings were taking their place. Few priests were visible, and few beggars." This latter statement indicates that for Du Bois, economic progress was intimately tied to the place of religion within any society. The extent of religious popularity and religious influence in any state, he implied, would mark the economic prosperity of that nation. The Soviet Union was now prosperous in large part because it was no longer as religious, and this prosperity marked it as a useful model for what the United States could become should Americans accept Marxism.[65]

Like Cyril Briggs, Hubert Harrison, and other black humanist and Marxist thinkers, W. E. B. Du Bois came to believe that religion and capitalism had been and were still intimately tied to colonialism, imperialism, and racism around the world. In 1945, he remarked that "the first impulsive recoil of religion and humanity from this horror of the slave trade to America was, in the face of the new wealth in crops, manufacture, and commerce, quickly *rationalized* into a new defense of poverty. The rich were envisaged as the white nations of the earth, armed with a new and miraculous technique; the congenital poor were the peoples of the tropics born to be slaves and fulfill their destiny and the glory of God by working for the comfort and luxury of the whites." Historically, Du Bois argues, Christianity had been a powerful force justifying the colonization of America, the enslavement of Africans, and the rise of capitalism in the Western world. To Du Bois, religion was also key to the rise of racism during the colonial era. "New patterns of contempt for human beings," he claimed, "were based on a doctrine of the inferiority of most men, which was announced as a scientific law and spread by the education of youth and the teachings of religion." These patterns that Du Bois explored were still all too familiar in his time and were perhaps even more widespread than they had been during the eighteenth and nineteenth centuries. His solution to the colonialism and imperialism that had exploited Africans and Asians was the establishment of planned economies that would recognize that no people need live in poverty; the production of goods should not depend on private profit but on public needs; chance and privilege should not determine how goods and services are distributed; and that all people should have access to free health care and education.[66]

For Du Bois, the Soviet Union represented a model society because it had succeeded in throwing off the vestiges of the religious beliefs that had had such a detrimental effect around the world. This assertion was especially true in the area of education, as he argued that "the greatest gift of the Soviet Union to modern civilization was the dethronement of the clergy and the refusal to let religion be taught in the public schools." To the extent that people received an adequate education, he noted, they would throw off their belief in miracles and a benevolent deity who rules the world. Indeed, among the principal dangers of modern society were those individuals who "allow their children to learn fairly tales and so-called religious truth, which in time the children come to recognize as conventional lies told by their parents and teachers for the children's good. One can hardly exaggerate the moral disaster of this custom." Instead of a religious education teaching children orthodox Christian creeds, Du Bois called for both the state and the church to foster "hearty research into real ethical questions" such as "When is it right to lie? Do low wages mean stealing? Does the prosperity of a country depend upon the number of its millionaires?" These ideas that Du Bois articulated from the late 1930s to the 1950s represent both his growing disenchantment from Christianity and his increasing identification as a communist. As his biographer David Levering Lewis observes, by the late 1930s, "Du Bois's distaste for the vibrant evangelism of black religious observance was so palpable that he might well have invented the tag line about religion being the opiate of the people had not Marx supplied it." He still continued to identify as an agnostic, but it was an agnosticism with no significant differences from atheism.[67]

After the ravages of the Great Depression and the failure of the Double V campaign (victory against fascism abroad and racism at home) to bring about any marked improvement in black life, Du Bois came to believe that socialism and communism offered the best opportunity for African Americans to improve their economic and political situations. When the Depression first hit "and thousands of workers, black and white, were starving in the 30's," he recounted, "I began to awake and see in the socialism of the New Deal, emancipation for all workers, and the labor problem, which included the Negro problem." No longer was the problem of the twentieth century solely the problem of the color line, as he had proclaimed in *The Souls of Black Folk* in 1903. It was now also the problem of class, and, as he would argue in 1958, African Americans must recognize that "no system of reform offers such real emancipation as socialism. The capitalism which so long ruled Europe and North America was founded on Negro slavery in America, and that slavery will never completely disappear so long as private capitalism continues to survive."[68]

Du Bois recognized that there would be challenges to spreading socialism among the black population from established civil rights groups and from black churches. After forced retirement from Atlanta University in 1943, Du Bois returned to the NAACP, which he hoped might be an effective vehicle for advancing his political agenda, but he was disappointed. With some people charging the organization with being a communist front and the Cold War in its earliest stages, Walter White and Roy Wilkins exercised increased vigilance over the organization and would not let it be dragged into support of communism. In the late 1940s and early 1950s, Du Bois's opposition to the Marshall Plan, the North Atlantic Treaty Organization, and the Korean War "as instruments of capitalist imperialism were heresies" that most contemporary black leaders could not get behind. Moreover, Du Bois hoped that American blacks would be at the forefront of spreading worldwide socialism because of their greater educational opportunities, but he remarked with dismay that "'philanthropy,' disguised in bribes, and 'religion' cloaked in hypocrisy, strangled Negro education and stilled the voices of prophets. The yellow, brown, and black thinkers of Asia had forged ahead." As both Du Bois and his fellow African American humanist thinkers had stated many times before, religious dogma and religious institutions remained the primary obstacles to extending democracy to the economic realm.[69]

The thinkers and radical political activists mentioned throughout this chapter represent one of the most significant trends in African American religious and intellectual life during the early to mid-twentieth century. Hubert Harrison, A. Philip Randolph, Harry Haywood, Richard Wright, Grace P. Campbell, Louise Thompson Patterson, and W. E. B. Du Bois all tied strident critiques of capitalism with denunciations of religion. In their view, Christianity and capitalism went hand in hand to advance European and American imperialism and colonialism, which itself was an important foundation for racism at home. The fact that these freethinkers embraced Marxist ideology was no mere accident. It was probably their religious skepticism that made them predisposed to accept a worldview whereby historical change is primarily the result of economic relationships rather than the will of God. Some of them abandoned active participation in the Socialist and Communist parties, including Randolph and Wright, yet they nevertheless remained religious skeptics and remained committed to improving black economic life through labor organizing and other forms of political protest. Their activities, along with those of black Marxist freethinkers such as Langston Hughes and Richard B. Moore, laid the important groundwork for the long civil rights movement beginning in the 1920s. And even though adherence to Marxism among blacks declined precipitously during the Cold War era, during the mid-1960s, a new generation of thinkers would draw from their example to offer their own critical perspectives on religion and capitalism.

Civil Rights and Black Power

During the mid-1950s, future civil rights leader Stokely Carmichael began traveling with his father from their Italian neighborhood in the Bronx down to 145th Street in Harlem to get his hair cut by a black barber—an experience that initiated his political education. "There came into the shop old Garveyites," he recalled, "race men, street players, black Republicans *and* Black Muslims, nationalists of all descriptions, and the rappers, poets, and wordmen." While he never heard any discussion of the *Brown v. Board of Education* decision or the Emmett Till case at his Bronx junior high school during these years, the men at the barbershop discussed these issues at length. Later, while enrolled at the Bronx High School of Science, Stokely went to Harlem to visit his cousin Inez and encountered Richard B. Moore, among other Harlem street speakers. Moore, an atheist, communist, and one of the founders of the African Blood Brotherhood during the 1920s, was now a Pan-Africanist who remained active in Harlem's political scene. He and speakers including Queen Mother Audley Moore and Malcolm X became important influences on Stokely Carmichael, who became a freethinker and committed Pan-Africanist over the next decade. Carmichael noted that Harlem stepladder orators such as Richard B. Moore were "our secular prophets, they were keepers of the flame, holding aloft our heritage as African people in exile . . . ceaselessly exhorting us to keep historical and revolutionary faith with our ancestors' long history of struggle and resistance." Moore's influence on Stokely Carmichael demonstrates important continuities between freethought during the interwar period and the civil rights era. Activists such as Moore, Louise Thompson Patterson, W. E. B. Du Bois, and others mentored a new generation of radical political thinkers and religious skeptics. While this new generation did not always subscribe to the communist beliefs of their predecessors, many did adopt their combination of religious skepticism and radical politics.[1]

119

Black freethought also underwent significant changes during the 1960s and 1970s. For one, open discussion of religious skepticism became less taboo. While earlier black freethinkers sometimes waited decades to reveal their doubts about Christianity, those in the civil rights era were often open about their atheism and agnosticism during that same period. With increased access to education, the sheer numbers of black freethinkers also began to rise. Black secularists could be found in nearly every major political group and cultural movement, from the Student Non-Violent Coordinating Committee (SNCC) to the black arts movement to the Black Panther Party for Self-Defense. Many of the most prominent black political and cultural figures from this era were freethinkers, including Carmichael, James Forman, James Baldwin, Huey Newton, and Lorraine Hansberry. They often denounced Christianity in harsher terms than their predecessors had done and continued to chip away at the ties between religion, racism, and patriarchy in the United States. Their work both drew from that of their predecessors and inspired a new generation of freethinkers who would help institutionalize the movement and create organizations dedicated specifically to advancing the cause of black freethought.

The Long Civil Rights Movement

The civil rights and black power movements of the 1950s and 1960s had their roots in developments stretching back to the early twentieth century, some of which have been explored in chapters 2 and 3. Indeed, some scholars argue that there was no radical break in black political activity and that rather than looking at the 1960s as the civil rights era, we should see the fifty years from 1920 to 1970 as one continual civil rights movement. One organization that has come to be most associated with civil rights is the National Association for the Advancement of Colored People (NAACP), which was organized in 1910 but did not start to make serious inroads into the system of Jim Crow until the 1920s. It did so at that point by helping black activists develop organizational and leadership capabilities and slowly chipping away at the myth that black people were content with second-class citizenship and segregation. While there were some cracks in segregation during the 1930s, due in part to agitation from labor unions, other minorities, and liberals fighting New Deal opponents of this practice, the condition of most black people in the country changed little during the decade. However, the 1940s and the onset of World War II stimulated a new sense of militancy among African Americans. Membership in the NAACP increased tenfold during the war, and the Congress of Racial Equality (GORE) was founded to employ nonviolent direct action in order to challenge Jim Crow. At the beginning of the decade, in 1941, A. Philip Randolph organized a March-On-Washington Committee that threatened a massive march on the Capitol. In response, President Franklin D. Roosevelt issued Executive Order 8802, which set up the President's Committee on Fair Employment Practices and outlawed racially discriminatory practices in hiring by labor unions and companies with government contracts. The rise of Nazism and the decline of imperialism during this period also led to a decline in the respectability of racism, as did the publication of works such as Gunnar Myrdal's *An American Dilemma*. Additionally, independence movements in Africa immediately following the war showed African Americans that change was possible and that global white supremacy, including its local variant, was vulnerable.[2]

All of these trends culminated in the *Brown v. Board of Education* ruling by the U.S. Supreme Court in 1954 that outlawed segregation in public schools throughout the nation. What was initially a sense of optimism and hope turned to anger and despair when whites fought the ruling tooth and nail, subjecting young black children to racist violence when they tried to enter what had been all-white schools. This backlash and the lack of results from the ruling convinced many African Americans that they had to take more drastic action and could not rely on the courts or white politicians. Among these drastic actions was the Montgomery bus boycott, which began after Rosa Parks, an NAACP member, refused to give up her seat on a segregated bus line. E. D. Nixon, president of the Alabama NAACP, had long wished for some type of mass demonstration, so he quickly bailed out Parks after her arrest and set in motion plans for the boycott. Nixon soon contacted Jo Ann Robinson, president of the Women's Political Council in Montgomery, and the two quickly decided that Parks would make the perfect symbol for the boycott. Blacks in the city stopped riding the buses on Monday, December 5, 1955 and the boycott lasted for 381 days. On June 4, 1956, a federal court ruled that the segregation of bus lines was unconstitutional, a decision that the U.S. Supreme Court upheld in its *Browder v. Gayle* decision later that year. Their victory convinced African Americans that direct action and local activism could be effective tools in getting the federal government's assistance in the movement.[3]

The Montgomery bus boycott helped produce a new national leader of the civil rights movement and provided a new strategy for bringing about racial equality. Martin Luther King Jr. had just accepted an offer to become pastor of Dexter Avenue Baptist Church in Montgomery in October 1954. King became president of the Montgomery Improvement Association, which led the boycott, and his philosophy of nonviolence came to dominate one important wing of the civil rights movement. Shortly after the boycott's end, King and others formed the Southern Christian Leadership Conference (SCLC) to capitalize on the momentum gained in Montgomery and coordinate civil rights activity across the nation. While the goal of SCLC was to mobilize large protests across the nation, it did very little of that from its founding in 1957 until 1960. That year, King moved from Dexter Avenue Baptist Church to become copastor of his father's Ebenezer Baptist Church in Atlanta, a move that allowed him to devote more time to working with the SCLC.[4]

SNCC and the Move toward Secular Humanism

Along with CORE, the SCLC, and the NAACP, the Student Non-Violent Coordinating Committee emerged as a top civil rights organization during the early 1960s. SNCC grew out of the sit-in movement that began at the Woolworth lunch counter in Greensboro, North Carolina, in February 1960. The sit-ins increased rapidly, expanding across the state and along the Eastern Seaboard. By mid-April 1960, an estimated fifty thousand people had participated in sit-ins, with the vast majority of them being students. In contrast to black churches in the South, more than 90 percent of students at Greensboro area colleges supported sit-ins; this level of enthusiasm was replicated on many other campuses. Initially, many of these students were anticommunists and desired to assimilate into American society rather than completely upend it. As Clayborne Carson points out, "most student protesters aspired to middle class status and did not basically object to American society or its dominant political institutions." These students, as well as more-established civil rights leaders such as Ella Baker, desired to capitalize on the wave of protests by forming a new organization comprised primarily of young people. The founding conference of SNCC was thus held in April 1960 on the campus of Shaw University in Raleigh, North Carolina.[5]

Baker, the executive director of the SCLC, quickly emerged as the driving force behind the effort to form this new organization. Baker had spent her whole adult life trying to bring about radical change in the American political system. From 1930 to 1980, she involved herself in numerous causes ranging from Puerto Rican independence to apartheid in South Africa to prison conditions and poverty. But her most important cause always remained the black freedom struggle. Her biographer Barbara Ransby notes that she was a radical humanist who understood the need for structural changes in the legal system and political institutions but that this process "had to involve oppressed people, ordinary people, infusing new meanings into the concept of democracy and finding their own individual and collective power to determine their lives and shape the course of history." She played significant roles in the NAACP and the SCLC, where she had worked for three years prior to the formation of SNCC. Ransby points out that in all of her work, "Baker criticized unchecked egos, objected to undemocratic structures, protested unilateral decision making, condemned elitism, and refused to nod in loyal deference to everything 'the leader' had to say." These ideas would be foundational in the origins of SNCC and similarly influenced the Students for a Democratic Society and the women's movement of the 1960s and 1970s.[6]

Baker had three primary goals in helping to organize the Southwide Student Leadership Conference on Nonviolent Resistance to Segregation: to ensure that the momentum gained during the sit-in movement of the past few months did not die down; to assist the students and other protestors with gaining access to important skills and resources; and to provide an opportunity for the students to coalesce into the type of militant but democratic organization necessary to bring about lasting political change. One question that emerged during the event was whether a new organization should focus solely on desegregation or adopt a broader political agenda. Baker endorsed the latter option, believing that a myopic focus on desegregation was one of the central problems of the other major civil rights organizations. She was also adamant from the start that the students themselves should decide what direction to take rather than take their cues from more-established leaders such as Martin Luther King Jr., who was present at the conference. Ransby states that early on, the political ideology of the students was no more radical than that of King and the SCLC, but "Baker saw enormous promise in their courageous actions, their creativity, and their openness to new forms of struggle, and she wanted to give them the space and freedom for that potential to develop."[7]

SNCC's early character was a religious one driven by one of its most influential leaders, James Lawson. Lawson was a northerner who had been attending the Vanderbilt School of Theology before being expelled for taking part in the Nashville sit-ins. Of all the participants at the conference, Lawson was perhaps most familiar with the philosophy of nonviolent direct action. During the 1950s, he had been imprisoned for refusing to fight in the Korean War. Upon his release, he traveled to India and did missionary work for three years. While there, he had the chance to closely study Gandhian nonviolence; after his return to the United States, he held workshops for activists in Nashville. While many students at the Raleigh conference wanted to emphasize the action the new organization would take, Lawson insisted on first defining its philosophy. He successfully pushed for the adoption of a statement of purpose that articulated the religious foundations of nonviolent resistance. "We affirm the philosophical or religious ideal of nonviolence," it reads in part, "as the foundation of our purpose, the presupposition of our faith, and the manner of our action. Nonviolence as it grows from the Judaic-Christian tradition seeks a social order of justice permeated by love." For Lawson, love was the central idea of nonviolence and had the power to overcome hate and evil.[8]

While SNCC was initially dedicated to Christian principles and nonviolence, tensions existed early on between religious and secular activists. Even after the 1960 Raleigh conference, many people began to move away from Lawson and John Lewis's religious radicalism. In 1961, tensions would rise even higher as the members debated whether to focus on nonviolent direct action or engage in activities such as voter registration drives. Those who advocated the former approach opposed any move that would take the focus off desegregation. Indeed, many believed that the new calls for voter registration were a tool the Kennedy administration was using to redirect SNCC's militancy toward other goals. By the summer of 1961, however, the transition toward a more secular approach to politics was under way, largely due to the influence of Bob Moses. Moses had attended Hamilton College in New York, where he encountered the work of the French existentialist philosopher Albert Camus, whose humanism and individualism he found appealing. Moses began working for SNCC in the summer of 1960, and the following year he opened a voter registration school in McComb, Mississippi. By the time he did so, many of the original students who founded the organization were no longer involved, and SNCC was being run by staff members. Clayborne Carson points out that these staff members "saw their methods of achieving social change as differing dramatically from those of any other reform organization. While retaining some of the liberal and Christian beliefs, they had broken away from conventional liberalism and institutional religion by asserting an unwillingness to compromise their ideals."[9]

This break from institutional religion became pronounced in the life and career of James Forman. Forman was involved in SNCC from its inception and played a key role in its growth as a national civil rights organization, eventually becoming its executive secretary and "master propagandist," according to fellow activist Julian Bond. Forman, along with Ella Baker, helped SNCC solve its first internal crisis over whether to pursue voter registration or nonviolent direct action. In the coming years, he would prove even more crucial to the organization. He handled essential day-to-day tasks of running the national headquarters in Atlanta, including answering the phone and cleaning the toilets. He was also one of the primary fund-raisers for SNCC and directed the full-time staff. His hard work and dedication were essential to SNCC's early successes.[10]

Forman, whose political ideology was not grounded in Christian theology, as Lawson's was, but rather in secular humanism, began to move away from religion as a young man. He had started attending Catholic school in 1935 and was up for a prize for being the smartest kid in class the following year. Forman was tied with one other boy and lost because the other child was taking classes to become a Catholic, an injustice that sparked his animus toward religion. In class, a nun named Sister Clevidge also used him as an example of one who would go to purgatory and not heaven because he was not Catholic, something he later recounted caused him "great emotional turmoil." He soon transferred to public school, but his problems with religion did not end. During the summers, he stayed with his grandmother in Mississippi and had to attend her church, the Concord Baptist Church. When he was twelve, he attended a revival there, and—in an episode echoing the earlier experience of Langston Hughes (described in chapter 2)—Forman was seated on the mourner's bench, where some of his friends yelled out that they had gotten religion. "The older people shouted that they had got religion too," Forman recalled. "At the age of twelve, in a Baptist tradition and setting, I did not have the courage to tell my grandmother that I thought this was all nonsense. I simply observed what had been happening around me and knew that I, too, could fabricate some tears in this emotionally charged atmosphere. So I covered my face with my handkerchief and cried, 'Lord, have mercy!' It worked. I was taken off the mourner's bench and the people talked of how many children got saved that day by the grace of the Lord."[11]

His development toward atheism and secular humanism continued in college. In 1947, Forman entered Wilson Junior College in Chicago and started to develop serious questions about God. "How could he exist? What type of God was he that would allow all the injustices in the world? World wars? Killing? Prejudices? Define him. Hell was here on earth, man, for black people."[12] He would end up dropping out of school and serving in the army before a second stint in college, this time at Roosevelt College in Chicago, completed his journey toward atheism and secular humanism. While enrolled in a philosophy course there, he noted, "God finally died in my conscious mind. For the final examination, we had to write an essay discussing the most important thing we had learned from the course. This is the essence of what I wrote: The most important things that I have learned from this class are a number of intellectual arguments which disprove the myth that there is a God."[13]

For Forman, atheism was an essential component of his political activity, as he thought that belief in God was a major factor keeping blacks in a subordinate position in the United States. "When a people who are poor," he argued, "suffering with disease and sickness, accept the fact that God has ordained for them to be this way—then they will never do anything about their human condition. In other words, the belief in a supreme being or God weakens the will of a people to change conditions themselves. As a Negro who has grown up in the United States, I believe that the belief in God has hurt my people. We have put off doing something about our condition on this earth because we have believed that God was going to take care of business in heaven."[14] Since he no longer believed God would help people on earth, he took it as his responsibility to do his part to advance the condition of black people. His position is a significant one because unlike many black freethinkers who preceded him, Forman was actively opposed to Christianity and did not see many benefits of the faith. This trend began during the civil rights era and would accelerate among black secular thinkers in the decades to come.

Forman's political engagement began while he was still in college and intensified after he completed school. As the student body president at

Roosevelt, he was partially responsible for inviting speakers to campus. His choices were generally those who would speak about civil rights issues such as the Montgomery bus boycott. He later attended graduate school at Boston University, where he began to develop a more sophisticated political theory. He embraced nonviolence, about which he originally had doubts before reading the speeches and writings of Kwame Nkrumah, who employed nonviolent direct action against the British in the movement for Ghanian independence. And he began to develop the theory of leadership that would guide his political life, a theory that was similar to that of Ella Baker. He posited that black people needed committed activists to build organizations that would outlast their founders. "We did not need charismatic leadership," he argued, "for this most often led to a disintegration once the charismatic leader was gone. My goal was to build structures that would perpetuate revolutionary ideas and programs, not personalities."[15]

During his political career, Forman was intensely hostile to Christianity and eventually called for both Christian churches and Jewish synagogues to pay reparations to black people. In a speech delivered at the National Black Theatre in July 1969, Forman claimed that the dogma and practice of white Christian churches had been "one of the most consistent and effective control mechanisms operating upon us." He recounted the history of religious support for slavery during the nineteenth century and argued that Christianity was still complicit in promoting American tyranny over black people in the twentieth century. While his animus was nominally aimed at white churches, Forman criticized black religious adherence as well. He recalled remarks his mother made to him years ago that whites would get their just due in the afterlife and that even though blacks would be miserable on earth for sixty or seventy years, they would be rewarded in heaven. "As long as this kind of psychology and ideology is spread by the Christian churches, people will not go on to struggle for liberation." His goal, then, was to partially cripple religious institutions by forcing them to pay $500 million in reparations. He first called for this sum in "The Black Manifesto," which he presented to the National Black Economic Development Conference in April 1969. The number was later revised to $3 billion "because of the control the churches have on the southern 'Negro' colleges." Forman demanded more money from churches to transform historically black colleges and universities into "truly black universities."[16]

Forman's call for reparations from churches and synagogues reflects his growing acceptance of socialism as a solution to problems of race and class in the United States. He believed that activists should distance themselves from those people trying to support black capitalism, as Marcus Garvey had done during the 1920s, because capitalism was intimately connected to racism at home and colonialism in Africa. As he stated in "The Black Manifesto," the fight of the Black Economic Development Conference "is against racism, capitalism, and imperialism, and we are dedicated to building a socialist society inside the United States where the total means of production and distribution are in the hands of the state." To ensure that the state would then be responsive to the needs of black people, the government must be led by "revolutionary blacks who are concerned about the total humanity of this world." In this call, Forman placed himself squarely in the decades-long tradition of black freethinkers embracing socialism and communism as an answer to racial inequality in the United States. And he likewise developed an internationalist perspective linking the fate of blacks in America to those throughout the African diaspora.[17]

Forman's socialist vision for reparations posited nine primary ways of spending the funds recouped from churches and synagogues. He wanted to create a southern land bank to help form cooperative farms and assist those people who lost housing due to participating in civil rights activities. This latter goal had been a concern for Forman since at least 1960, when he worked in Fayette County, Tennessee, organizing labor unions to send money and supplies and look into buying land for sharecroppers kicked off their farms for voting. Forman also called for the creation of four publishing houses that would be located in Detroit, Los Angeles, Atlanta, and New York City and could provide needed venues for the work of black activists, artists, and intellectuals. In a similar vein, he wanted to create four television networks specifically for black people that would be located in major markets. Other goals for the funds included a research center, a job training center, a union for welfare recipients, a National Black Labor Strike and Defense fund, and the International Black Appeal, an organization that would help fund cooperative black businesses. His final goal was for the creation of a black university, one that would be funded by money from religious institutions but would not be under their control in any way. To achieve their ends, Forman called for "the total disruption of selected church-sponsored agencies operating anywhere in the United States and the world." He hoped white Christians and Jews would peacefully acquiesce to their demands but posited that if they did not, "we declare war, and we are prepared to fight by whatever means necessary."[18]

The Black Power Movement

James Forman was one of the earliest supporters of "Black Power" as an ideology and as a movement in the United States. While SNCC started out promoting nonviolence and racial integration, it would move away from these positions around 1966, when the call for Black Power swept the nation. Unlike SNCC activists such as John Lewis, as well as leaders of the other major civil rights organizations, Forman approved of the term "Black Power." He notes that "to achieve that power, poor black people had to take power from the racist, exploitative masters of the society, who are white. Revolutionary warfare is the ultimate weapon by which this is achieved. Therefore 'Black Power' was more than a slogan to me. It was a concept pointing the way to a revolutionary ideology." Before heading to a march in Meredith, Mississippi, in 1966, Willie Ricks, a young SNCC field secretary, came to him and asked what he thought about the chant "Black Power." Forman thought it was a great idea and decided to support him. They had already been using the phrase "power for poor black people," so Forman saw no problem with shortening it. While in front of the cameras on the final day of the Meredith march, Forman positioned himself behind Ricks and joined in the chant, helping to popularize the phrase.[19]

While the public articulation of Black Power would take off during the mid-1960s, the movement had its roots in both southern rural communities and northern urban areas dating back to the end of World War II. Many of the main ideas of Black Power are reflected in the life and activism of Robert F. Williams. Williams grew up in North Carolina and served in World War II. Upon his return to Monroe, North Carolina, in 1946, he employed armed resistance to Ku Klux Klan activities. He left for nearly a decade and joined the local NAACP branch when he went back in 1955. He soon became the branch's president and worked to build it up over the next few years, primarily from the working class around Monroe and especially from former veterans, who were unlikely to subscribe to nonviolence. Timothy Tyson notes that against the backdrop of "white lawlessness and political stalemate in 1959 and early 1960, Robert Williams . . . stressed black economic advancement, black pride, black culture, independent black political action, and what he referred to as 'armed self-reliance.'" These five goals would come to characterize the Black Power movement from its inception. Williams ended up having to flee to Cuba, and while there in 1962, he published his book *Negroes with Guns*, which would heavily influence the work of Huey Newton, a key proponent of Black Power in his own right and eventual founder of the Black Panther Party.[20]

Other notable figures in the emerging Black Power movement included Malcolm X, LeRoi Jones, and Sonia Sanchez. Malcolm X and the Nation of Islam were important forerunners to Black Power, as the sect emphasized economic uplift and displayed a militant rhetoric that few other groups did. Malcolm X also anticipated some of the cultural themes of the movement in his 1962 speech entitled "Who Taught You to Hate Yourself?" Here he asks his listeners: "Who taught you to hate the texture of your hair? Who taught you to hate the color of your skin, to such extent that you bleach to get like the white man? Who taught you to hate the shape of your nose and the shape of your lip? Who taught you to hate yourself, from the top of your head to the soles of your feet? Who taught you to hate your own kind?"[21] The poet and writer LeRoi Jones (Amiri Baraka) would likewise articulate a powerful cultural message that spoke to key concerns of Black Power activists. He was drawn to radical politics after meeting Fidel Castro shortly following the Cuban Revolution in July 1960. The death of Malcolm X in 1965 helped push Jones to more-revolutionary political activity. The day after Malcolm's assassination, February 22, 1965, Jones announced plans to create the Black Arts Repertory Theater and School (BARTS). He aimed to use black art as a vehicle for political revolution, which in itself was not new but did coincide with the resurgence of black nationalism during the 1960s. The poet Sonia Sanchez joined BARTS, and her poetry would profoundly influence Black Power activists. Jones, Sanchez, and others recruited young intellectuals for their project that represents an important yet underexamined shift in black radical politics, one that helped educate and politicize poor and working-class blacks in Harlem. The varied efforts of Black Power activists "accelerated America's reckoning with its own uncomfortable, often ugly, racial past, and in the process spurred a debate over racial progress, citizenship, and democracy that would scandalize as much as it would change the nation," according to Peniel Joseph.[22]

The person who would become most associated with Black Power in the mid-1960s was Stokely Carmichael. It was he, along with Willie Ricks, who began using the phrase during a rally in Greenwood, Mississippi, on June 16, 1966. Carmichael spent his early years in Trinidad before moving to the Bronx in 1952. He enrolled in the prestigious Bronx High School of Science in 1956 and quickly became involved in leftist politics. He befriended a white student named Gene Dennis who had said on the first day of school that his summer reading included Karl Marx's *Capital*. Gene's father worked for the Communist Party, USA (CPUSA), and Gene himself was a communist. Carmichael soon began attending meetings of the Young Communist League with Gene Dennis and could be often seen at youth marches and rallies focused on topics ranging from antipoverty to education to civil rights and anti–nuclear proliferation. Reflecting back on this time forty years later, Carmichael noted that his work with the student Left did not spark his interest in politics, but it did focus it in a particular direction, "the tradition of European radical writing and revolutionary theory. For the first time I encountered a systematic radical analysis, a critical context and vocabulary that explained and made sense of history."[23]

As his last statement suggests, his time at Bronx Science led Carmichael to sever his traditional religious notions and pushed him toward secular humanism. Adopting the materialist approach to history of Marx, Friedrich Engels, Vladimir Ilyich Lenin, and other thinkers he read in study groups for the Young Communist League was a critical factor in his rejection of religion. But perhaps even more important was the curriculum at Bronx Science, which Carmichael stated was "heavily focused on Western rationalism, scientific materialism, and the scientific method, all of which I found logical and thus intellectually satisfying." Because of this curriculum, Carmichael claimed, "my religious feelings gradually lessened." Also, important in his growing rejection of religion was likely the influence of those stepladder speakers in Harlem such as Richard B. Moore, whom he heard on visits to the barbershop and when seeing his cousin Inez.[24]

Despite his own growing rejection of Christianity, Carmichael was never comfortable openly proclaiming his atheism and actively opposing religion the way his SNCC colleague James Forman did. Indeed, the reason Carmichael never actually joined the Young Communist League, despite attending its meetings for years, was because of the open atheism of most of its members. Carmichael was uncomfortable with and even offended by these young people's anti-God jokes. His own devotion to religion was waning, but he knew that was not the case for most black people in the United States, and he "did not want to be alienated from my people because of Marxist atheism." His commitment to civil rights activism increased during his time in high school and accelerated after he started college at Howard University in 1960. Carmichael came to believe that if he was going to be a serious civil rights activist, "then any talk of atheism and the rejection of God just wasn't gonna cut it. I just knew that." His first trips into the South confirmed this in his mind, as most political meetings took place in churches and opened with prayer. Carmichael's position goes against the dominant trend of black freethought becoming increasingly radical during the civil rights and Black Power movements and demonstrates the continuing diversity among African American secular thinkers.[25]

Secularism and the Black Panther Party

The same year that Stokely Carmichael began calling for Black Power in the South, Huey Newton and Bobby Seale formed the Black Panther Party, an organization that contributed significantly to black freethought during this era. Newton and Seale formed the party to oppose American imperialism abroad and police brutality at home. The two first met in 1962 at Merritt College in Oakland, where Newton impressed Seale with his knowledge of E. Franklin Frazier's book *Black Bourgeoisie*. In 1964, Newton went to jail for six months, and when he got out, he joined the Soul Students Advisory Council, which was a part of the Revolutionary Action Movement, a Philadelphia based anti-imperialist and black nationalist organization. According to Joshua Bloom and Waldo Martin, the Revolutionary Action Movement posited a tenet that would become central to the political ideology of the Black Panther Party: "RAM argued that black America was essentially a colony and framed the struggle against racism by blacks in the United States as part of the global anti-imperialist struggle against colonialism." From the start, then, we can see that the key underpinnings of the Black Panther Party's politics shared similar concerns to those of black freethinkers in the early twentieth century: anti-imperialism, black nationalism, and opposition to racism.[26]

In short order, Newton and Seale developed the Ten Point Platform and Program of the Black Panther Party to clearly articulate the new organization's main goals. These included, first, freedom and self-determination for black communities, including the control of all institutions within those communities; second, full employment; and third, reparations for both slavery and racist violence. The fourth and fifth points noted a desire for decent housing and education "that exposes the true nature of this decadent American society." They wanted blacks to especially be exposed to African and African American history and culture courses. Free health care, including expanded access to preventive care as well as health education, was part of their sixth point's demand. The seventh point, the one that many people would come to associate with the Black Panthers, was their call for an end to police brutality and the murder of black people in the United States. Tied to this demand was, in the eighth point, their insistence on an end to all wars of aggression abroad. Newton argued that "as the aggression of the racist American Government escalates in Vietnam, the police agencies of America escalate the repression of Black people throughout the ghettos of America." Thus, it was especially important to end colonialist and imperialist wars. The ninth point demanded the release of black and oppressed people from American jails because they usually did not receive trials by juries of their peers. And the tenth point reiterated earlier ones in stating that "we want land, bread, housing, education, clothing, justice, peace and people's community control of modern technology."[27]

Huey Newton was one of several Black Panther Party leaders who embraced freethought. Unlike black freethinkers including James Forman and Richard Wright, Newton did not have a contentious or unpleasant relationship with religion as a youth. His father was the pastor of the Bethel Baptist Church in Monroe, Louisiana, where Huey was born in 1942, and assisted at various Oakland churches after they moved there in 1945. Newton states of his father that he "swelled up proud to see him up there leading church services, moving the congregation with his messages. All of us shared the dignity and respect he commanded." After they moved to Oakland, they regularly attended the Antioch Baptist Church, a storefront congregation, where Huey was a member of the Baptist Young People's Union, the Young Deacons, and the junior choir. Engaging in these activities and attending church gave Huey and his family "a feeling of importance unequaled anywhere else in our lives," especially when compared with school in Oakland, where Newton always felt alienated and targeted by his white teachers. His early religiosity was so pronounced that Newton even contemplated becoming a minister like his father.[28]

Like James Forman's, Newton's religious beliefs shifted after taking philosophy courses at Oakland City College (later Merritt College) in 1959. After reading existentialist thinkers such as Camus, Jean-Paul Sartre, and Søren Kierkegaard, Newton realized he had been moving toward existentialist belief for some time. He also began to question his religious upbringing and belief in God. "In trying to find God and understand Him as a philosophical existential being," he explained, "I began to question not only the Christian definition of God, but also the very foundation of my religion. I saw that it was based on belief alone, the soundness of which was never questioned." These questions troubled him because of his intensely religious background. "I felt damned," he recounted, because doubting the truth of Christianity was a heresy that went against all the principles by which he was raised. Newton also started to feel Sartre's concept that human beings are condemned to be free. Without the protection of religion and comforts such as prayer, "eventually you, and you alone, have to deal with troubling questions. This always leads to anxiety. There is nothing, so you are free—and terrified." While Newton realized the anguish that comes along with human existence, especially an existence without God, he also started to realize the possibilities in creating his own path in life.[29]

Huey Newton believed that human beings created religions out of ignorance because they had no way of explaining natural phenomena in the world. "We know nothing about God, really, and that is why as soon as the scientist develops or points out a new way of controlling a part of the universe, that aspect of the universe is no longer God." For example, people used to believe that thunder resulted from God clapping his hands together. "As soon as we found out that thunder was not God, we said God has other attributes but not *that* one," he wrote. Thus, for Newton, the steady advance of science would eventually make belief in God obsolete. "As man approaches his development and becomes larger and larger," he posited, "the church therefore becomes smaller and smaller because it is not needed any longer." While he likely did not know it, his conception of God and religion was similar to that of Zora Neale Hurston, who had argued that human beings created religions out of fear of the unknown and that once they mastered those fears, they would no longer need God.[30]

Huey Newton and other party leaders developed one of the central slogans of the Black Panthers, "All Power to the People," on the idea of man as God. Newton states, "I have no other God but man, and I firmly believe that man is the highest or chief good." If you must be truthful and honest with anyone, it is God, "and if each man is God, then you must be true to him." His idea of the relationship between God and mankind is similar to that of Amiri Baraka, who wrote, "God is man idealized. Religion is the aspiration of man toward an idealized existence." For both of them, black people's acceptance of God and Christian theology has meant that they downplayed seeking power in this world for rewards that would supposedly come in the afterlife. In a similar vein to Friedrich Nietzsche, whom he read in college, Newton argued that Christianity was a religion of outcasts and oppressed people. While early Christians had been able to exercise Nietzsche's will to power, that was not the case with blacks in the United States, who continually looked for justice in the promised land. "The phrase 'All Power to the People' was meant to turn this around, to convince Black people that their rewards were due in the present, that it was in their Power to create a Promised Land *here and now*." Newton's religion and politics, then, were based on secular humanism. For black people to recognize their true potential and become equal citizens around the world, he believed, they needed to slough off the idea of God and take responsibility for their own destinies.[31]

Newton and Bobby Seale, along with other Black Panther Party leaders, quickly embraced communism as a first step toward solving racism. Newton first read Marx at Oakland City College and was soon convinced "of the benefits of collectivism and a collectivist ideology." This collectivism was reflected in many of the goals of the party, as articulated in the Ten Point Platform. Newton came to see racism and capitalism as inextricably linked, although he harbored no notions that racism would suddenly disappear after the communist revolution. "Never convinced that destroying capitalism would automatically destroy racism," he noted, "I felt, however, that we could not destroy racism without wiping out its economic foundation." One of the aspects of communism that likely attracted Newton most was its materialism. As we have seen, leading communist thinkers in both the nineteenth and twentieth centuries rejected belief in God and argued that human progress would come about through a revolution that overthrew capitalism rather than by divine intervention. Communism thus intersected perfectly with Newton's developing critique of religious belief and his idea that Christianity in particular had kept black people in a subordinate position. When new Black Panther Party branches started opening up in other cities, the writings of Marx became required reading for anyone who wanted to join the organization.[32]

Newton and Seale were notably drawn to revolutionary Marxist theorists who posited the importance of guerrilla warfare to enacting social and political change. These theorists included Frantz Fanon, whose *Wretched of the Earth* was also required reading for Black Panther Party members; the Latin American revolutionary Che Guevera; and the communist leaders Fidel Castro of Cuba, Vladimir Ilyich Lenin of the Soviet Union, and Mao Zedong of China. Mao's writings were critical in Newton and Seale's intellectual development and to their party's ideology. Mao claimed that guerrillas were both political theorists and military commanders and that both groups could gain support for the revolution through their participation in armed struggle while also raising the consciousness of the people through their words and actions. Castro likewise noted the importance of the guerrilla to revolutionary warfare, while Fanon argued that using violence to oppose colonialism could empower human beings and allow them to re-create themselves in the existentialist sense. Newton and Seale likewise agreed with Lenin's notion that a vanguard consisting of a small number of people could precipitate revolution. Their views in this respect were shared by the rank and file. When Elaine Brown first joined the Black Panther Party in Los Angeles in 1968, Ericka Huggins told her and other new recruits that "we were now in the vanguard of revolution. Our job was to encourage the revolution that would bring true freedom to black people. The goal of the revolution was to overthrow the racist U.S. government and to institute socialism in the United States of America." These notions about the efficacy of guerrilla fighters were particularly salient in the context of the Vietnam War, which saw guerrilla warfare being used to great effect by the North Vietnamese.[33]

Like Huey Newton, Eldridge Cleaver, the party's minister of information, was influenced by the role of Marxist theory in Chinese and Korean indigenous movements. According to Peniel Joseph, Cleaver "proposed adopting a vision of class struggle that intimately considered African American experiences and the long history of racial subordination that confounded conventional Marxist rhetoric and practice." While the Black Panthers admired Marx, they did not rigidly adhere to all of his ideas. Indeed, Cleaver argued that unemployed black people could be the vanguard of the communist revolution and that the Black Panther Party could move beyond Marx's notion that the industrial working class had to be at the forefront of a revolution. Cleaver joined the party shortly after it was formed and edited its newspaper the *Black Panther*. When Newton and Seale were imprisoned, Cleaver took over leadership of the Panthers and played a significant part in the party's embrace of white radicals, a position which no other Black Power organization took during the 1960s and one that put them at odds with cultural nationalist groups such as the Us organization, founded by Ron Karenga (now known as Maulana Karenga).[34]

In addition to being a committed Marxist, Cleaver was a freethinker who discarded his religion while incarcerated. Cleaver first entered prison in California in 1954 for marijuana possession, and he recalled that during a later stint at Folsom Prison, his group of fellow inmates was "espousing atheism. Unsophisticated and not based on any philosophical rationale, our atheism was pragmatic. I had come to believe that there is no God; if there is, men do not know anything about him. Therefore, all religions were phony—which made all preachers and priests, in our eyes, fakers, including the ones scurrying around the prison who, curiously, could put in a good word for you with the Almighty Creator of the universe but could not get anything down with the warden or parole board—they could usher you through the Pearly Gates *after you were dead*, but not through the prison gate *while you were still alive and kicking*." His complaint about religion was a common one among freethinkers dating back to the nineteenth century and would gain new currency during the civil rights era and the growing national prominence of black religious figures such as Martin Luther King Jr. Another problem Cleaver had with the prison ministers was their role in preparing inmates for death row. "Such men of God," Cleaver argued, "are powerful arguments in favor of atheism." He began to bolster his atheist belief by reading the works of other freethinkers, including Thomas Paine, Voltaire, and Marx.[35]

Despite his espousal of atheism, Cleaver at times affiliated himself with various religions for political and pragmatic purposes. When he was locked up in a youth institution, he attended Roman Catholic Mass every Sunday. All inmates had to go to one religious service, and that was where the blacks and Mexicans went, while whites went to the Protestant chapel. Later on, while confined in solitary in Folsem, he read Thomas Merton's autobiography *The Seven Storey Mountain*, of which he noted, "I was tortured by that book because Merton's suffering, in his quest for God, seemed all in vain to me. At the time, I was a Black Muslim chained in the bottom of a pit by the Devil. Did I expect Allah to tear down the walls and set me free? To me, the language and symbols of religion were nothing but weapons of war." Even though he had joined the Nation of Islam, he did not believe in its theology. He likely joined because he was attracted to the black nationalism of the group as well as its emphasis on cooperative economics and uplifting of black people more broadly. After the death of Malcolm X, the rift between his followers and those of Elijah Muhammad became more apparent. Cleaver chose Malcolm's side because he believed more strongly in the slain leader's politics and style of leadership. Speaking about adherence to the ideas of the Nation of Islam,

Cleaver posited that "it was not the Black Muslim movement itself that was so irresistibly appealing to the true believers. It was the awakening into self-consciousness of twenty million Negroes which was so compelling." Malcolm captured the voice and desires of black people better than any man of his time; even if he had been a Quaker, Seventh-Day Adventist, Catholic, "or a Sammy Davis-style Jew, and if he had continued to give voice to the mute ambitions in the black man's soul, his message would still have been triumphant," Cleaver contended. Like Zora Neale Hurston, Eldridge Cleaver did not personally believe in God but nevertheless participated in religious rituals for self-affirmation and a feeling of community.[36]

Another leader of the Black Panther Party who shared Cleaver's non-belief and distrust of ministers was David Hilliard. Hilliard spent his early years in Rockville, Alabama, before moving to Oakland at the age of eleven. It was there that he first met Huey Newton and became good friends with the future party founder. Like Cleaver, Hilliard was drawn to the Nation of Islam as a teenager, largely due to the influence of Malcolm X. Hilliard commented that Malcolm X, "with his razor-sharp mind and wit—speaks my language. He's no *saditi* [snob]." Hilliard attended a few meetings and even began lecturing his black friends to stop dating white women, one of the rules of being a member of the Nation of Islam. He never converted, however, because his friends on the street would not go to these gatherings, and he wanted to hang out with them. In addition, he noted, "the Nation of Islam is a living contradiction for me. I respect their personal discipline, but like to drink, dress up, and party." Instead, Hilliard ended up embracing the political message of Malcolm X rather than his theological beliefs. Shortly after Newton and Seale founded the Black Panther Party, Newton approached Hilliard and told him about the organization. Hilliard had been reading Malcolm X's autobiography and learning his philosophy of self-defense, so the Black Panther Party was incredibly appealing to him. He became one of the first members and soon rose to chief of staff and ran many of the party's day-to-day activities, including editing and selling the *Black Panther*, raising funds, and assisting party members who were arrested by providing bail and obtaining legal counsel.[37]

Hilliard developed a contempt for ministers similar to that of Eldridge Cleaver. He liked certain aspects of the rhetorical style and ability to move people that Martin Luther King Jr. had but completely disagreed with his and other black ministers' championing of nonviolence. Hilliard stated that King is "a preacher, and I've never overcome my contempt for our local ministers who would accept tithes from their poor, hard-working spellbound congregations." Those ministers "preached false glory," and in Hilliard's mind, King was even worse because "there's not false glory, there's *no* glory in getting your brains beat out." The black community, Hilliard argued, would be much better off if parishioners held on to their tithes and instead purchased guns or weapons to defend themselves. Hilliard went even further in a speech before the National Committee of Black Churchmen in Berkeley, California. Here he referred to the assembled crowd of preachers as "a bunch of bootlicking pimps and motherfuckers." He threatened the preachers that if they did not come around to supporting the Black Panthers' agenda, the Panthers would be forced to "off" some of them. Hilliard's views were extreme even for the Panthers; however, the spirit of his statement speaks to the visceral anticlericalism common among many participants in the Black Panther Party.[38]

Black Panthers across the country shared Hilliard's nonbelief and anticlericalism for many of the same reasons. Clark Squire, a member of the party in New York City, had grown up in rural Texas where the "respected class of blacks" included teachers and preachers who attempted to indoctrinate young African Americans into the values of American democracy by teaching them about free enterprise, due process, and constitutional rights. "All of this in the face of poverty, disease, fighting, killing, and exploitation running amok in the black community," Squire claimed. "We never heard one word from 'respected' blacks about those evil conditions—either their cause or their cure." Because of this situation, Squire never could respect the middle-class black leaders, including preachers, in his community. Like Hilliard and Newton, he "had a lot more respect for the bloods off the block because they were much less hypocritical, less brainwashed . . . and were more willing to fight." Similarly, Curtis Powell, another Black Panther from New York City, returned there from a trip to Africa in 1967 and was looking to become more politically engaged but was turned off by many groups' religious adherence. Referring to the Nation of Islam, he posited, "I dug the Muslims some, but except for Malcolm they were too spooky. I couldn't relate at all to the thing about Yacub," the mad scientist who Black Muslims claimed was responsible for creating the white race.[39]

Lumumba Shakur, Black Panther leader in New York City, had a similar reaction to the Nation of Islam as Powell did. During a visit with his father in 1962 while incarcerated in New York, Shakur indicated that he liked Malcolm X's philosophy and considered himself both a black nationalist and a Muslim but "could not relate to praying." He was released from prison just before he turned twenty-two, in December 1964, after having served a five-year sentence. Knowing that Malcolm X had just split from the Nation of Islam and formed the secular Organization for Afro-American Unity (OAAU), Shakur knew he would join the organization. He did so largely because the OAAU "would emphasize black nationalism instead of religion. I could relate to black nationalism instantly because I had a problem relating to religion." He began an activist career shortly after his release and often ran into trouble with ministers. The OAAU floundered after the death of Malcolm X, so Shakur and his friend Sekou from prison began checking out the various nationalist groups in New York. Finding none that suited their needs, they got together with other black nationalists in Queens to organize the Grass Root Front. "Our aim was to take the anti-poverty programs from the hands of the religious pimps and preachers," he asserted, "and guarantee the grass-root people control of the anti-poverty programs." The group ended up splitting because Sekou, Shakur, and others were staunchly opposed to religion and ministerial influence, while others did not share their beliefs. Shakur's reference to preachers as "pimps" was a common one among Black Panthers of the era and indicates the deep sense of disrespect that many of them wanted to convey to the public. Shakur suggested that black preachers were little better than white authorities and even collaborated with them to maintain power and influence.[40]

The *Black Panther* newspaper served as an organ to promote similar views of religion by party members, especially those of women. In her poem "Free by Any Means Necessary," Sarah Webster Fabio links her political vision with that of Malcolm X and expresses her support for a humanist approach to politics. She posits that "the pen / has always / been a white /weapon; it / must be wrested / from the oppressor's / hands by/ black power." She goes on to indicate that this "wresting" will have the effect of creating new and positive images of black people, a goal of black artists and writers dating back to the nineteenth century. Fabio also claims that the Black Panthers "are the holy men / of our time; / they are the / last practitioners/ of the judeo-christian / ethic." All other ministers and so-called holy men, she argues, "have turned their / priesthoods into a mafia / protecting, not man / but status quo." Like Cleaver and Hilliard, Fabio believed that Christian ministers were not looking out for the interests of black people but rather upholding an oppressive, capitalist system that perpetuated racism at home and imperialism abroad. Her solution, like that of many black radicals in 1968, involved freeing Huey Newton, Bobby Seale, and other incarcerated party members. She ends the work by stating that the American power structure should "Free black panthers. / Free humanism / Free black men / Free goodness & honor / Free Huey, now, and Free us all." Her inclusion of humanism is significant because it suggests her belief that without humanism, black people could never truly be free.[41]

Evette Pearson denounced the ties between religion and racism in even harsher terms in a letter/poem published in the *Black Panther* the following year. Pearson begins her piece "In White America Today" by arguing that the descendants of "god-fearing racists" who murdered countless Native Americans to have a place to worship the Christian God are now also trying to wipe out black men in America, partially through birth control pills and sending young blacks to Vietnam. Pointing out the hypocrisy of white Christians, Pearson writes, "In white America today, god-fearing racists are buying guns, black man. The guns are to blow your brains out after they pray to the god that ordered black Adam out of the garden of eden. He'll whisper a prayer, give your wife a pill; deny your daughter medication, put your son on the front lines, and piously blow your brains out." In addition to pointing out the hypocrisy of Christians in America, she is also subtly attacking the philosophy of nonviolence by noting that blacks are getting killed even by those who consider themselves religious. Pearson then offers a mock version of the Lord's Prayer that similarly seeks to undermine the cultural power and respect for Christianity:

> Our father, (says white America)
> which art in heaven   ·
> how I love this game.
> Of all the blessings
> you've given me—
> this game of pain
> is closest to my heart.
> I said I'd pray and pray
> you gave me the U.S.A.
> I joined the Trustee Board
> You let me kill the Injuns, lord.
> You blessed me with slaves
> You blessed me with fools—

Then the niggers started going to schools.
Integration! Freedom!
Now it's revolution!
But I know
the lord is good
Your grace is sufficient to silence niggers—for good.
AMEN!

Her solution was a form of regressive gender politics whereby black women need to reject birth control pills to "replenish the earth with healthy black warriors." In her view, black people must increase their number because there is a revolution coming, and before they are wiped out by whites, they need to prepare by having as many children as possible.[42]

Pearson's piece speaks to the ambiguities of the Black Panthers' ideas on gender. While black freethinkers in the early twentieth century such as Zora Neale Hurston, W. E. B. Du Bois, and Nella Larsen combined a critique of religion with a critique of patriarchy and sexism, such was not always the case during the civil rights era. One result of the police harassment and political repression the Panthers faced was that they sometimes practiced communal living, which led to conflicts over gender roles. According to Bobby Seale, in such situations, if there is cooking to be done, both men and women do it, and they both do the dishes as well. "The sisters don't just serve and wait on the brothers," Seale claimed. While this was the ideal approach, it was not always followed in practice, and sexism sometimes thrived within the party. One woman who spoke up about gender inequities was Roberta Alexander. According to her, the party debated topics such as women holding leadership positions, women engaging in armed self-defense, women doing the majority of the typing, and even whether or not women should have sex with the men for the sake of the revolution. For the most part, these conflicts were relegated to the sidelines within the party, at least until 1970.[43]

That year Huey Newton put forth an open letter that spoke to issues of gender equality and heterosexism within the Black Panther Party. On August 15, 1970, Newton urged the party to support the burgeoning women's rights movement as well as the gay liberation movement. Newton argued that party members should stop using terms such as "faggot" and "punk" to denounce their opponents, a practice that was widespread. While Eldridge Cleaver had previously been dismissive of calls for gender equality among the Black Panthers, he eventually came around as well, in large part owing to the incarceration of party member Ericka Huggins. Her husband, John, was killed in a shootout with Karenga's Us organization in Los Angeles, after which she moved to New Haven, Connecticut. She soon became the head of a Black Panther chapter in that city, which made her a target of the Federal Bureau of Investigation. She was arrested and charged with conspiracy, spending two years in prison awaiting trial before the charges were dropped for lack of evidence. Her bravery during this ordeal made Cleaver reconsider his position on gender equality. "The incarceration and suffering of Sister Erica," he wrote, "should be a stinging rebuke to all manifestations of male chauvinism within our ranks. That we must purge our ranks and our hearts, and our minds, and our understanding of any chauvinism, chauvinistic behavior, or disrespectful behavior toward women." Huggins's ordeal, in his view, meant that the party must recognize "that a woman can be just as revolutionary as a man and that she has equal stature" with men. A few years later, when Newton was in forced exile in Cuba, Elaine Brown proved Cleaver's words to be true when she took over the leadership of the party, partially through her control of its stockpile of weapons.[44]

Women were at the forefront of the party's "survival programs," programs that expressed both the humanist and socialist vision of the Black Panthers. Perhaps the most well known of these programs was the Free Breakfast for Children Program, launched in the fall of 1968. Bobby Seale heard that local high school teachers were considering creating a free lunch program, so he pushed for the breakfast program instead (an initiative that Eldridge Cleaver derided as "sissy" at the time). Seale believed this program could expose the fact that the government was failing to provide necessary social services in poor communities and also believed it would be a great recruiting tool. Ruth Beckford, a member of the Panther Advisory Committee and a community activist, was at the forefront of planning and organizing the program. She helped arrange food donations and managed the staff. She likewise recruited women in the Parent–Teacher Association to cook breakfast and helped raise money. Beckford's leadership represents a broader trend in the party after 1968—namely, the greater participation of women in the party, who helped to broaden its appeal across classes and generations. The Free Breakfast for Children Program quickly spread across the country, with one estimate stating that by November 1969, twenty-nine branches were serving breakfast to more than 22,000 children each weekday. An editorial in the *Black Panther* shortly before this date stated in clear terms the program's goal and its relation to Huey Newton's vision for the party: "The Free Breakfast for Children Program is a socialistic program, designed to serve the people. All institutions in a society should be designed to serve the masses, not just a 'chosen few.' In America, this program is revolutionary."[45]

Another critical survival program that expressed the humanist and socialist vision of the Black Panther Party was the free community-based medical clinics. After more branches of the party began opening up in the late 1960s, headquarters required all of them to operate these free clinics. The party developed a health politics based on the World Health Organization's 1948 charter, which states, "Health is a state of complete physical, mental and social well-being and not merely the absence of disease or infirmity. . . . Health is one of the fundamental rights of every human being without distinction of race, religion, political belief, economic or social condition." Additionally, the charter noted that attaining health for all people is an essential component of promoting world peace. Editorials in the *Black Panther* in the late 1960s and early 1970s defined health in similar terms, noting that it was the government's responsibility to provide health care and that health care was a fundamental right of all human beings. Some of the central health problems the Black Panthers were trying to combat include lack of access to health care, segregated health care facilities, lack of access to medical training and accreditation for blacks, and neglect by health care officials. The party developed a perspective on health that Alondra Nelson terms "social health": "As a praxis, social health linked medical services to a program of societal transformation. The Panthers' clinics, for example, were imagined as sites of social change where preventive medicine was dispensed alongside extramedical services (e.g., food banks and employment assistance) and ideology via the Party's political education (PE) classes." Free clinics became a "survival program" for the community, in a literal sense, but also for the party, as they helped broaden its appeal throughout the country.[46]

The survival program that had the longest-lasting impact reflected the Black Panther Party's educational efforts. One of Newton's main justifications for the Free Breakfast Program for Children was that it would allow kids to receive a better education, something impossible to do when dealing with hunger. The party critiqued educational institutions from its inception. Newton wrote of his own education in Oakland that he "did not have one teacher who taught me anything relevant to my own life experience. . . . All they did was try to rob me of the sense of my own uniqueness and worth, and in the process they nearly killed my urge to inquire." The party set up "liberation schools" for children and teenagers in San Francisco, Richmond, and Berkeley, California, starting in 1969. These schools were initially similar to after-school and summer programs. Both party members and volunteers from the community taught at them. At first, issues with funding made the schools hard to maintain, but the first permanent school opened its doors on June 25, 1969, in Berkeley. Education at these schools focused on issues of class, culture, and the necessity of forming interracial alliances. And the schools likewise inculcated the humanist perspective of the party. As one teacher from the San Francisco liberation school noted of its goals, "we are teaching the young brothers and sisters what 'Power to the People' means and we, the teachers, know that power belongs to the people and that youth makes revolution."[47]

Along with the liberation schools, the party established the Intercommunal Youth Institute (IYI) in 1971, a school that likewise expressed the humanistic vision of the Black Panthers. The IYI, later renamed the Oakland Community School, was in operation until 1982, making it the longest-lasting of all Black Panther Party programs. The school was led by Elaine Brown and Ericka Huggins and reflected important changes in educational pedagogy, including having a curriculum that was student-centered. The motto of the school spoke to Huey Newton's problem with his own education that stifled his desire to learn: "Learning *how* to think, not *what* to think." It was common for Huggins to walk up and down the hallways of the school and observe teachers to ensure that they were not putting students down or stifling their freedom of expression. Punishments might include yoga or breathing exercises, and students had a say in the type of discipline other students received for infractions such as missing homework. As Donna Murch argues, among Huggins's most urgent concerns "was countering the authoritarian model of education that black children, their parents, and the school's teachers had received."[48]

A Humanist Critique of Black Theology

Along with the Black Panther Party, another significant outgrowth of the Black Power movement of the late 1960s was the creation of a black theology of liberation. Just as the theology of nineteenth-century thinkers such as Henry Highland Garnett and Maria Stewart emerged from the secular antislavery movement, so too would the twentieth-century iteration of black theology emerge from a similarly secular movement. The drive toward creating a black theology began at a meeting of ministers and academics, who in 1966 formed the National Committee of Negro Churchmen, which was later changed to the National Conference of Black Churchmen. James H. Cone, the man who has come to be most associated with the movement, notes that "the idea of 'black theology' emerged when a small group of radical black clergy began to reinterpret the meaning of the Christian faith from the standpoint of the black struggle for liberation." While black thinkers had certainly articulated a theology of liberation dating back to the eighteenth century, there was no systematic black theology that people in the 1960s could draw from and only a handful of black theologians and religious historians in academia, according to Cone.[49]

There are five main sources of this school of theology that Cone outlines in his seminal 1970 book *A Black Theology of Liberation*: black experience, black history, black culture, scripture, and the Christian tradition. As Anthony Pinn notes, "the latter two are to be read and interpreted through a hermeneutic of suspicion—recognition that white Americans have manipulated these two for their own purposes such as the safeguarding of white supremacy and African American inferiority." Along with these major tenets, a key aspect of black theology, according to Cone, is "the blackness of God, and everything implied by it in a racist society. . . . There is no place in black theology for a colorless God in a society where human beings suffer precisely because of their color." This blackness on the part of the divine meant that he identified with black people and was a God of the oppressed. As such, God would ultimately bring about justice and equality for African Americans.[50]

Black theologians such as Cone, Albert Cleage, Major Jones, J. Deotis Roberts, and others took seriously the critiques of black freethinkers that the black church was too otherworldly and was an ineffective institution for advancing racial justice. Henry James Young agreed with James Forman's argument that the belief that God will intervene in history and ensure freedom can be detrimental for blacks. "Even today that black man continues to wait, eschatologically," Young wrote, "for God's omnipotent intervention and eradication of oppression. As a result, black Americans have not utilized at the maximum capacity their physical, intellectual, and spiritual faculties toward freedom and liberation." The goal of black theology, then, was to merge the political organization and concerns of Black Power activists with the gospel. For Cone, black theology "is a theology of the black poor, reconstructing their hopes and dreams of God's coming liberated world."[51]

Cone's earliest iteration of black theology was not without its critics. Religious historians such as Gayraud Wilmore argued that Cone should rely less on European theologians such as Karl Barth and more on African American sources, including slave narratives, spirituals, and protest literature. Cornel West's 1982 work *Prophesy Deliverance!* which examined radical black religion stretching back to the eighteenth century, was an attempt to do just as Wilmore suggested. J. Deotis Roberts also critiqued Cone for his lack of attention to reconciliation. In embracing Black Power and even the use of violence to end racial discrimination, Roberts believed that Cone's approach would further alienate whites rather than bring the races together. African American women pointed to the all-male orientation of black theology to argue that it was a sexist system of thought. Without the inclusion of black women's sources and experiences in black theology, they argued, it would remain inadequate to the task of ensuring freedom and equality for all. Gender oppression was as important as racial oppression, black women argued. During the 1970s and 1980s, women such as Rev. Dr. Pauli Murray, Katie G. Cannon, and Francis Beale developed a womanist theology that spoke to the intersecting oppressions of race and gender.[52]

William R. Jones proffered perhaps the harshest assessment of black theology in his 1973 book *Is God a White Racist? A Preamble to Black Theology*. Jones grew up in Louisville, Kentucky, and studied philosophy at Howard University. He received a Master of Divinity degree from Harvard University in 1958 and was ordained by the Unitarian Universalist Society of Wellesley Hills, Massachusetts, that same year, after which he served as Assistant Minister and Director of Religious Education at the First Unitarian Church in Providence, Rhode Island for two years. Jones went on to complete his doctorate in religious studies at Brown University with a doctoral dissertation entitled "On Sartre's Critical Methodology." According to Lewis R. Gordon, what Jones found compelling about the thought of Sartre and other existentialists "was their quest for radical self-critique, a practice they extended to the study of thought and society." Six years later, his concern would lead him to write *Is God a White Racist?* when he was teaching at Yale Divinity School. He would later move to become professor of religious studies at Florida State University, where he also founded the African American Studies program and served as a community minister from 1977 to 2012.[53]

For Jones, this book personified his ideas of black liberation and also reflected his conversion from the evangelical Christianity of his youth to secular humanism. He notes that after a long period of reading and searching, "I found myself wrestling with these agonizing choices: Should I hold fast to those Christian truths that my family upbringing imprinted on my being as absolute, infallible, and divinely ordained? Or should I incarnate the verities I was unearthing in the humanist existentialism of de Beauvoir, Camus, Fanon, and Sartre and adopt the critique of black theism that I was reconstructing from a variety of sources in the black religious tradition?" He eventually settled on the latter option. At first, Jones believed that to get rid of oppression, he had to challenge all religion, just as many of his contemporaries in the Black Power movement were doing. He soon changed his mind, however, and came to believe that he just had to challenge "mis-religion," a framework he adopted from Carter G. Woodson, who posited the binary of education and "mis-education" in his classic work *The Mis-Education of the Negro*. Thus, *Is God a White Racist?* "comprised a constructive. criticism of the black church and black theology that blended deconstruction and reconstruction." The deconstructive task was exposing the religious ideas that supported the oppression of black people, or "Whiteanity," as he called it, while the constructive task involved "formulating a new God category that was not at cross-purposes with the demands of a liberation theology."[54]

In the first part of the book, Jones makes his case for divine racism. The first premise of this idea was that God divides humanity into an in-group and an out-group and does not value all people equally. He notes that to speak of divine racism is to attack a central category of Western theology—namely, the benevolence and goodness of God. In this study, he engaged in a type of work similar to what freethinkers had been employing since the early years of the twentieth century. Jones notes that one way to approach the problem of divine racism is to say that God is the sum of his acts, which "requires that whatever motive or character is assigned to God must be based on His past or present acts or both. Further, one is not permitted to speak of a divine motive of character that is different from his actual performance relative to man." While believers might attribute evil and suffering to Satan or say that God is using evil to bring about good, Jones says that the existence of evil is reflective of God's character. Furthermore, suffering in the Bible is often directed at particular ethnic groups, leading one to question whether God is a white racist. "Black theology," Jones writes, "precisely because of the prominence of ethnic suffering in the black experience, cannot operate as if the goodness of God for all mankind were a theological axiom." Indeed, the central ideas of black theologians, including black theology as a theology of liberation, blacks being God's chosen people, and black theology's critique of the Christian tradition, imply the issue of divine racism.[55]

Jones's solution to the problems of black theology was to replace it with a new theology he termed "humanocentric theism." Drawing from the work of the Jewish existentialist Martin Buber, Jones posits as the central idea of humanocentric theism an exalted status given to man based on the perceived will of God. Rather than viewing God as jealous of man and trying to limit his capacities, as indicated in the biblical story of the Tower of Babel, Jones argues that God wants mankind to reach its highest heights. Other important facets of this framework include "its affirmation of a delegated ontological status to man as a co-creator of essential features of human existence; its emphasis upon the activity, choice, and freedom of man; and the reinterpretation of the concept of divine sovereignty and omnipotence." This theology was similar to secular humanism, an idea that the work of the religion professor Howard Burkle supports. Jones believed that humanocentric theism would be a valuable framework for black theodicy for four primary reasons. First, he argued that it would better allow for the freedom of mankind, which was essential to any liberation theology. Second, he believed that it did a better job of refuting notions of divine racism than black theology did by "removing God's overruling sovereignty from human history." Third, Jones noted that no longer could whites point to God's will as reason for keeping blacks in a subordinate status. If human beings are completely responsible for their own fates, then racism was solely the fault of humans. And fourth, Jones believed that humanocentric theism could be a middle ground between fundamentalist religion and atheism. This latter concern likely stemmed from his position as a Unitarian Universalist minister. While he had rejected the God of his youth, the same God that most black people continued to believe in, he still felt the need to affirm a spiritual dimension to human existence. Nevertheless, his theology had an important influence on freethinkers during his time and played an important role in Anthony Pinn's construction of a secular humanist theology two decades later.[56]

The Black Arts Movement

Whereas black theology and humanocentric theism represent religious manifestations of Black Power ideology, the black arts movement can be seen as its literary outgrowth. Most scholars date the movement from 1965 to roughly 1976. Some of its main themes were similar to the Harlem Renaissance: black cultural nationalism, an appreciation of African culture, and the literary use of black music. However, it had some important differences from the earlier movement, including the prevalence of antiwhite language and a greater appreciation for the black vernacular. Additionally, artists of the black arts movement often renounced respectability politics to a much greater degree than writers such as Langston Hughes, Nella Larsen, and Zora Neale Hurston had done. But one common thread in both movements was the importance of a secular perspective among many of its key participants. Writers such as Lorraine Hansberry, James Baldwin, and Nikki Giovanni used their plays, poems, essays, and novels to critique Christianity and explore the possibilities of black life without religion.[57]

Although Lorraine Hansberry passed away just before the black arts movement began, her writing anticipated some of its key themes, including an appreciation for African culture, a questioning of respectability politics, and an exploration of black atheism. Hansberry was born in Chicago in 1930 to Carl and Nantille Hansberry. Her father founded one of Chicago's first black banks and a real estate company worth more than $250,000 that owned property housing four thousand families. Black freethinkers and radicals such as W. E. B. Du Bois, Langston Hughes, and Paul Robeson were frequent guests in their home. Carl Hansberry's political activism shaped Lorraine's later embrace of radicalism. He, along with the NAACP, challenged racially exclusionary housing covenants that would not allow them to move from the South Side to Hyde Park. He won the Supreme Court case *Hansberry v. Lee* in 1943, but it did little good because there was no way to enforce the decision. Lorraine reflected about this "victory" later in life that "my father was typical of a generation of Negroes who believed that the 'American way' could successfully be made to work to democratize the United States." She thus rejected her father's liberalism and instead embraced the socialism and humanism of Du Bois and Robeson.[58]

Hansberry developed her political ideology while working with Du Bois and Robeson's newspaper, *Freedom*. She joined the anti-imperialist and anticapitalist publication after dropping out of college in 1951.

She started out as a receptionist and typist but soon became the associate editor, remaining with the paper until it folded in 1955. During that time, she wrote twenty-two articles and reviews on the arts, African culture and politics, and women's rights. An article on the latter topic displayed her appreciation for Simone de Beauvoir's existentialist feminism. She argued that Beauvoir's *The Second Sex* "may very well be the most important work of this century," which was an especially bold claim, given that many black thinkers attributed that honor to Du Bois's *Souls of Black Folk*. The opposition to *The Second Sex* by many women was telling in Hansberry's view because it indicated that the very nature of their oppression, outlined in the book, prevents them from seriously grappling with its ideas. In her view, the oppression that Beauvoir outlined at length in her work was a direct result of Christianity. "I have remarked heavily upon the sociological roots of the comparative equality of American women," she posited, "because such sources are not to be confused as having come from some benevolent features of our principal religious ethic drawn as it was from the Judeo-Christian doctrines of the Mediterranean which set woman as firmly as ever in the encasement of subservient immanence." Like her mentor Du Bois, with whom she was studying African history and politics during this time, Hansberry came to believe that religion and feminism were incompatible.[59]

Hansberry develops this perspective on religion in her most well-known play, *A Raisin in the Sun. Raisin* debuted in 1959 and was an instant success, winning the New York Drama Critics Circle award for best play that year. The play is set on the South Side of Chicago sometime between the end of World War II and 1959. It focuses on the Younger family shortly after the death of the patriarch, Walter Younger Sr. The family is waiting on $10,000 in life insurance money, and much of the drama revolves around what will be done with the funds. Walter Younger Jr. would like Mama to give him the money to invest in a liquor store, while Mama wants to use the money to buy a house in a white neighborhood and support the medical career of her daughter Beneatha. Beneatha is a modern woman who embraces feminism, anticolonialism, and atheism. While many people urge her to marry her middle-class suitor George Murchison, she decides to wait until her schooling is complete, putting her career ahead of middle-class domesticity. And when Mama remarks to her that she will be a doctor if God wills it, Beneatha replies, "God hasn't got a thing to do with it." She goes on to express her frustration that God gets all the credit for human achievements, asking whether or not God would be paying her tuition. Mama is incredulous at this statement, noting that she took her and Walter to church every Sunday, and that Beneatha had not been brought up to speak so disrespectfully about God. "Mama, you don't understand. It's all a matter of ideas, and God is just one idea I don't accept. It's not important. I am not going out and be immoral or commit crimes because I don't believe in God. It's just that I get tired of Him getting credit for all the things the human race achieves through its own effort. There simply is no blasted God—there is only man and it is *he* who makes miracles."[60]

Beneatha expresses Hansberry's own humanist sentiments. As she noted in an interview with Mike Wallace shortly after the play came out, "Beneatha is me, eight years ago." For Hansberry, human beings have the capacity for morality through the use of reason and do not need to believe in God in order to be good people. And when human beings achieve something in the world, she contended, people should recognize them rather attribute their accomplishments to an unseen deity. "We don't need mysticism to exalt man," she claimed in one interview. "Man exalts himself by his achievements . . . and his power to rationalize—or excuse me—his power to reason." Her perspective on religion was similar to that of Zora Neale Hurston and Huey Newton— namely, that people attribute to God the aspects of nature and human life they do not understand. Unlike Hurston, however, Hansberry did not see this as a weakness but rather a strength of human beings. It was just a strength that she herself did not need. After an interviewer pointed out the sustenance that Mama gets from her faith in *Raisin*, Hansberry responded that "this is one of the glories of man, the inventiveness of the human mind and the human spirit; whenever life doesn't seem to give an answer, we create one. And it gives us strength. I don't attack people who are religious at all, as you can tell from the play; I rather admire this human quality to make our own crutches as long as we need them. The only thing I am saying is that once we can *walk*, you know—then drop them."[61]

Along with her critique of religion, *Raisin* also reflects Hansberry's anticolonialism and anti-imperialism. When Mama indicates that she gives money to her church to help save Africans from heathenism, Beneatha replies, "I'm afraid they need more salvation from the British and French." She eventually rejects her black American suitor George in favor of a Nigerian student named Joseph Asagai. At one point in the play, Beneatha puts on an African robe and headdress and starts doing an African folk dance to a Nigerian record. And when Asagai teases her about her relaxed hair and calls her an assimilationist, Beneatha cuts it off in favor of a natural, something that would become increasingly widespread among women in the Black Power movement. Cheryl Higashida points out that Hansberry was one of a handful of black feminist writers, including Alice Childress, Paule Marshall, Rosa Guy, and Audre Lorde, who "developed feminist positions and aesthetics that in turn rearticulated internationalist discourses linking the struggles of First World minorities with Third World anticolonialisms and nationalisms."[62]

While Hansberry would come under fire for *Raisin's* seemingly integrationist message, the play in fact represents a radical, socialist political vision. Mama purchases a home in a white neighborhood where it is clear they are not wanted. In fact, shortly after she makes the initial payment, the family receives a visit from Karl Lindner of the Clybourne Park Improvement Association. Lindner quickly tells them "a man, right or wrong, has the right to want the neighborhood he lives in a certain kind of way," and he offers to buy back their house at a profit to Mama. After much back-and-forth, the family decides to move into the house and is packing up at the end of the play. Critics such as Harold Cruse harshly denounced Hansberry for this ending. According to Cruse, "in this drive for integration the Negro working class is being told in a thousand ways that it must give up its ethnicity and become human, universal, full-fledged American." As Ben Keppel argues, however, "Hansberry understood integration to be the removal of all barriers to the construction of solidarity among the children of the American working class—both white and black." Her own experiences growing up in segregated Chicago neighborhoods and schools convinced her that class solidarity would be impossible without the possibility of integration.[63]

Hansberry also did not place an unmediated faith in integration, as many of her critics suggested. The fate of the Youngers is anything but clear at the end of the play. While they are moving into a white neighborhood, they know they may have to defend themselves from racist violence similar to what they might encounter in the Jim Crow South. Lindner hints at this possibility when he tells Walter that "people can get awful worked up when they feel that their whole way of life and everything they've worked for is threatened." In this sense, Hansberry implicitly attacks the American Dream, which tells people they can succeed if they work hard. For the Youngers, the only way they were able to succeed was with the death of Walter Sr., and this success was far from certain. Thus, rather than being a simple integrationist play celebrating American democracy, Hansberry uses *A Raisin in the Sun* to expose the contradictions within the black community that would come to the fore during the 1960s and to provide a framework for her anti-imperialist and anticolonialist political vision.[64]

Like Lorraine Hansberry, James Baldwin had a literary career that predated the black arts movement by more than a decade; however, he would briefly emerge as one of its principal figures during the mid-1960s. Indeed, Amiri Baraka, while giving Baldwin's eulogy in 1987, claimed that Baldwin's 1964 play *Blues for Mister Charlie* was the beginning of the movement. Baldwin was born in Harlem on August 2, 1924 to Emma Berdis Jones. Only nineteen at the time of her son's birth, Jones had recently migrated to Harlem from Deals Island, Maryland, as part of the Great Migration. When he was three years old, James took the last name of his stepfather, David Baldwin. James Baldwin grew up in an intensely religious household. David Baldwin was a Baptist minister who preached at various storefront congregations in Harlem. They sometimes attended the Abyssinian Baptist Church, and in 1937, James joined the Mount Calvary of the Pentecostal Faith Church, which was located on Lenox Avenue and headed by Mother Horn. He soon switched congregations and began attending the Fireside Pentecostal Assembly at 136th Street and Fifth Avenue. There he became a preacher at the age of fourteen.[65]

From the beginning of his time at Fireside Pentecostal Assembly, Baldwin was in a spiritual crisis of sorts. He joined the church because he wanted a sense of belonging and got that from the start. When he first encountered the pastor, she asked him whose little boy he was, which was the same phrase "used by pimps and racketeers on the Avenue when they suggested, both humorously and intensely, that I 'hang out' with them." Baldwin notes that he "unquestionably wanted to be *somebody's* little boy," so he replied that he was hers. He soon underwent a religious conversion when he was involuntarily thrown to the floor one day and swept up in religious emotion. The saints in his church surrounded him in a Pentecostal ritual known as "pleading the blood" whereby they helped the young convert's soul throw off demons and Satan and accept Jesus as savior. Despite this conversion experience, however, Baldwin never truly accepted Jesus as his savior and never believed that trusting in God would bring about his salvation. In recalling his conversion experience, Baldwin contended, "God—and

I felt this even then, so long ago, on that tremendous floor, unwill-ingly—is white. And if His love was so great, and if He loved all His children, why were we, the blacks, cast down so far? Why?"[66]

Written more than a decade before William R. Jones published *Is God a White Racist?*, Baldwin's autobiographical work *The Fire Next Time* raised many of the same questions that the philosopher and theo-logian later explored in his work. Baldwin thought he would get bored being a regular church member, and he wanted to best his father, so he began preaching and did so for three years. He soon came to see, however, that the principles and rituals of the black church did not differ markedly from those of white Christian churches. These princi-ples were blindness, loneliness, and terror. His reading and schoolwork soon forced him to confront the uncomfortable truth that the Bible was not divinely inspired but written by humans. And he also began to realize that the Word was spread by men and women who were not always divinely inspired. "Being in the pulpit was like being in the the-atre," he claimed. "I was behind the scenes and knew how the illusion worked. . . . I knew how to work on a congregation until the last dime was surrendered—it was not very hard to do—and I knew where the money for 'the Lord's work' went. I knew, though I did not wish to know it, that I had no respect for the people with whom I worked." Baldwin's defection from Christianity differs from that of many of the individuals in this book because as a preacher, he was the consummate insider. But it was that insider status that eventually pushed him away from the church because he felt guilty taking what little money the poor and working-class people who attended his church had. When Baldwin began taking fewer preaching engagements at the age of seventeen, his father asked him if he'd rather write than preach, to which Baldwin replied, simply, yes.[67]

Like most black freethinkers of his era, Baldwin eventually adopted a secular humanist perspective and came to believe that Christianity would not be an effective tool for achieving racial equality and politi-cal power for black people. After three years of preaching, he posited that "the blood of the Lamb had not cleansed me in any way whatever. I was just as black as I had been the day I was born. Therefore, when I faced a congregation, it began to take all the strength I had not to stam-mer, not to curse, not to tell them to throw away their Bibles and get off their knees and go home and organize, for example, a rent strike." In noting that despite his conversion he was as black as when he was born, Baldwin argued in effect that God was powerless to remove the

stain of sin and worldliness from him. Furthermore, God was powerless to help poor people achieve economic equality and they could only
do so through their own efforts. This may have been because God was
white, as he claimed to believe earlier, or because God simply didn't
exist. The results were the same either way. When he taught Sunday
school for the young black children in his church, Baldwin began to
feel as though he was "committing a crime in talking about the gentle
Jesus, in telling them to reconcile themselves to their misery on earth
in order to gain the crown of eternal life. Were only Negroes to gain
this crown? Was Heaven, then, to be merely another ghetto?"[68]

Baldwin also embraced secular humanism because of what he saw
as the hypocrisy of the church. While ministers preached about love,
he believed the church was actually "a mask for hatred and self-hatred
and despair" because there was no love in it. He also started to believe
that the church was hypocritical on a number of fronts. At one point
a minister told him that he was never to give up his seat to a white
woman on a bus or train because a white man would never do the same
for a black woman. "Well, that was true enough, in the main—I saw
his point," Baldwin stated. "But what was the point, the purpose, of
my salvation if it did not permit me to behave with love toward others,
no matter how they behaved toward me?" Baldwin here professes a
belief in the Golden Rule, which enjoins Christians to do unto others
as they would have others do unto them. Unfortunately, in his opinion,
too few Christians actually practiced the Golden Rule. It might seem
that Black Christians, having been discriminated against for much if
not all of their lives, would be more cognizant of this rule, but Baldwin claimed that the opposite was true, a situation that made the faith
unpalatable to him. He eventually concluded that "whoever wishes to
become a truly moral human being . . . must first divorce himself from
all the prohibitions, crimes, and hypocrisies of the Christian church. If
the concept of God has any validity or any use, it can only be to make
us larger, freer, and more loving. If God cannot do this, then it is time
we got rid of Him."[69]

While he rejected Christian theology and belief, like many other
black freethinkers, Baldwin could never completely divorce himself
from the church. Despite his misgivings about Christianity, he continued to admire the joy and ability to face suffering prevalent among
black Christians. He also claimed "there is no music like that music, no
drama like the drama of the saints rejoicing, the sinners moaning, the
tambourines racing, and all those voices coming together and crying

holy unto the Lord." While he gave up formal preaching in church, he would continue to use the sermonic form in some of his works, including *Go Tell It on the Mountain*, *The Fire Next Time*, and *Blues for Mister Charlie*. Baldwin's sermons actually functioned to negate the power of institutions such as the government and the church and to empower those on the margins, including black people. Michele Elam argues that while sermons are generally geared toward the soul's salvation and the expansion of the church, "Baldwin uses the structure of the sermon to create collectivity, and by extension political agency, through bearing witness to shared experiences of disenfranchisement." Baldwin thus became something of a secular preacher who continued to employ the rhetoric, rhythms, and drama of sermons in his essays and fictional writing, especially in his early works.[70]

Perhaps the most critically acclaimed of his fictional works was his novel *Go Tell It on the Mountain*; this novel reflected Baldwin's experiences with and ambivalence toward Christianity. Baldwin conceived of this novel in the early 1940s, when he was seventeen years old. In 1944, he first met his fellow black freethinker Richard Wright. Baldwin traveled to Wright's Brooklyn apartment and gave him fifty pages of the manuscript, then titled *Crying Holy*. Wright read the draft, offered comments, and helped Baldwin procure a $500 grant from the Eugene F. Saxon Memorial Trust. Despite this influx of cash, it took Baldwin nearly a decade to publish the novel, which came out in 1953. It is an autobiographical work about a fourteen-year-old boy names John Grimes whose father, Gabriel, was a preacher and whom everyone thought would become one as well. The novel takes place on the Saturday of John's fourteenth birthday. The action moves between the past and the present, showing the many hypocrisies in Gabriel's claim to being a saint. Before Gabriel married John's mother, for example, he had cheated on his wife Deborah with a woman named Esther. After Esther got pregnant, Gabriel sent her up North, where she had her child and died shortly thereafter. In the present day, John's older brother Roy, who is more worldly than John, gets stabbed in a fight. That evening, John ends up in a service at his father's Temple of the Fire Baptized. As he is contemplating turning his life over to God, John asks questions such as, "Why did his mother weep? Why did his father frown? If God's power was so great, why were their lives so troubled?" Despite these brief misgivings, the final chapter details John's conversion experience, one that likely mirrored Baldwin's conversion at the same age.[71]

While *Go Tell It on the Mountain* might be seen as an affirmation of Pentecostalism and black Christianity, it is also an indictment of certain aspects of the faith. For one, John's father is a walking contradiction, as we learn regarding his infidelities. When Gabriel was cheating on his first wife, his brother-in-law Frank says to his wife Florence, "I thought you said you brother was a preacher," to which she replies, "being a preacher ain't never stopped a nigger from doing his dirt." Gabriel also does not seem to have the Christian love in his heart that one might expect of a preacher who claims to be saved. "His father said that all white people were wicked," John narrates, "and that God was going to bring them low. He said that white people were never to be trusted, and that they told nothing but lies, and that not one of them had ever loved a nigger." Even John's eventual acceptance of and conversion to Christianity has hints of revenge and spite toward his father. He notes at one point that if he accepted Jesus as his savior, then he would not have to fear his earthly father anymore. "Then he and his father would be equals, in the sight, and the sound, and the love of God. Then his father could not beat him any more, or despise him any more, or mock him any more—he, John, the Lord's anointed." John gives the reader a sense that his conversion is just as much about one-upping his father as it is about the love of God and the desire to join the community of saints. John's conversion can also be read as an indictment of black Christianity because John ultimately subjugates himself to the larger group. And like Baldwin himself, John in his conversion may have ushered in a false consciousness that will blind him to the political and social realities of his world.[72]

Baldwin's 1964 play *Blues for Mister Charlie* similarly criticizes and questions black people's acceptance of Christianity. The play is loosely based on the case of Emmett Till, the fourteen-year-old black youth from Chicago who was murdered in Mississippi in 1954 after whistling at a white woman. Baldwin's play takes place in Plaguetown, U.S.A., and he notes in the beginning that "the plague is race, the plague is our concept of Christianity," and this plague can destroy all human bonds of affection.[73] The work opens with the body of a young black man named Richard being dumped in the weeds by a white store owner named Lyle. There are two parts of the town, WHITETOWN and BLACK-TOWN. The first part of the play takes place in the latter, with nearly all of the action located in the church, led by Meridian, Richard's father. Baldwin thus recognizes the centrality of the church in black life but questions this centrality throughout the work. Early on, Lorenzo, a black student, is in the church cussing, and when someone points out he is in a sacred space, he responds,

> Well, I wish to God I was in an arsenal. I'm sorry Meridian, Mother Henry—I don't mean that for you. I don't understand you. I don't understand Meridian here. It was his son, it was your grandson, Mother Henry, that got killed, butchered! Just last week, and yet, here you sit—in this—this—the house of this damn almighty God who don't care what happens to nobody, unless, of course, they're white. Mother Henry, I got a lot of respect for you and all that, and for Meridian, too, but that white man's God is *white*. It's that damn white God that's been lynching us and burning us and castrating us and raping our women and robbing us of everything that makes a man a man for all these hundreds of years. Now, why we sitting around here, in *His* house? If I could get my hands on Him, I'd pull him out of heaven and drag Him through this town at the end of a rope.[74]

Baldwin here reiterates the point he made in *The Fire Next Time* that if there is a God, he must not care about black people. At the same time, he implicitly questions the existence of God altogether. He also displays the anger and contempt that many young people started to feel by the mid-1960s and the increasing restlessness regarding nonviolence that would lead to the rise of Black Power just two years later. A young woman named Juanita remarks to Lorenzo that if he carried out his threat, he'd be no better than white people. Lorenzo replies, "I don't want to be better than they are, why should I be better than they are? Better at being a doormat, better at being a corpse? Sometimes I just don't know. We've been demonstrating—*non-violently*—for more than a year now and all that's happened is that now they'll let us into the crummy library downtown."[75]

The main characters in the play either profess an open disbelief in God or raise serious questions about individual and collective belief in Christianity. At one point the play flashes back to when Richard had come back south after living in New York City, where he worked as a musician. Richard's grandmother, Mother Henry, says to him that the most important things to her growing up were taking care of her husband and raising her children to be God-fearing. Richard then tells her, "you know I don't believe in God, Grandmama." Her reply is reminiscent of Mama's response to Beneatha in *A Raisin in the Sun*: "You don't know what you talking about. Ain't no way possible for you not to believe in God. It ain't up to you." Richard wonders: if his own beliefs aren't up to him, who are they up to? Mother Henry argues, "it's up to the life in you. . . . *That* knows where it comes from, *that* believes in God." Baldwin raises a similar critique here of religious adherence as he does in *Go Tell It on the Mountain*: young black people are often forced to accept doctrines by the larger community, a move that stifles their individuality and restricts their options in life.[76]

James Baldwin's writing speaks to some of the key themes of the Black Power and black arts movements, but he did not completely embrace black nationalism because of his views on gender and sexuality. Andrew Shin and Barbara Judson point out that Baldwin developed "a vision of the homosexual as the chief instrument of cultural renovation. Indeed, bodily pleasure between men functions as a paradigm for the body politic—two men lying together spoon-fashion becomes an image of the just society." Baldwin began exploring themes of homoerotic desire in his first novel, *Go Tell It on the Mountain*. Early in the text, Baldwin introduces the reader to Elisha, John's seventeen-year-old Sunday school teacher. "John stared at Elisha all during the lesson, admiring the timbre of Elisha's voice, much deeper and manlier than his own, admiring the leanness, and grace, and strength, and darkness of Elisha in his Sunday suit." Toward the end of the novel, when John is undergoing his conversion experience, Elisha stays up for hours praying and "pleading the blood" for John. During John's ordeal, "in his heart there was a sudden yearning tenderness for holy Elisha; desire, sharp and awful as a reflecting knife, to usurp the body of Elisha, and lie where Elisha lay." John's reflections are likely similar to Baldwin's own at a young age, although it was not until he was twenty-four years old that Baldwin admitted to himself that he was gay. Baldwin went on to treat homosexuality as a valid form of love in novels such as *Giovanni's Room* (1956) and *Just Above My Head* (1979). Baldwin's notions of the body and sex are used to critique the subjugation and control that Christianity places on its adherents. At the same time, however, his ideas about sex draw from his evangelical heritage in positioning sexual desire and awakening as akin to a religious conversion. As Clarence Hardy argues, "Baldwin's vision of love is a bracing one. From the rigors of childbirth to the funk after sex, Baldwin sees our fleshy bodies as the very vehicles of love and grace. For Baldwin, true grace could not come any other way."[77]

James Baldwin's explorations of homosexuality in his fiction both alienated him from writers of his time period and freed future writers to explore similar themes in their work. In one letter, Richard Wright wrote derogatively about Baldwin's sexuality, "Yes, he can write. But he's a faggot." Wright and Baldwin had fallen out over two essays Baldwin wrote critiquing Wright's works "Many Thousands Gone" and "Alas, Poor Richard." Eldridge Cleaver similarly criticized Baldwin (and many others) for homosexuality in his book *Soul on Ice*. Cleaver believed that black homosexuals were even worse than Uncle Toms, who are just trying to survive; instead, gay blacks are intellectual sycophants who hate themselves. Cleaver decried the fact that Baldwin's characters in his novels "all seem to be fucking and sucking in a vacuum." Of Wright and Baldwin, Wright was the superior writer and social critic in Cleaver's eyes. "Baldwin has a superb touch when he speaks of human beings," Cleaver claimed, "when he is inside of them—especially his homosexuals—but he flounders when he looks beyond the skin; whereas Wright's forte, it seems to me, was in reflecting the intricate mechanism of a social organization, its functioning as a unit." Cleaver's criticism was especially damaging to Baldwin's reputation among writers of the black arts movement, many of whom shared his homophobic attitude. Baldwin's examination of the intersections of sexuality and religion, however, inspired writers of the 1970s and "opened the floodgate for contemporary anti-Christian, nonbiblically based black American literature," according to Sondra A. O'Neale. Black writers including Ntozake Shange, Toni Morrison, Alice Walker, and others portrayed characters with more expansive views of black identity and spirituality than had been the norm prior to the 1960s.[78]

One writer of the black arts movement whom Baldwin likely influenced was Nikki Giovanni. The two of them sat down for a conversation on the television program *Soul!* that was taped in London and aired in the United States on December 15 and 22, 1971. Their discussion was a wide-ranging one, touching on the vocation of the writer, feminism, and religion. Giovanni blasphemously remarked to Baldwin, "I never wanted to be the most moral person in the world. I would like—I would sell my soul—You know what I mean? What does it profit a man to gain the world and lose his soul? The world! You know what I mean? The world. That's what it profits him." While Giovanni had professed a belief in God two years earlier in an interview with Charles Hobson and Sheila Smith, by 1971 she showed a complete disregard for the traditional teachings of Christianity. To say that she would sell her soul to gain the world is in effect saying she does not believe she has a soul, or if she does, God is powerless over where it goes after she dies. Baldwin remarked that since he left the church, he had only gone back for fund-raisers and political meetings, to which she replied that she had grown up in a Baptist church and really enjoyed it. She noted further, however, "I can't dig theology, but the music and the energies of the church" she appreciated. Her religious views, then, are very similar to Baldwin's, as he continued to be influenced by his Pentecostal upbringing even while critiquing the theology and function of the church.[79]

Giovanni's lack of respect for religious ideas in her youth was reflected in much of her early work, which offered a powerful challenge to the politics of respectability. In her autobiography *Gemini*, published the same year as the discussion with Baldwin, Giovanni claimed that "the weak have made cleanliness next to godliness and God a green faggot who fucked nature and set the world in motion. The weak have made weakness a religion. The weaker you are the more you have a right to drain the strong." By saying God "fucked nature" to create the world, she is arguing against notions of the deity as a chaste being far removed from humanity, as the story of the Virgin Birth would have people believe. But later she indicates a lack of belief in God, noting, "God is dead. Jesus is dead. Allah is dead." With no more gods, she posits, humans need to begin celebrating other humans much more than they have, especially those who are still alive rather than just those who have died. Instead of writing songs and poems about Martin Luther King Jr., Malcolm X, and others, we need to "give a kind word to [Charles] Mingus, the Aylers, Aretha [Franklin], Ameer Baraka, Adam Powell."[80]

Giovanni's poetry also supported the main thrusts of the Black Power movement. She believed herself to be a revolutionary whose task it was to usher black people away from an acceptance of Western culture. Like members of the Black Panther Party, Giovanni also believed in the use of violence as an effective means of achieving revolution. One important twist in her ideology was that she believed "the revolution isn't to show what we're willing to die for; Black people have been willing to die for damned near everything on earth. It's to show what we're willing to kill for."[81] This attitude is reflected in the poem that has perhaps been anthologized more than any of her other works and is worth quoting at length:

Nigger
Can you kill
Can you kill
Can a nigger kill a honkie
Can a nigger kill the Man
Can you kill nigger
Huh? nigger can you
kill
Do you know how to draw blood
Can you poison
Can you stab-a-Jew
Can you kill huh? nigger
Can you kill
Can you run a protestant down with your
'68 El Dorado
(that's all they're good for anyway)
Can you kill
Can you piss on a blond head
Can you cut it off
Can you kill
A nigger can die
We ain't got to prove we can die
We got to prove we can kill
They sent us to kill
Japan and Africa
We policed europe
Can you kill
Can you kill a white man
Can you kill the nigger
in you
Can you make your nigger mind
die[82]

Here she indicates a desire for black men to be willing to kill whites for
their freedom rather than passively accept violence from white people.
But she also wants black people to kill the "nigger" and "Negro" within
them. This desire reflects a broader goal of the black arts movement—
namely, embracing use of the term "black" over "Negro" and especially
rejecting the racist use of the term "nigger," which is seen as an acqui-
escence to white supremacy. Giovanni also makes a subtle dig at the

ties between white supremacy and religion when she calls for black people to "run a protestant down with your '68 El Dorado." The Protestant to which she refers is almost certainly a white Christian who has held black people in subjugation. Being willing to kill one of them would be an affirmation of black humanity, in her view.[83]

Giovanni's rhetoric and ideology were common among other participants in the black arts movement, including women poets such as Sonia Sanchez and June Jordan. Cheryl Clarke argues that during the movement, "African Americans dreamed a different world and imagined a different black community where their rich heritage and culture would be honored." Women poets such as Giovanni fused their art and activism into a powerful critique of the status quo. This era was also the first time that black women poets openly discussed sexuality in frank terms, something that we have seen was also an important concern of freethinkers such as James Baldwin. Rejecting Western culture also included rejecting the Victorian sexual codes forbidding premarital sex and even openly discussing one's sexual life. For Giovanni, Baldwin, and other freethinkers of this era, sexual liberation went hand in hand with liberation from Christianity.[84]

This notion of sexual liberation would be an important concern of the burgeoning women's rights movement of the 1970s. While she was not a participant in the black arts movement, Florynce "Flo" Kennedy shared many of the same concerns and critiques of sexism as Nikki Giovanni. In her irreverently titled 1976 essay "Nobody Ever Died from a Blow Job," Kennedy argued for the legalization of prostitution and noted that "neither the feminists nor the church nor the government nor anybody else" has the right to tell women what they can and cannot do with their bodies. In an earlier piece, Kennedy compared the plight of women and blacks in American society and claimed that their oppression is similar because both groups encourage religion "and recognition of the divine right of the dominants are dramatized and applauded by society." For black feminists and freethinkers, then, religion was clearly the root cause of both black people's and women's oppression, and the only way to achieve a just society was to denounce Christianity and replace it with secular humanism. This perspective gained increasing currency during the 1960s and would continue to be a central concern of black freethinkers in the decades following the civil rights and Black Power movements.[85]

In the years following the civil rights movement, freethought remained prominent in African American literature, especially among women writers, including Octavia Butler. Black women are often the main characters in her works, and for some of them, such as Lilith Iyapo in her novel *Dawn*, God is simply a nonfactor. Lilith wakes up on an alien spacecraft hundreds of years after Earth has become uninhabitable. In attempting to navigate her new life, not once does Lilith consider why God put her in this situation or whether God will get her out. In Butler's short story "The Evening and the Morning and the Night," fifteen-year-old Lynn comes to disbelieve in God because both her parents died as a result of an incurable disease, Duryea-Gode Disease (DGD), and she knew she would someday as well. While in college, Lynn muses to herself, "two DGD parents—both religious, both as opposed to abortion as they were to suicide. So they had trusted God and the promise of modern medicine and had a child? But how could I look at what happened to them and trust anything?" For Lynn, as for nineteenth-century slaves and twentieth-century blacks enduring segregation and racist violence, the suffering in the world precluded the possibility of God's existence.[1]

Butler was an atheist who believed that human beings created religion and gods because they could not figure out how to live in harmony with one another. "At the moment there are no true aliens in our lives," she once wrote. There are "no gods or devils, no spirits, angels, or gnomes. Some of us know this. Deep within ourselves we know it. We're on our own, the focus of no interest except our consuming interest in ourselves." She proffered a humanist vision for life on earth, noting that "our only help is ourselves and one another." The reality of our being alone is too much for most people, she claimed; as a result, we have created aliens, both in outer space and among different peoples. These aliens are the various gods that human beings have imagined, she contended, a process that is a sign of weakness. "Sometimes we just need someone to talk to, someone we can trust to listen and care, someone who knows us as we really are and as we rarely get to know one another, someone whose whole agenda is us. Like children, we do still need great and powerful parent figures and we need invisible friends."[2]

Freethought was also a central theme in the work of Alice Walker, one of the most important writers of the twentieth century. Walker grew up in rural Georgia and entered Spelman College in 1961. While the leaders at Spelman desired to cultivate religion and respectability among its women, Walker bristled at her treatment there and became more skeptical of religion. She asserts, "as a freshman my feelings were very anti-religion and anti-church. I was brought up in a very rigidly church-going home." One of her professors, Staughton Lynd, a Quaker, helped her realize "that I was not being a sinner by not believing every-thing that had been tossed at me in church over the years." She started to attend Quaker meetings with Lynd and enjoyed them because every-one there was free to believe, or not believe, whatever they wished. And after the meetings, their discussions revolved around the civil rights movement and how to stop the war in Vietnam.[3]

Walker eventually became an atheist and a pagan. In a 1973 inter-view, she stated that she had seemingly spent her whole life rebelling against the church and "the truth is probably that I don't believe there is a God, although I would like to believe it. Certainly I don't believe there is a God beyond nature. The world is God. Man is God. So is a leaf or snake." For Walker, everything on earth is divine. In everyday life, she claimed, "I worship the Earth as God—representing everything—and Nature as its spirit." Perhaps the main reason she came to disbelieve in Christianity was the seeming cruelty of the faith. She wondered how the God of the Bible could be so cruel as to curse all humanity because two people ate a piece of fruit thousands of years ago. And she also bris-tled at the way religion was used to justify slavery and the oppression of women. "I try to imagine my mother and the other women calling on God as they gave birth, and I shudder at the image of Him they must have conjured. He was someone, after all, they had been taught, who said black people were cursed to be drawers of water and hewers of wood." Given this image, Walker argued, blacks' continued adher-ence to Christianity was harmful for their own self-esteem. "It is fatal to love a God who does not love you," she proclaimed. "A God created specifically to comfort, lead, advise, strengthen, and enlarge the tribal borders of someone else. We have been beggars at the table of religion that sanctioned our destruction." Human beings thus deserve to wor-ship a loving God, and Earth or Mother Nature is the natural choice, she concluded.[4]

Walker's earliest writings display the influence of her religious skepticism. Her short story "The Diary of an African Nun" is set in Uganda and critiques the religious colonization of African peoples. "At twenty I earned the right to wear this dress, never to be without it, always to bathe myself in cold water even in winter, and to wear my mission-cropped hair well covered." Walker's irony is clear; while the nun may have achieved her childhood goal of joining the Roman Catholic order, she has suffered because of it and will continue to do so. Every night she sits in her room until seven and then goes to bed. "Through the window I can hear the drums," she notes, "smell the roasting goat's meat, feel the rhythm of the festive chants." But she cannot participate in her people's culture because of her new religion. Additionally, she has to be an active agent in suppressing Ugandan religion and culture. "The drums will soon, one day, be silent. I will help muffle them forever. To assure life for my people in this world I must be among the lying ones and teach them how to die. I will turn their dances into prayers to an empty sky, and their lovers into dead men." Catholics denounced Walker for this story, including the Rev. Donald J. O'Leary, who wrote a letter critical of Walker in the journal *Freedomways*. Walker's reply reflected her growing humanist vision and belief that creeds are less important than actions. "Rev. O'Leary apparently believes that faith in his God and in the teaching of the Catholic church are both prerequisites for good works," she claimed. "I am more in sympathy with the Peace Corps. I would ask that missionaries offer help where help is needed without demanding conversion, celibacy, or the shunning of artificial methods of birth control."[5]

Walker's first novel, *The Third Life of Grange Copeland*, features an atheist as its main character and sharply critiques religion's role in black culture. Grange Copeland is an abusive alcoholic early in the novel and usually comes home drunk every Saturday night, brandishing his gun and threatening to kill his wife and his son Brownfield. On Sunday mornings, however, "Grange would make his way across the pasture and through the woods, headlong, like a blind man, to the Baptist church, where his voice above all the others was raised in song and prayer." While Grange attended church dutifully, he makes it clear later in the novel that he became an atheist when he was eight years old and remained one into adulthood. In the familiar story of the mourner's bench, Grange wanted to get saved during a revival service because his Uncle Buster promised him a whipping if he remained unconverted. During the service, Grange looked over and noticed that his Uncle Buster, drunk in church, had fallen asleep. A fly was hovering right near Uncle Buster's mouth, so Grange made a deal with God. "He said to himself that if the fly got inside Uncle Buster's mouth, *and if Uncle Buster swallowed it*, he would jump right up, claim he had found the Holy Ghost and join the church. He had decided the Holy Ghost was not coming on its own." The fly did go into Uncle Buster's mouth, and he swallowed it to prevent others from seeing it fly out. Grange thus jumped up, shook the preacher's hand, and ostensibly converted to Christianity." Like the conversions of Langston Hughes, Richard Wright, and James Forman under similar circumstances, Grange Copeland's was a feigned one. Grange posits that "he was a member of the church but did not believe in God. For how could any God with self-respect, he wanted to know, bargain with a boy of seven or eight, who proposed such a nasty deal and meal." Walker uses this story in part to critique the hypocrisy of religious people, who claim to be moral but do things like show up at church drunk. And she likewise condemns efforts of black Christians to force others to convert, especially with threats of physical abuse. Human beings should be absolutely free to choose their religious beliefs or to have no beliefs at all, she implies.[6]

Walker's nontraditional religious views influenced her most well-known work, *The Color Purple*. Published in 1982, this book focuses on a poor young black girl named Celie during the early 1900s. Celie endures repeated sexual abuse at the hands of her stepfather before being forced into a loveless and abusive marriage at the age of fourteen. She is separated from her sister and her children but finds a sense of sisterhood with her husband's sometime lover Shug Avery. Shug helps Celie stave off abuse from her husband and find a sense of identity and independence by the end of the book. With *The Color Purple*, Walker became the first black woman awarded a Pulitzer Prize, and the novel's 1985 film adaptation was nominated for multiple Academy Awards. As with her first novel, Walker saw this book as a critique against traditional Christian ideas of God. "*The Color Purple* is a book about learning to believe in your own god or goddess," she posited, "whatever is sacred to you. It is not about what other people are telling you. You get rid of the Charlton Heston-type God, you get rid of Yahweh." She especially objected to Christians telling people they were sinners damned to hell without faith in Jesus. Her solution was for people to "begin to be a child of what you actually are, a child of the earth. That is why at the end, Celie understands that if God is anything, God is everything."[7]

After publishing *The Color Purple*, many of Walker's writings and activities were geared toward various social justice causes, including vegetarianism, ecology, the environment, indigenous history and culture, and opposition to war. In 1993, she published *Warrior Marks* and produced a documentary by the same name to battle female genital mutilation (FGM). Her efforts helped raise critical awareness of FGM throughout the world and succeeded in reducing the practice in multiple African nations. Walker also made several humanitarian trips to Cuba to deliver medicine and discuss difficult issues such as racism and homophobia with government officials, including Fidel Castro. And she was also active in the movement to abolish apartheid in South Africa and in the animal rights movement. These efforts led the American Humanist Association to award her its Humanist of the Year award in 1997. This prize was established in 1953 "to recognize a person of national or international reputation who, through the application of humanist values, has made a significant contribution to the improvement of the human condition." Walker joined the ranks of prominent freethinkers such as Isaac Asimov, Bill Nye, and Richard Dawkins as winners of this prize. She was the first black woman so honored and just the second African American (A. Philip Randolph won the prize in 1970).[8]

Alice Walker's work has also played a significant role in the creation of "womanist theology," one of the central developments in black religious studies since the 1980s. Walker coined the term "womanism" and posits that a "womanist" is, in part, "a woman who loves other women, sexually and/or nonsexually. Appreciates and prefers women's culture, women's emotional flexibility . . . and women's strength." Furthermore, a "womanist is to feminist as purple to lavender." For Walker, it was important that black women create their own terms. While black feminism was a necessary correction to the feminism of white women, it did not go far enough, in her view. Black women theologians formulated womanist theology out of Walker's term to center the voices and lives of black women in theological discourse. This move was not without its critics, however, as some argued against using a secular term for theology. Cheryl J. Sanders, a Pentecostal minister and theologian, opposed using the word "womanism" because Walker's definition of the term is not theistic, Walker herself is not a Christian, and Walker's support for lesbianism was troubling to her. The advocates for using womanism, including scholars such as Katie G. Cannon, Delores S. Williams, and Jacquelyn Grant, won out. In a similar vein to the secularism of the

Black Power movement and its role in the creation of black theology, Walker's secular formulation has had a significant impact on the study and methodology of African American religion since the late 1980s.[9]

The freethinker Anthony Pinn has likewise made significant contributions to our scholarly understanding of black theology. At roughly the same time that Walker won the Humanist of the Year award, Pinn began publishing works aimed at broadening understanding of African American religion to include humanism. His 1998 book *Varieties of African American Religious Experience*, for example, asks, "How does theology address traditions that fall outside the Christian context, traditions that are contrary to, if not hostile toward, the basic claims of Christian faith?" For Pinn, it was necessary that black theology include traditions such as voodoo, Yoruba religion, Islam, and humanism. Doing so can push us to reconsider what the very term "religion" means, he argues. More recently, Pinn has been concerned with the creation of an African American humanist theology that does not take the existence of God as a given. His book *The End of God-Talk* contends that "God has never been anything more than a symbol—an organizing framework for viewing and living life in 'relationship too. . . .' This symbol has run its course, and it is no longer capable of doing the heavy lifting required for the contemporary world." Pinn also uses alternative sources for theological reflection, including African American literature, visual arts such as photography, and material culture. He does so because there are no sacred texts for black humanism, and the best way to construct a black humanist theology is to use the ethical principles of other black humanists, including individuals explored in this book such as Frederick Douglass and Richard Wright. Pinn's scholarly work has positioned him as the foremost academic working on black freethought in the United States. He has also played a significant role in the freethought movement itself. He is a frequent speaker at freethought venues such as the American Humanist Association's annual conference and has organized numerous talks, symposia, and conferences exploring black secularism. Additionally, Pinn published a memoir detailing his path away from being an ordained Methodist minister to embracing atheism, *Writing God's Obituary.*[10]

In addition to the continued influence of freethought on African American literature and theology, the key development in this movement has been its institutionalization starting in the late 1980s. Prior to this time, a small number of African Americans had participated in secular organizations such as the American Humanist Association,

American Atheists, and the Freedom From Religion Foundation. They likewise took part in the Ethical Culture Society and religious sects such as the Unitarian Universalists, which includes a significant number of nontheistic members and ministers. But blacks always remained a small minority within these organizations and rarely occupied national leadership positions. Additionally, the main priorities of these organizations—separation of church and state and the promotion of a secular nation—are also goals of black freethinkers but not their primary goals. Many began looking for ways to participate in the freethought movement in a way that could incorporate their racial identities as well as their nonreligious ones.[11]

Norm Allen Jr. formed the first black freethought organization in 1989, African Americans for Humanism (AAH), in order to increase awareness of humanism within the black community. It provided support for black atheists and those who were on the fence about religion and were looking for a rational approach to life. Additionally, AAH aimed to "solve many of the problems that confront African-Americans through education and self-reliance, thereby affirming that autonomy and freedom of choice are basic human rights." Other central goals of AAH included challenging religious ideas that have been at the heart of problems in the black community; emphasizing the importance of a "humanist moral education"; highlighting the contributions of black humanists in world history; promoting happiness on earth by sharing ideas; and "fighting against racism in every form." It worked toward these goals through multiple forums, including its blog, social media outlets such as Facebook and Twitter, national and regional conferences, and campus branches around the country.[12]

Black Atheists of America and Black Nonbelievers share many of the goals of AAH. Ayanna Watson founded Black Atheists of America in 2011 to bridge "the gap between atheism and the black community." As a minority within a minority, black atheists often confront ostracism from both whites and other blacks. Black Atheists of America thus hopes to create a stronger freethought movement by encouraging black atheists to openly proclaim their atheism and by supporting them when they do so. Among their programs is Science Cubed[3], which aims to promote equal access to scientific education by donating supplies to science programs across the country. Mandisa Thomas founded Black Nonbelievers in 2011. This group aims to connect "with other Blacks (and allies) who are living free of religion and other beliefs, and might otherwise be shunned by family and friends. Instead of accepting dogma, we seek to determine truth and morality through reason and evidence." Like Black Atheists of America, one of its specific goals is to support those blacks who might be hesitant to openly express their religious skepticism. The mission of the organization is to provide fellowship for black nonbelievers; provide a supportive and nurturing environment for black atheists coming out; promote atheist pride; and organize black atheists for charitable causes. Black Nonbelievers started in Atlanta and now includes branches in thirteen other cities as well.[13]

Along with these national groups, local organizations such as Black Skeptics of Los Angeles (BSLA) have similarly influenced the growth of black freethought. Founded in 2010, BSLA provides resources and education for atheists, humanists, and nonbelievers of color. Unlike other black freethought groups, it explicitly embraces Latino freethinkers in its mission statement, reflecting the prominence of the Latino community within Los Angeles. The group also aims to promote the work of black skeptics and humanists through outreach and educational efforts and social justice initiatives. BSLA's initiatives include organizing an annual conference and speaker discussion panels on topics ranging from humanism to feminism to educational access. In 2013, it created the First in the Family Humanist Scholarship to support high school students from underprivileged backgrounds who are engaged in social justice efforts in their communities. This scholarship is supported by organizations such as the Freedom From Religion Foundation and by donations from individual humanists and atheists. In providing this scholarship, BSLA is taking on one of the functions that churches often serve in black communities by supporting access to education. As BSLA member Sikivu Hutchinson notes in her work *Moral Combat*, "making black secular community relevant to African Americans will require more than an emphasis on science literacy and critical thinking." It will require a commitment of black secularists to move beyond a separation of church and state and work to address the myriad problems facing communities of color.[14]

The national and local freethought organizations reflect the growth of black secularism and articulate some of the primary goals of the "new black atheists." Since the mid-1990s, the number of black "nones," or those with no religious affiliation, has nearly doubled. As of 2014, blacks made up 3 percent of atheists, 3 percent of agnostics, and 9 percent of "nones" in the United States. New black atheists are not content to personally reject religion but instead have a goal of spreading freethought to the broader black community. Sikivu Hutchinson and Mandisa Thomas, for example, argue that religion hurt the black community by promoting sexism, patriarchy, and homophobia. They claim that black churches have failed to address drug addiction, housing inequities, health disparities, lack of employment opportunities, and other pressing social problems facing black Americans. Rather than attempting to apply religious solutions such as abstinence-only education to a problem such as teenage pregnancies, black atheists call for more sex education and access to birth control. Today new black atheists are more likely than ever to be women. While there have been prominent black women freethinkers like Zora Neale Hurston, Nella Larsen, Lorraine Hansberry, and Alice Walker, until recently it has been much more likely for men to openly embrace skepticism. New black atheists reject the politics of respectability that have held sway in the black community since the early 1900s. The politics of respectability demand that black women be chaste, temperate, industrious, and socially conservative. Above all, they must be religious. They must always portray the race in the best light.[15]

With women leading the contemporary freethought movement, the politics of respectability and its antifeminist tendencies are being undermined. As Hutchinson argues, "for many black atheist women, atheism's appeal lies in its deconstruction of the bankrupt mores, values, and ideologies that prop up patriarchy, sexism, heterosexism, racism, white supremacy, imperialism, and economic injustice."[16] As it has in the past, feminism remains an essential part of the new black atheists' humanism. New black atheists think that it is not enough to deny the existence of God, teach evolution in schools, or fight for the separation of church and state. They want to bring worldly solutions to practical problems. Many have embraced Black Lives Matter, a movement that is notably unaffiliated with black religious institutions. In doing so, they believe they will improve the lot of blacks in particular but will also be promoting a more just, more democratic, and less racist American society.

Black Freethinkers has argued that freethought has played a critical yet heretofore unexamined role in black cultural, political, and intellectual life. Black freethinkers have held a wide array of religious opinions, ranging from deism to paganism to atheism and agnosticism. What has united them is a commitment to reason, to improving life in this world, and to challenging racial inequality. Many of the most well-known thinkers and leaders in black communities throughout the United States have rejected the idea of God and instead embraced secular humanism as the best method for fighting racism, sexism, imperialism, and capitalism. While small in number when compared to black Christians, black freethinkers have been no fringe sect but rather people operating at the center of black life since the nineteenth century. It is time we see this vibrant intellectual tradition for what it is: one of the most significant in African American history.

NOTES

Introduction

1. Charles C. Jones, *The Religious Instruction of the Negroes. In the United States* (Savannah: Thomas Purse, 1842), 127.

2. William E. Channing, *Slavery* (Boston: James Munroe, 1835), 100, 108; Curtis J. Evans, *The Burden of Black Religion* (Oxford: Oxford University Press, 2008), 28, 44–45; Eugene Macdonald, "Colored Preachers," *Truth Seeker* 10, no. 26 (June 30, 1883): 409. This paragraph and three others in this introduction are adapted from my article "Slavery and African American Irreligion," *Journal of Southern Religion* 18 (2016): jsreligion.org/vol18/cameron.

3. *Executive Sessions of the Senate Permanent Subcommittee on Investigations of the Committee on Government Operations*, vol. 2, *Eighty-Third Congress: First Session, 1953* (Washington, D.C.: U.S. Government Printing Office, 2003), 980; Pew Research Center Religious Landscape Study, "Racial and Ethnic Composition," accessed July 31, 2017, http://www.pewforum.org/religious-landscape-study/racial-and-ethnic-composition/.

4. Sylvia R. Frey and Betty Wood, *Come Shouting to Zion: African American Protestantism in the American South and British Caribbean to 1830* (Chapel Hill: University of North Carolina Press, 1998), 63–148; Albert J. Raboteau, *Slave Religion: The "Invisible Institution" in the Antebellum South* (Oxford: Oxford University Press, 1978), 116, 120–21, 132; Mechal Sobel, *Trabelin' On: The Slave Journey to an Afro-Baptist Faith* (Princeton, N.J.: Princeton University Press, 1979), 101; Paul Harvey, *Through the Storm, Through the Night: A History of African American Christianity* (Lanham, Md.: Rowman and Littlefield, 2011), 21–48; Edward E. Curtis IV, *Muslims in America: A Short History* (Oxford: Oxford University Press, 2009), 1–46; Michael Gomez, *Exchanging Our Country Marks: The Transformation of African Identities in the Colonial and Antebellum South* (Chapel Hill: University of North Carolina Press, 1998); Yvonne P. Chireau, *Black Magic:*

Religion and the African American Conjuring Tradition (Berkeley: University of California Press, 2003).

5. Daniel L. Fountain, *Slavery, Civil War, and Salvation: African American Slaves and Christianity, 1830–1870* (Baton Rouge: Louisiana State University Press, 2010), 1–3, 8; Anthony B. Pinn, *Varieties of African American Religious Experience* (Minneapolis: Augsburg Fortress Publishers, 1998); Anthony B. Pinn, *Introducing African American Religion* (London: Routledge, 2013); Anthony B. Pinn, *The End of God-Talk: An African American Humanist Theology* (Oxford: Oxford University Press, 2012); Norm Allen Jr., ed. *The Black Humanist Experience: An Alternative to Religion* (Amherst, N.Y.: Prometheus Books, 2003); Sikivu Hutchinson, *Moral Combat: Black Atheists, Gender Politics, and the Values Wars* (Los Angeles: Infidel Books, 2011); Sikivu Hutchinson, *Godless Americana: Race and Religious Rebels* (Los Angeles: Infidel Books, 2013); Donald R. Barbera, *Black and Not Baptist: Nonbelief and Freethought in the Black Community* (New York: iUniverse, 2003); Candace R. M. Gorham, *The Ebony Exodus Project: Why Some Black Women Are Walking Out on Religion—and Others Should Too* (Durham, N.C.: Pitchstone Publishing, 2013).

6. Herbert M. Morais, *Deism in Eighteenth Century America* (1934; repr., New York: Russell and Russell, 1960); Kerry Walters, *Revolutionary Deists: Early America's Rational Infidels* (New York: Prometheus Books, 2011); Christopher Grasso, "Skepticism and American Faith: Infidels, Converts, and Religious Doubt in the Early Nineteenth Century" *Journal of the Early Republic* 22 (2002): 465–508; Eric R. Schlereth, *An Age of Infidels: The Politics of Religious Controversy in the Early United States* (Philadelphia: University of Pennsylvania Press, 2013); Susan Jacoby, *Freethinkers: A History of American Secularism* (New York: Owl Books, 2004), 17; Evelyn A. Kirkley, *Rational Mothers and Infidel Gentlemen: Gender and American Atheism, 1865–1915* (Syracuse, N.Y.: Syracuse University Press, 2000); James Turner, *Without God, Without Creed: The Origins of Unbelief in America* (Baltimore: Johns Hopkins University Press, 1985), xii.

7. James Turner, *Without God, Without Creed*; Charles Taylor, *A Secular Age* (Cambridge, Mass.: Harvard University Press, 2007); Jonathan S. Kahn and Vincent W. Lloyd, eds. *Race and Secularism in America* (New York: Columbia University Press, 2016), 10. Throughout this book I use sociologist José Casanova's framework of secularism as ideology, of which there are two main parts—philosophical-historical and political. The first of these secularisms posits religion as a relic of a bygone era, while the second sees religion as an irrational force that should be eliminated from the public sphere. Most black secularists posited a political secularism. See

José Casanova, "The Secular, Secularizations, Secularisms," in *Rethinking Secularism*, ed. Craig Calhoun, Mark Juergensmeyer, and Jonathan Vanantwerpen (Oxford: Oxford University Press, 2011), 66–67.

8. Hutchinson, *Moral Combat*, 119–22.

9. Judith Weisenfeld, "On Jordan's Stormy Banks: Margins, Center, and Bridges in African American Religious History," in *New Directions in American Religious History*, ed. Harry S. Stout and D. G. Hart (New York: Oxford University Press, 1997), 418.

10. Erik S. McDuffie, *Sojourning for Freedom: Black Women, American Communism, and the Making of Black Left Feminism* (Durham, N.C.: Duke University Press, 2011), 40.

11. William R. Jones, *Is God a White Racist? A Preamble to Black Theology* (1973; repr., Boston: Beacon Press 1998), 185.

Chapter 1

1. Nathaniel Paul, "Emancipation Address," in *Jim Crow New York: A Documentary History of Race and Citizenship, 1777–1827*, ed. David N. Gellman and David Quigley (New York: New York University Press, 2003), 228, 231.

2. Charles W. Akers, *Called unto Liberty: A Life of Jonathan Mayhew, 1720–1766* (Cambridge, Mass.: Harvard University Press, 1964), 46–47, 60–65; Jonathan Mayhew, *Seven Sermons Upon the Following Subjects* [. . .] (Boston: Rogers and Fowle, 1749), 15.

3. Mayhew, *Seven Sermons*, 38, 107.

4. Louis P. Masur, ed. *The Autobiography of Benjamin Franklin, with Related Documents* (Boston: Bedford/St. Martin's, 2003), 73. For Ebenezer Gay, Charles Chauncy, and the growth of Arminianism in colonial America, see Robert J. Wilson III, *The Benevolent Deity: Ebenezer Gay and the Rise of Rational Religion in New England, 1696–1787* (Philadelphia: University of Pennsylvania Press, 1984); and Charles Chauncy, *Twelve Sermons on the Following Seasonable and Important Subjects* . . . (Boston: Kneeland, 1765), 183, 194.

5. Henry F. May, *The Enlightenment in America* (Oxford: Oxford University Press, 1976), 21; Kerry Walters, *Revolutionary Deists: Early America's Rational Infidels* (New York: Prometheus Books, 2011), 7–8.

6. Thomas Paine, *The Age of Reason* (1794; repr., New York: Barnes and Noble, 2006), 3–4, 6.

7. Thomas Paine, *Common Sense and Related Writings*, ed. Thomas P. Slaughter (Boston: Bedford/St. Martin's, 2001), 82; Paine, *The Age of Reason*, 30.

8. Walters, *Revolutionary Deists*, 179–86.

9. Elihu Palmer, *The Examiners Examined; Being a Defence of the Age of Reason* (New York: L. Wayland and J. Fellows, 1794), 16, 84; Herbert M. Morais, *Deism in Eighteenth Century America* (1934; repr., New York: Russell and Russell, 1960), 131–33.

10. Eric R. Schlereth, *An Age of Infidels: The Politics of Religious Controversy in the Early United States* (Philadelphia: University of Pennsylvania Press, 2013), 174, 196, 197, 209–13; Lori D. Ginzberg, "'The Hearts of Your Readers Will Shudder': Fanny Wright, Infidelity, and American Freethought," *American Quarterly* 46 (1994): 195–226; Helen Lefkowitz Horowitz, *Rereading Sex: Battles over Sexual Knowledge and Suppression in Nineteenth-Century America* (New York: Alfred A. Knopf, 2002), 45–68.

11. Schlereth, *An Age of Infidels*, 10; For more on freethought during the revolutionary and early national periods, see Christopher Grasso, *Skepticism and American Faith: From the Revolution to the Civil War* (New York: Oxford University Press, 2018).

12. This emphasis on suffering as a key feature of slavery is evident in the earliest slave narratives, especially in titles including John Jea's *The Life, History, and Unparalleled Sufferings of John Jea* (Portsea, England, 1811).

13. Kirsten Fischer, *Suspect Relations: Sex, Race, and Resistance in Colonial North Carolina* (Ithaca, N.Y.: Cornell University Press, 2002), 161.

14. Harriet Jacobs, *Incidents in the Life of a Slave Girl. Written by Herself*, ed. Lydia Maria Child (Boston: printed by the author, 1861), 44, http://docsouth.unc.edu/fpn/jacobs/jacobs.html.

15. Jacobs, *Incidents in the Life of a Slave Girl*, 24.

16. Austin Steward, *Twenty-Two Years a Slave, and Forty Years a Freeman; Embracing a Correspondence of Several Years, while President of Wilberforce Colony, London, Canada West* (Rochester: William Alling, 1857), 96–97, http://docsouth.unc.edu/fpn/steward/steward.html.

17. Henry Bibb, *Narrative of the Life and Adventures of Henry Bibb, an American Slave, Written by Himself. With an Introduction by Lucius C. Matlack* (New York: printed by the author, 1849), 13, 15, http://docsouth .unc.edu/neh/bibb/bibb.html.

18. Daniel Payne, *Recollections of Seventy Years* (Nashville: A. M. E. Sunday School Union, 1888), 19–20, 27, 28, http://docsouth.unc.edu /church/payne70/payne.html. Virginia's laws in this era display a similarly renewed hostility to slave education. An 1838 law, for instance, stated that any free blacks who left the state to be educated would not be allowed to return; see June Purcell Guild, *Black Laws of Virginia: A Summary of the*

Legislative Acts of Virginia Concerning Negroes from Earliest Times to the Present (Richmond: Whittet and Shepperson, 1936), 112.

19. Frederick Douglass, *Narrative of the Life of Frederick Douglass, An American Slave, Written by Himself* (Boston: American Anti-Slavery Society, 1845), 1, 33, http://docsouth.unc.edu/neh/douglass/douglass.html.

20. Charles Ball, *Slavery in the United States: A Narrative of the Life and Adventures of Charles Ball* [. . .] (New York: John S. Taylor, 1837), 164–65, http://docsouth.unc.edu/neh/ballslavery/ball.html; Jacobs, *Incidents in the Life of a Slave Girl*, 113.

21. Catherine Adams and Elizabeth H. Pleck, *Love of Freedom: Black Women in Colonial and Revolutionary New England* (Oxford: Oxford University Press, 2010), 4, 106–7; Christopher Cameron, *To Plead Our Own Cause: African Americans in Massachusetts and the Making of the Antislavery Movement* (Kent, Ohio: Kent State University Press, 2014), 12; Allan Kulikoff, "How Africans Became African Americans," in *Major Problems in African-American History*, vol. 1, *From Slavery to Freedom, 1619–1877*, ed. Thomas C. Holt and Elsa Barkley Brown (Boston: Wadsworth, 2000), 191; Walter Johnson, *Soul by Soul: Life Inside the Antebellum Slave Market* (Cambridge, Mass.: Harvard University Press, 1999), 5–6; Bibb, *Narrative of the Life and Adventures of Henry Bibb*, 108.

22. Robert Pierce Forbes, *The Missouri Compromise and Its Aftermath: Slavery and the Meaning of America* (Chapel Hill: University of North Carolina Press, 2007), 34, 38; Daniel Walker Howe, *What Hath God Wrought: The Transformation of America, 1815–1848* (Oxford: Oxford University Press, 2007), 125–28; Gordon S. Wood, *Empire of Liberty: A History of the Early Republic, 1789–1815* (Oxford: Oxford University Press, 2009), 357.

23. Nathan O. Hatch, *The Democratization of American Christianity* (New Haven, Conn.: Yale University Press, 1989), 3, 103–4; Howe, *What Hath God Wrought*, 164–87.

24. Allen Dwight Callahan, *The Talking Book: African Americans and the Bible* (New Haven, Conn.: Yale University Press, 2006), 83–137. For the role of the Exodus story in northern black religious and political thought, see Eddie S. Glaude Jr., *Exodus! Religion, Race, and Nation in Early Nineteenth-Century Black America* (Chicago: University of Chicago Press, 2000).

25. Guild, *Black Laws of Virginia*, 107; Albert J. Raboteau, *Slave Religion: The 'Invisible Institution' in the Antebellum South* (Oxford: Oxford University Press, 1978), 212–15, 231.

26. Ball, *Slavery in the United States*, 165; For the appeal of Catholicism among slaves in the United States, see Raboteau, *Slave Religion*, 271–75.

27. John C. Willis, "From the Dictates of Pride to the Paths of Righteousness: Slave Honor and Christianity in Antebellum Virginia," in *The Edge of the South: Life in Nineteenth-Century Virginia*, ed. Edward L. Ayers and John C. Willis (Charlottesville: University Press of Virginia, 1991), 37–38, 42; Daniel Fountain, *Slavery, Civil War, and Salvation: African American Slaves and Christianity, 1830–1870* (Baton Rouge: Louisiana State University Press, 2010), 1; Yvonne P. Chireau, *Black Magic: Religion and the African American Conjuring Tradition* (Berkeley: University of California Press, 2003), 12, 14.

28. Raboteau, *Slave Religion*, 258. Part of this section was adapted from my article: Christopher Cameron, "Slavery and African American Irreligion," *Journal of Southern Religion* 18 (2016): jsreligion.org/vol18/cameron.

29. Steward, *Twenty-Two Years a Slave*, 99.

30. Ball, *Slavery in the United States*, 165.

31. Bibb, *Narrative of the Life and Adventure of Henry Bibb*, 22–23; Peter Randolph, *Sketches of Slave Life: Or, Illustrations of the "Peculiar Institution"* (Boston: printed by the author, 1855), 31–32, 30.

32. William Wells Brown, *Narrative of William W. Brown, a Fugitive Slave. Written by Himself* (Boston: American Anti-Slavery Society, 1847), reprinted in *I Was Born a Slave: An Anthology of Classic Slave Narratives*, vol. 1, *1772–1849*, ed. Yuval Taylor (Chicago: Lawrence Hill Books, 1999), 691.

33. Cotton Mather, *The Negro Christianized: An Essay to Excite and Assist that Good Work, the Instruction of Negro-Servants in Christianity* (Boston: B. Green, 1706), 21; Christine Leigh Heyrman, *Southern Cross: The Beginnings of the Bible Belt* (Chapel Hill: University of North Carolina Press, 1997), 24, 155–58; A. T. Holmes, "The Duties of Christian Masters (1851)," in *Defending Slavery: Proslavery Thought in the Old South, A Brief History with Documents*, ed. Paul Finkelman (Boston: Bedford/St. Martin's, 2003), 106; Thornton Stringfellow, "The Bible Argument: Or, Slavery in the Light of Divine Revelation (1860)," in Finkelman, *Defending Slavery*, 123.

34. John R. McKivigan, *The War against Proslavery Religion: Abolitionism and the Northern Churches, 1830–1865* (Ithaca, N.Y.: Cornell University Press, 1984), 15, 14, 30.

35. W. Brown, *Narrative of William W. Brown*, 702; Bibb, *Narrative of the Life and Adventures of Henry Bibb*, 23–24; Jacobs, *Incidents in the Life of a Slave Girl*, 115.

36. Jacobs, *Incidents in the Life of a Slave Girl*, 115.

37. Jacobs, *Incidents in the Life of a Slave Girl*, 36; Solomon Northup, *Twelve Years a Slave. Narrative of Solomon Northup* [. . .] (Auburn, N.Y., 1854), 136.

38. Raboteau, *Slave Religion*, 121–22; Charles C. Jones, *The Religious Instruction of the Negroes. In the United States* (Savannah: Thomas Purse, 1842), 125.

39. Daniel Payne, "Slavery Brutalizes Man," *Lutheran Herald and Journal of the Fort Plain, N.Y., Franckean Synod* 1, no. 15 (August 1, 1839): 113.

40. Ezra Greenspan, *William Wells Brown: An African American Life* (New York: W. W. Norton, 2014), 174, 175.

41. William Wells Brown, *Clotel or, The President's Daughter* (1853; New York: Penguin Books, 2004), 44–45, 46, 50, 51.

42. Greenspan, *William Wells Brown*, 175; W. Brown, *Clotel*, 57, 72–73, 74.

43. Brown, *Clotel*, 77, 78, 79.

44. Scott C. Williamson, *The Narrative Life: The Moral and Religious Thought of Frederick Douglass* (Macon, Ga.: Mercer University Press, 2002), 3, 57; Douglass, *Narrative*, 57, 60–61. For a view of the Second Coming, see Matt. 24:42–44 (AV). My interpretation in this and the following two paragraphs draws from Zachary McLeod Hutchins, "Rejecting the Root: The Liberating, Anti-Christ Theology of Douglass's *Narrative*," *Nineteenth-Century Literature* 68, no. 3 (December 2013): 307–8.

45. Douglass, *Narrative*, 67–68, 70, 71–72.

46. Douglass, *Narrative*, 71; Hutchins, "Rejecting the Root," 306–7, 308–9.

47. James A. Colaiaco, *Frederick Douglass and the Fourth of July* (New York: Palgrave Macmillan, 2006), 71, 126–27.

48. Quoted in Waldo E. Martin Jr., *The Mind of Frederick Douglass* (Chapel Hill: University of North Carolina Press, 1984), 137.

49. Martin, *Mind of Frederick Douglass*, 136.

50. Martin, *Mind of Frederick Douglass*, 147.

51. Martin, *Mind of Frederick Douglass*, 159.

52. Douglass, *Narrative*, 54

53. Frederick Douglass, *My Bondage and My Freedom*, in *The Frederick Douglass Papers*, ser. 2, *Autobiographical Writings*, vol. 2, *My Bondage and My Freedom*, ed. John W. Blassingame, John R. McKivigan, and Peter P. Hinks (New Haven, Conn.: Yale University Press, 2003), 130; Frederick Douglass, "What to the Slave Is the Fourth of July?" in *Narrative of the Life of Frederick Douglass, An American Slave: Written by Himself, with Related Documents* 2nd ed., ed. David W. Blight (Boston: Bedford/St. Martin's, 2003), 164; Colaiaco, *Frederick Douglass and the Fourth of July*, 18.

54. Quoted in Herbert Aptheker, "An Unpublished Frederick Douglass Letter," in Anthony B. Pinn, *By These Hands: A Documentary History of African American Humanism* (New York: NYU Press, 2001), 79, 80, 77.

55. Frederick Douglass, "A Liberal Selection," *Boston Investigator* 40, no. 6 (June 29, 1870): 266.

56. Maria Diedrich, *Love Across Color Lines: Ottilie Assing and Frederick Douglass* (New York: Hill and Wang, 1999), 228, 229.

57. The Iconoclast, "Fred. Douglass on the Supernatural," *Boston Investigator* 40, no. 33 (December 14, 1870): 261; for the Free Religious Association, see Sidney Warren, *American Freethought, 1860–1914* (New York: Gordian Press, 1966), 34; Frederick Douglass to Mr. Potter, 15 May 1874, in Frederic May Holland, *Frederick Douglass: The Colored Orator* rev. ed. (New York: Haskell House, 1969), 334–35; Free Religious Association, *The Free Religious Association: Proceedings at the Forty-sixth Annual Meeting* (Boston: Free Religious Association, 1913), 5.

58. William L. Van Deburg, "Frederick Douglass: Maryland Slave to Religious Liberal," in Pinn, *By These Hands*, 90; Robert G. Ingersoll, *The Works of Robert G. Ingersoll, in Twelve Volumes*, vol. 7, Dresden ed., *Interviews* (New York: Dresden Publishing, 1908), 136–37; Susan Jacoby, *The Great Agnostic: Robert Ingersoll and American Freethought* (New Haven, Conn.: Yale University Press, 2013), 107, 111–12.

59. Cincore quoted in Leigh Eric Schmidt, *Village Atheists: How America's Unbelievers Made Their Way in a Godly Nation* (Princeton, N.J.: Princeton University Press, 2016), 140, 141; for Cincore's attendance at national freethought conventions and reference to him as the "colored Bob Ingersoll," see Samuel P. Putnam, *400 Years of Freethought* (New York: Truth Seeker, 1894), 661; "infidel slime" quotation from *Christian Recorder*, December 25, 1890.

60. Lord A. Nelson, "A Colored Brother's Enthusiasm," *Freethought*, March 24, 1888, 150; R. S. King, "'Is There a God?' Asks a Colored Brother," letter to the editor, *Truth Seeker* 31, no. 51 (December 17, 1904): 809; Schmidt, *Village Atheists*, 141.

61. "Negroes Praised Him: What Prominent Colored Men of Washington Said of Robert G. Ingersoll," *Truth Seeker* 26, no. 16 (April 20, 1901): 246.

62. Daniel Smith Lamb, *Howard University Medical Department: A Historical, Biographical and Statistical Souvenir* (Washington, D.C.: R. Beresford, 1900), 238; Julius J. Chilcoat, "From a Colored Physician," letter to the editor, *Liberal Review* 1, no. 1 (February 1904): 58.

63. Mr. Carr, "The Negro's Viewpoint of the Negro Question," *Truth Seeker* 30, no. 21 (May 23, 1903): 326.

64. Carr, "Negro's Viewpoint," 327.

65. J. M. Benjamin, "Negro Question Not a Burning One," *Truth Seeker* 30, no. 50 (December 12, 1903): 790; W. L. Dolphyn, "Must Lynch Them," *Truth Seeker* 30, no. 40 (October 3, 1903): 634; S. Rittenberg, "Lynching Excused," *Truth Seeker* 26, no. 24 (June 17, 1899): 378.

66. Charles D. McBride, "The Hose Murder," *Truth Seeker* 26, no. 30 (July 29, 1899): 474–75; H. Sandberg, "The Crime of Lynching," *Truth Seeker* 28, no. 44 (November 2, 1901): 697; J. W. Mehaffey, "Where Was God?" *Boston Investigator* 62, no. 47 (February 22, 1893): 2.

67. Hugh O. Pentecost, "How We Treat Negroes," *Truth Seeker* 30, no. 23 (June 6, 1903): 354; Will S. Andres, "Impromptu Thoughts," *Boston Investigator* 60, no. 24 (September 17, 1890): 2; "Harvard's Colored Class-Day Orator," *Boston Investigator* 60, no. 13 (July 2, 1890): 4.

68. Eugene Macdonald, "Colored Preachers," *Truth Seeker* 10, no. 26 (June 30, 1883): 409; Eugene Macdonald, "The Negro Problem," *Truth Seeker* 30, no. 10 (March 7, 1903): 148. For a fuller treatment of race and freethought in Great Britain and the United States, see Nathan Alexander, *Race in a Godless World: Atheism, Race, and Civilization in Britain and the United States, c. 1850–1914* (New York and Manchester: New York University Press and Manchester University Press, 2019).

Chapter 2

1. Wallace D. Best, *Langston's Salvation: American Religion and the Bard of Harlem* (New York: New York University Press, 2017), 5; Josef Sorrett, *Spirit in the Dark: A Religious History of Racial Aesthetics* (New York: Oxford University Press, 2016), 6, 20.

2. Michael Lackey, *African American Atheists and Political Liberation: A Study of the Sociocultural Dynamics of Faith* (Gainesville: University Press of Florida, 2007), 16.

3. James R. Grossman, *Land of Hope: Chicago, Black Southerners, and the Great Migration* (Chicago: University of Chicago Press, 1989), 3–19; David Levering Lewis, *When Harlem Was in Vogue* (New York: Oxford University Press, 1979), 21; Historian Steven Hahn notes that the push for emigration from 1915 to 1930 closely resembles the grassroots emigrationism of black southerners in the 1870s. See his *A Nation under Our Feet: Black Political Struggles in the Rural South from Slavery to the Great Migration* (Cambridge, Mass.: Harvard University Press, 2003), 467. For more on the Great Migration, see Isabel Wilkerson, *The Warmth of Other Sons: The Epic Story of America's Great Migration* (New York: Vintage, 2010).

4. Grossman, *Land of Hope*, 57, 94–95, 144–45; Wallace D. Best, *Passionately Human, No Less Divine: Religion and Culture in Black Chicago, 1915–1952* (Princeton, N.J.: Princeton University Press, 2005), 2, 51, 83–86, 100; Davarian Baldwin, *Chicago's New Negroes: Modernity, The Great Migration, and Black Urban Life* (Chapel Hill: University of North Carolina Press, 2007), 155–91; For more on how the Great Migration impacted urban northern religious life, see Milton C. Sernett, *Bound for the Promised Land: African American Religion and the Great Migration* (Durham, N.C.: Duke University Press, 1997), 122–79.

5. David Levering Lewis, ed. *The Portable Harlem Renaissance Reader* (New York: Penguin Books, 1994), xiii, xxii; Jeffrey B. Ferguson, *The Harlem Renaissance: A Brief History with Documents* (Boston: Bedford/ St. Martin's, 2008), 1–2, 6–8; Lewis, *When Harlem Was in Vogue*, 48; The Harlem Renaissance was the cultural and intellectual center of the broader New Negro Renaissance, which influenced black literature and art throughout the North and South, primarily touching urban areas such as Chicago, Detroit, Memphis, and New Orleans. For the worldwide influence of the movement, see Davarian Baldwin and Minkah Makalani, eds., *Escape from New York: The New Negro Renaissance Beyond Harlem* (Minneapolis: University of Minnesota Press, 2013).

6. Arnold Rampersad, *The Life of Langston Hughes*, vol. 1, *1902–1941: I, Too, Sing America* (New York: Oxford University Press, 1986), 50–51; Ferguson, *Harlem Renaissance*, 7–8.

7. Lewis, *Portable Harlem Renaissance Reader*, xxx–xxxi; W. E. B. Du Bois, "Criteria of Negro Art," *Crisis* 32 (October 1926): 296; Langston Hughes, "The Negro Artist and the Racial Mountain," *Nation* 122, no. 3181 (June 23, 1926): 692.

8. James Turner, *Without God, Without Creed: The Origins of Unbelief in America* (Baltimore: Johns Hopkins University Press, 1985), 119.

9. James Turner, *Without God, Without Creed*, 136; Lewis, *Portable Harlem Renaissance Reader*, xiv.

10. Lackey, *African American Atheists and Political Liberation*, 121.

11. N. J. Demerath, "Irreligion, A-Religion, and the Rise of the Religion-Less Church: Two Case Studies in Organizational Convergence," *Sociological Analysis* 30, no. 4 (1969): 192–93; Alain Locke, "Moral Training in Elementary Schools," *Teacher.* 8, no. 4 (April 1904): 96–97; David Weinfeld, "Isolated Believer: Alain Locke, Baha'i Secularist," in *New Perspectives on the Black Intellectual Tradition*, ed. Keisha Blain et al. (Evanston, Ill.: Northwestern University Press, 2018), 87.

12. Alain Locke, "The True Nature of a Church," March 1, 1904, and Alain Locke to Mary Locke, 3 November 1906, box 52, folder 15, both in Alain Locke Papers, Moorland-Springarn Research Center, Washington, D.C.; Weinfeld, "Isolated Believer," 87–88.

13. Winston James, *A Fierce Hatred of Injustice: Claude McKay's Jamaica and his Poetry of Rebellion* (London: Verso, 2000), 18–28; U. Theo McKay to Claude McKay, 26 April 1929, box 5, folder 143, Claude McKay Papers, Beinecke Rare Book and Manuscript Library, Yale University, New Haven, Conn. (hereafter cited as Beinecke Library); Claude McKay, *My Green Hills of Jamaica and Five Jamaican Short Stories*, ed. Mervyn Morris (Kingston, Jamaica: Heinemann Educational Book [Caribbean], 1979), 19.

14. McKay, *My Green Hills of Jamaica*, 41, 42, 44; C. A. Wilson, *Men with Backbone: And Other Pleas for Progress*, 2nd ed. (Kingston, Jamaica: Educational Supply Company, 1913), 69, 74; James, *Fierce Hatred of Injustice*, 29–30.

15. Rampersad, *The Life of Langston Hughes*, 13–17.

16. Charles H. Lippy, *Introducing American Religion* (London: Routledge, 2009), 80.

17. Langston Hughes, *The Big Sea* (New York: Hill and Wang, 1940), 19, 20.

18. Hughes, *The Big Sea*, 20, 21.

19. For Kierkegaard's fideism, or argument that religious truth is subjective and should not be subject to the same types of proofs as other kinds of truth, see his "Truth Is Subjectivity" in *Philosophy of Religion: Selected Readings*, 2nd ed., ed. Michael Peterson et al. (New York: Oxford University Press, 2001), 94–97.

20. Hughes, *The Big Sea*, 21–22; Rampersad, *Life of Langston Hughes*, 17. For the *Appeal to Reason*, see Elliot Shore, *Talkin' Socialism: J. A. Wayland and the Role of the Press in American Radicalism, 1890–1912* (Lawrence: University Press of Kansas, 1988). For Emanuel Haldeman-Julius and American freethought, see Susan Jacoby, *Freethinkers: A History of American Secularism* (New York: Owl Books, 2004), 263–66. I discuss the connections between socialism, communism, and black freethought in chapter 3.

21. Hughes, *The Big Sea*, 25–26.

22. Hughes, *The Big Sea*, 42.

23. Zora Neale Hurston, *Dust Tracks on a Road*, in *Folklore, Memoirs, and Other Writings* (New York: Library of America, 1995), 755.

24. Hurston, *Dust Tracks on a Road*, 755, 754.

25. Hurston, *Dust Tracks on a Road*, 754; Roy Jackson, *The God of Philosophy: An Introduction to the Philosophy of Religion*, 2nd ed. (Durham, U.K.: Acumen, 2011), 67–74.

26. Hurston, *Dust Tracks on a Road*, 759, 763; Ludwig Feuerbach, *The Essence of Christianity* (London: John Chapman, 1854) https://archive.org /details/a581696600feneuoft. A closer contemporary of Hurston's, Sigmund Freud, was also influenced by Feuerbach, believing that God is a mental projection human beings create to deal with psychological problems in this world. See Sigmund Freud, *The Future of an Illusion* (1927; repr., New York: W. W. Norton, 1989).

27. Hurston, *Dust Tracks on a Road*, 763, 764; Friedrich Nietzsche, *Beyond Good and Evil: Prelude to a Philosophy of the Future*, trans. Walter Kaufmann (1886; repr., New York: Vintage Books, 1989), 60; Will Durant, *The Story of Philosophy: The Lives and Opinions of the Greater Philosophers* (New York: Simon and Schuster, 1951), 315.

28. Richard Wright, *Black Boy (American Hunger)* (1945; repr., New York: HarperCollins, 1998), 26. For anecdotes and jokes about the preacher and fried chicken in black folklore, see Psyche A. Williams Forson, "'Suckin' the Chicken Bone Dry': African American Women, Fried Chicken, and the Power of a National Narrative," in *Cooking Lessons: The Politics of Gender and Food*, ed. Sherrie A. Inness (Lanham, Md.: Rowman and Littlefield, 2001), 182.

29. Wright, *Black Boy*, 39, 40.

30. Wright, *Black Boy*, 102.

31. Wright, *Black Boy*, 103, 104; Michel Fabre, *The Unfinished Quest of Richard Wright* (1973; Urbana: University of Illinois Press, 1993), 33.

32. Wright, *Black Boy*, 104.

33. Wright, *Black Boy*, 104, 136.

34. Wright, *Black Boy*, 112.

35. Wright, *Black Boy*, 113–15.

36. Wright, *Black Boy*, 151; Qiana J. Whitted, *"A God of Justice?" The Problem of Evil in Twentieth-Century Black Literature* (Charlottesville: University of Virginia Press, 2009), 55–56.

37. Wright, *Black Boy*, 153, 155.

38. Alain Locke, "The New Negro," in *The New Negro: Voices of the Harlem Renaissance*, ed. Alain Locke (1925; repr., New York: Simon and Schuster, 1992), 11, 15.

39. Langston Hughes claimed that Locke was one of the "midwives" of the Harlem Renaissance, the other two being Jessie Redmond Fauset and Charles Johnson. See Arnold Rampersad, introduction to Locke, *New*

Negro, xi; Christopher Buck, *Alain Locke: Faith and Philosophy* (Los Angeles: Kalimát Press, 2005), 22, 23.

40. Alain Locke, "Pluralism and Intellectual Democracy," in *The Philosophy of Alain Locke: Harlem Renaissance and Beyond*, ed. Leonard Harris (Philadelphia: Temple University Press, 1989), 58, 59.

41. Alain Locke et al., "Is There a Basis for Spiritual Unity in the World Today?" *Town Meeting: Bulletin of America's Town Meeting of the Air* 8, no. 5 (June 1, 1942): 6, 7, 8.

42. Peter Smith, *An Introduction to the Baha'i Faith* (Cambridge: Cambridge University Press, 2008), 32, 52–53; Buck, *Alain Locke*, 43; Weinfeld, "Isolated Believer," 85.

43. Buck, *Alain Locke*, 6; Alain Locke, "Unity through Diversity: A Bahá'í Principle," in Leonard Harris, *Philosophy of Alain Locke*, 137; Weinfeld, "Isolated Believer," 88–90.

44. Ferguson, *Harlem Renaissance*, 17–18; Leonard Harris, *Philosophy of Alain Locke*, 6.

45. Langston Hughes, "Song for a Dark Girl," *Crisis* 25 (October 1922): 267; Ferguson, *Harlem Renaissance*, 95.

46. Langston Hughes, "Litany," in *Selected Poems of Langston Hughes* (New York: Vintage, 1990), 24.

47. Hughes, "Who But the Lord?" in *Selected Poems*, 196; Whitted, "A God of Justice?" 22.

48. Langston Hughes, "Goodbye, Christ" in *The Collected Poems of Langston Hughes*, ed. Arnold Rampersad and David Roessel (New York: Vintage, 1994), 166.

49. Cary D. Wintz and Paul Finkelman, eds. *Encyclopedia of the Harlem Renaissance*, 2 vols. (New York: Routledge, 2004), 1:110–11.

50. Hughes, *The Big Sea*, 275, 276–77. For the riot at Becton's funeral, see "5,000 Riot to See Harlem Funeral," *New York Times*, May 31, 1933, L13.

51. Hughes, *The Big Sea*, 277–78.

52. Lackey, *African American Atheists and Political Liberation*, 16.

53. Hurston, *Dust Tracks on a Road*, 764.

54. Hurston, *Dust Tracks on a Road*, 764. For the philosophy of materialism, see Ted Honderich, ed. *The Oxford Guide to Philosophy* (Oxford: Oxford University Press, 2005), 564–66. In her materialism, Hurston again posited a similar philosophy as Friedrich Nietzsche, who argued strongly against the one hundred-year tradition of German idealism; see Nietzsche, *Beyond Good and Evil*, 22–23. Emerson quoted in Ralph Waldo Emerson, *Nature*, in *The American Transcendentalists: Essential Writings*, ed. Lawrence Buell

(New York: Modern Library, 2006), 60. Emerson likely would not have considered himself a freethinker, but his theology was extremely unorthodox for his time, and his writings have inspired countless freethinkers throughout American history. The best exploration of his thought is Robert D. Richardson, *Emerson: The Mind on Fire* (Berkeley: University of California Press, 1995). For more on transcendentalism, see Philip F. Gura, *American Transcendentalism: A History* (New York: Hill and Wang, 2008).

55. Hurston, *Dust Tracks on a Road*, 755.

56. Hurston, *Dust Tracks on a Road*, 764; Zora Neale Hurston, *Mules and Men*, in Hurston, *Folklore, Memoirs, and Other Writings*, 1–267; Cheryl A. Wall, "Mules and Men and Women: Zora Neale Hurston's Strategies of Narration and Visions of Female Empowerment," *Black American Literature Forum* 23, no. 4 (Winter 1989): 662, 672.

57. Thadious M. Davis, *Nella Larsen, Novelist of the Harlem Renaissance: A Woman's Life Unveiled* (Baton Rouge: Louisiana State University Press, 1994), xiii, 51–89, 121–22.

58. Nella Larsen, *Quicksand* (1928; Mineola, N.Y.: Dover Publications, 2006), 2, 3, 16, 17, 4.

59. Larsen, *Quicksand*, 31.

60. Larsen, *Quicksand*, 105, 106.

61. Larsen, *Quicksand*, 120, 121.

62. Larsen, *Quicksand*, 123.

63. Thelma E. Berlack, "New Author Unearthed Right Here in Harlem," *Amsterdam News* (New York), May 23, 1928, 16; Nella Larsen Imes to Carl Van Vechten, 12 November 1926, James Weldon Johnson Collection, Beinecke Library; Davis, *Nella Larsen*, 172, 59.

64. E. Merril Root, "Ebony Hour-Hand, Pointing to Midnight," *Christian Century*, October 18, 1928, 1262; Davis, *Nella Larsen*, 280.

65. Ann duCille, *The Coupling Convention: Sex, Text, and Tradition in Black Women's Fiction* (New York: Oxford University Press, 1993), 87; Cheryl Wall, "Passing for What? Aspects of Identity in Nella Larsen's Novels," *Black American Literature Forum* 20, no. 1–2 (Spring–Summer 1986): 109; Thadious M. Davis, introduction to "Nella Larsen," *The Gender of Modernism: A Critical Anthology*, ed. Bonnie Kime Scott (Bloomington: Indiana University Press, 1990), 211.

66. Hurston, *Mules and Men*, 36.

67. Hurston, *Mules and Men*, 142; Wall, "Mules and Men and Women," 668; Tera W. Hunter, *To 'Joy My Freedom: Southern Black Women's Lives and Labors after the Civil War* (Cambridge, Mass.: Harvard University Press, 1997), 180, 183.

68. Zora Neale Hurston, *Their Eyes Were Watching God* (1937; repr., New York: HarperCollins, 2006), 86.

69. Henry Louis Gates Jr., afterword to Hurston, *Their Eyes Were Watching God*, 195–200; duCille, *Coupling Convention*, 110, 120. For more on Alice Walker, see the afterword to the present volume.

70. Yoshinobu Hakutani, introduction to *Critical Essays on Richard Wright*, ed. Yoshinobu Hakutani (Boston: G. K. Hall and Co., 1982), 3; Alain Locke, review of *Their Eyes Were Watching God*, by Zora Neale Hurston, *Opportunity*, June 1, 1938, quoted in Henry Louis Gates Jr. and A. K. Appiah, eds. *Zora Neale Hurston: Critical Perspectives Past and Present* (New York: Amistad, 1993), 18; Richard Wright, review of *Their Eyes Were Watching God*, by Zora Neale Hurston, *New Masses*, October 5, 1937, 22–23.

71. Richard Wright, "How 'Bigger' Was Born," in *Native Son* (1940; repr., New York: HarperCollins, 1993), 439.

Chapter 3

1. Harry Haywood, *Black Bolshevik: Autobiography of an Afro-American Communist* (Chicago: Liberator Press, 1979), 1.

2. Michael Newman, *Socialism: A Very Short Introduction* (Oxford: Oxford University Press, 2005), 6–7; Jack Ross, *The Socialist Party of America: A Complete History* (Lincoln: University of Nebraska Press, 2015), 3–30.

3. David McLellan, *Marxism and Religion: A Description and Assessment of the Marxist Critique of Christianity* (New York: Harper and Row, 1987), 1, 2; Peter Singer, *Marx: A Very Short Introduction* (Oxford: Oxford University Press, 2000), 21–27.

4. V. I. Lenin, "Socialism and Religion," in *Collected Works*, vol. 10, *November 1905–June 1906*, ed. and trans. Andrew Rothstein (Moscow: Foreign Languages Publishing House, 1962), 83, 84.

5. Michael Burleigh, *Sacred Causes: The Clash of Religion and Politics, from the Great War to the War on Terror* (New York: HarperCollins, 2007), 53–54, 326–28; Jane Degras, ed. *The Communist International 1919–1943 Documents*, vol. 2, *1923–1928* (London: Oxford University Press, 1960), 38.

6. Cornelius L. Bynum, "'An Equal Chance in the Race for Life': Reverdy C. Ransom, Socialism, and the Social Gospel Movement, 1890–1920," *Journal of African American History* 43, no. 1 (Winter 2008): 7; Anthony B. Pinn, *Introducing African American Religion* (London:

Routledge, 2013), 154–56; Robin D. G. Kelley, *Hammer and Hoe: Alabama Communists during the Great Depression* (Chapel Hill: University of North Carolina Press, 1990), 107–8.

7. For Harrison's early life, see Jeffrey B. Perry, *Hubert Harrison: The Voice of Harlem Radicalism, 1883–1918* (New York: Columbia University Press, 2009), 21–51; Hubert Harrison to Frances Reynolds Keyser, 20 May 1908, in Hubert Harrison, *A Hubert Harrison Reader*, ed. Jeffrey B. Perry (Middletown, Conn.: Wesleyan University Press, 2001), 37, 38. On Huxley, see Jennifer Michael Hecht, *Doubt: A History* (San Francisco: HarperCollins, 2003), 406–8.

8. Hubert Harrison, "Paine's Place in the Deistical Movement," *Truth Seeker* 38, no. 6 (February 11, 1911): 87.

9. Hubert Harrison, "The Negro a Conservative: Christianity Still Enslaves the Minds of Those Whose Bodies It Has Long Held Bound," *Truth Seeker* 41, no. 37 (September 12, 1914): 583.

10. Harrison, "Negro a Conservative."

11. Hubert Harrison, "The Duty of the Socialist Party," *New York Call*, December 13, 1911, 6.

12. Gompers quoted in Harrison, *Hubert Harrison Reader*, 79; Sally Miller, "For White Men Only: The Socialist Party of America and Issues of Gender, Ethnicity and Race," in "New Perspectives on Socialism I," special issue, *Journal of the Gilded Age and Progressive Era* 2, no. 3 (July 2003): 296–97; Hubert Harrison, "The Negro and the Labor Unions," in *When Africa Awakes: The "Inside Story" of the Stirrings and Strivings of the New Negro in the Western World* (New York: Porro Press, 1920), 22.

13. Hubert Harrison, "The White War and the Colored Races," in Harrison, *Hubert Harrison Reader*, 204, 206.

14. Richard B. Moore, "Hubert Henry Harrison," in *Dictionary of American Negro Biography*, ed. Rayford W. Logan and Michael R. Winston (New York: W. W. Norton, 1982), 293; Claude McKay, *A Long Way from Home* (New York: Lee Furman, 1937), 41; William Pickens, "Hubert Harrison: Philosopher of Harlem," *Amsterdam News* (New York), February 7, 1923, 12.

15. Hubert Harrison, "The Liberty League of Negro-Americans: How it Came to Be," in Harrison, *Hubert Harrison Reader*, 87; Hubert Harrison, "Declaration of Principles," in Harrison, *Hubert Harrison Reader*, 91, 92.

16. Cynthia Taylor, *A. Philip Randolph: The Religious Journey of an African American Labor Leader* (New York: New York University Press, 2006), 8–9, 25–27; Manning Marable, "A. Philip Randolph and the Foundations of Black American Socialism" *Radical America* 14, no. 2 (March-April 1980): 11.

17. Jervis Anderson, A. *Philip Randolph: A Biographical Portrait* (1972; repr., Berkeley: University of California Press, 1986), 25, Randolph quoted at 25.

18. Marable, "A. Philip Randolph," 11; A. Philip Randolph and Chandler Owen, editorial, *Messenger*, November 1917, 21.

19. Walter Everette Hawkins, "Too Much Religion," *Messenger*, November 1917, 27.

20. Walter Everette Hawkins, "Here and Hereafter," *Messenger*, November 1917, 27.

21. "The Mob Victim," *Messenger*, July 1918, 27.

22. Rachel Scharfman, "On Common Ground: Freethought and Radical Politics in New York City, 1890–1917" (Ph.D. diss., New York University, 2005), 88, 163; A. Philip Randolph and Chandler Owen, "Woman Suffrage and the Negro," *Messenger*, November 1917, 6.

23. David Levering Lewis, *W. E. B. Du Bois: Biography of a Race, 1868–1919* (New York: Henry Holt, 1993), 525–26; Theodore Kornweibel Jr. *"Seeing Red": Federal Campaigns against Black Militancy, 1919–1925* (Bloomington: Indiana University Press, 1998), 77–79; Anderson, A. *Philip Randolph*, 106–7; Ross, *Socialist Party of America*, 201; For more on the *Messenger*, see Theodore Kornweibel Jr. *No Crystal Stair: Black Life and the Messenger, 1917–1928* (Westport, Conn.: Greenwood Press, 1975).

24. Miller, "For White Men Only," 300; Kornweibel, *"Seeing Red,"* 94–95. For more on Randolph's organizing activities throughout his career, see Andrew E. Kerste and Clarence Lang, eds. *Reframing Randolph: Labor, Black Freedom, and the Legacies of A. Philip Randolph* (New York: New York University Press, 2015).

25. On Garvey's program see Angela Jones, ed. *The Modern African American Political Thought Reader: From David Walker to Barack Obama* (New York and London: Routledge, 2013), 231; Marable, "A. Philip Randolph and the Foundations of Black American Socialism," 12; Taylor, A. *Philip Randolph*, 56–57.

26. Mark Solomon, *The Cry Was Unity: Communists and African Americans, 1917–1936* (Jackson: University Press of Mississippi, 1998), 3–14; Joyce Moore Turner, *Caribbean Crusaders and the Harlem Renaissance* (Urbana: University of Illinois Press, 2005), 56–57; For more on the anticolonialism of the ABB, see Minkah Makalani, "Internationalizing the Third International: The African Blood Brotherhood, Asian Radicals, and Race, 1919–1922," *Journal of African American History* 96, no. 2 (Spring 2011): 151–78.

27. Solomon, *Cry Was Unity*, 16; Joyce Moore Turner, *Caribbean Crusaders*, 36; Cyril Briggs, "Christianity as Propaganda," *Crusader*, October 1920, 9; Cyril Briggs, "The Salvation of the Negro," *Crusader*, April 1921, 9.

28. W. Burghardt Turner and Joyce Moore Turner, eds. *Richard B. Moore, Caribbean Militant in Harlem: Collected Writings, 1920–1972* (Bloomington: Indiana University Press, 1988), 19–25, Moore quoted at 51.

29. Egbert Ethelred Brown, "From Montego Bay to Harlem: A Pilgrimage of Faith," 39, box 2, folder 6, Egbert Ethelred Brown Papers, 1914–1956, Schomburg Center for Research in Black Culture, New York, N.Y. (hereafter cited as Brown Papers).

30. Egbert Ethelred Brown, "'All My Mice Are Alive': The Religion of the Laboratory," 3, 7–8, box 2, folder 1; Egbert Ethelred Brown, "A Challenging Question: Should a Man Be Required to Give Up His Intelligence in Order to Be a Christian," 18–19, box 2, folder 3; Egbert Ethelred Brown, "Are Unitarians Christians?" 28–29, box 2, folder 1; all in Brown Papers.

31. Joyce Moore Turner, *Caribbean Crusaders*, 165, Moore quoted at 166. For more on the Harlem Unitarian Church, see Juan M. Floyd-Thomas, *The Origins of Black Humanism in America: Reverend Ethelred Brown and the Unitarian Church* (New York: Palgrave Macmillan, 2008).

32. Joyce Moore Turner, *Caribbean Crusaders*, 4, xv; W. Burghardt Turner and Joyce Moore Turner, *Richard B. Moore, Caribbean Militant in Harlem*, 28; Claude McKay, "A Negro Poet," in *The Passion of Claude McKay*, ed. Wayne Cooper (New York: Schocken Books, 1973), 48.

33. Winston James, *Holding Aloft the Banner of Ethiopia: Caribbean Radicalism in Early Twentieth-Century America* (London: Verso, 1998), 50–53, 71, 77.

34. Solomon, *Cry Was Unity*, 47–52, 68–70, 76; Mark Naison, *Communists in Harlem during the Depression* (Urbana: University of Illinois Press, 1983), 16–18; For the rise of American communism, see Robert Service, *Comrades!: A History of World Communism* (Cambridge, Mass.: Harvard University Press, 2010), 119–29.

35. Haywood, *Black Bolshevik*, 29, 31.

36. Marable, "A. Philip Randolph," 9; Davarian Baldwin, *Chicago's New Negroes: Modernity, the Great Migration, and Black Urban Life* (Chapel Hill: University of North Carolina Press, 2007), 13–14; Haywood, *Black Bolshevik*, 84, 92.

37. Haywood, *Black Bolshevik*, 96, 97–98.

38. Haywood, *Black Bolshevik*, 99, 107, 114.

39. Richard Wright, *Black Boy (American Hunger)* (1945; repr., New York: HarperCollins, 1998), 294–95, 316–17, 320–21; Cedric J. Robinson, *Black Marxism: The Making of the Black Radical Tradition* (Chapel Hill: University of North Carolina Press, 1983), 292–93.

40. Richard Wright, "Blueprint for Negro Writing," in *The Norton Anthology of African American Literature*, ed. Henry Louis Gates Jr. and Nellie Y. McKay (New York: W. W. Norton, 1997), 1382.

41. Robinson, *Black Marxism*, 296, 297; Richard Wright, "How 'Bigger' Was Born," in *Native Son* (1940; repr., New York: HarperCollins Publishers, 1993), 439.

42. Wright, *Black Boy*, 330–31; Fraser M. Ottanelli, *The Communist Party of the United States: From the Depression to World War II* (New Brunswick, N.J.: Rutgers University Press, 1991), 44; Robinson, *Black Marxism*, 304–5; In 1949, Wright included his story of leaving the CPUSA in the edited collection: Richard Wright, *The God That Failed*, ed. Richard H. Crossman (New York: Harper and Row, 1949).

43. LaShawn Harris, "Running with the Reds: African American Women and the Communist Party during the Great Depression," *Journal of African American History* 94, no. 1 (Winter 2009): 21–26, 30–31; Miller, "For White Men Only," 285–89. For more on black female communists, see Erik S. McDuffie, *Sojourning for Freedom: Black Women, American Communism, and the Making of Black Left Feminism* (Durham, N.C.: Duke University Press, 2011).

44. LaShawn Harris, "Running with the Reds," 32–34; Audley "Queen Mother" Moore interview with Cheryl Gilkes in Ruth Edmonds Hill, ed. *The Black Women Oral History Project* (Westport, Conn.: Meckler, 1991), 132. For the growing conservatism of black churches, see Gayraud S. Wilmore, *Black Religion and Black Radicalism: An Interpretation of the Religious History of African Americans* (Maryknoll, N.Y.: Orbis Books, 1973), 163–95.

45. McDuffie, *Sojourning for Freedom*, 25–34.

46. McDuffie, *Sojourning for Freedom*, 40; "Some Women I Have Known Personally, Campbell, Grace," box 1, Essays on Women folder, Hermina Dumont Huiswood Papers, Tamiment Library and Robert F. Wagner Labor Archives, New York University, New York, N.Y.

47. McDuffie, *Sojourning for Freedom*, 44, 45–46.

48. McDuffie, *Sojourning for Freedom*, 41–42.

49. James, *Holding Aloft the Banner of Ethiopia*, 174, 175; Joseph G. Tucker, "Special Report," September 29, 1923 Department of Justice File 61-23-248, quoted in James, *Holding Aloft the Banner of Ethiopia*, 174.

50. Louise Thompson Patterson, Memoirs, chapter 1, draft b, "Childhood/West," 23–25, box 19, folder 16; Memoirs, chapter 2, draft B, "Pine Bluff/Hampton," 16, box 19, folder 18; Langston Hughes to Louise Thompson, n.d., box 17, folder 12; all in Louise Thompson Patterson Papers, Emory University Manuscripts, Archives, and Rare Book Library, Atlanta, Georgia (hereafter cited as Patterson Papers).

51. McDuffie, *Sojourning for Freedom*, 63.

52. McDuffie, *Sojourning for Freedom*, 42, 64; Louise Thompson Patterson, Memoirs, chapter 3, "Harlem in the 1920s," 11, box 19, folder 20, Patterson Papers.

53. Louise Thompson Patterson, Memoirs, chapter 5, "Return to U.S./Scottsboro," 2–4, Box 20, folder 4, Patterson Papers; McDuffie, *Sojourning for Freedom*, 75; W. B. Turner and Joyce Moore Turner, *Richard B. Moore, Caribbean Militant in Harlem*, 60.

54. Patterson, "Return to U.S./Scottsboro," 2–4; Louise Thompson Patterson, Memoirs, chapter 6, draft, "Harlem Riot of 1935," 8, 17, 9, box 20, folder 5, Patterson Papers; Harris, "Running with the Reds," 36–37.

55. Lewis, *W. E. B. Du Bois: Biography of a Race*, 48–50.

56. Lewis, *W. E. B. Du Bois: Biography of a Race*, 65; W. E. B. Du Bois, *The Autobiography of W.E.B. Du Bois: A Soliloquy on Viewing My Life from the Last Decade of Its First Century* (New York: International Publishers, 1968), 111, 127; George Frederick Wright, *The Logic of Christian Evidences* (Andover, Mass.: Warren F. Draper, 1883).

57. Du Bois, *Autobiography*, 285, 186–87, 183; Lewis, *W. E. B. Du Bois: Biography of a Race*, 66.

58. Lewis, *W. E. B. Du Bois: Biography of a Race*, 142; Du Bois, *Autobiography*, 197. For Du Bois's role in the creation of sociology as an academic discipline, see Aldon Morris, *The Scholar Denied: W. E. B. Du Bois and the Birth of Modern Sociology* (Oakland: University of California Press, 2015).

59. Lewis, *W. E. B. Du Bois: Biography of a Race*, 409–10; Brian L. Johnson, *W. E. B. Du Bois: Toward Agnosticism, 1868–1934* (Lanham, Md.: Rowman and Littlefield, 2008), 66, 84.

60. W. E. B. Du Bois, "The Negro Church," *The Crisis: A Record of the Darker Races* 4, no. 1 (May 1912): 24, 25.

61. W. E. B. Du Bois, "The Church and the Negro," in W. E. B. Du Bois, *Du Bois on Religion*, ed. Phil Zuckerman (Walnut Creek, Calif.: AltaMira Press, 2000), 99; Frederick Douglass, "What to the Slave Is the Fourth of July?" in *Narrative of the Life of Frederick Douglass, An American Slave: Written by Himself, with Related Documents*, 2nd ed., ed. David W. Blight (Boston: Bedford/St. Martin's, 2003), 164.

62. W. E. B. Du Bois, "The Color Line and the Church," in Du Bois, *Du Bois on Religion*, 169, 170.

63. B. Johnson, *W. E. B. Du Bois: Toward Agnosticism*, 111; Corliss Lamont, *The Philosophy of Humanism* (1949; repr., New York: Continuum, 1990), 36, 37.

64. Lewis, *W. E. B. Du Bois: Biography of a Race*, 143–44, 525–26; David Levering Lewis, *W. E. B. Du Bois: The Fight for Equality and the American Century, 1919–1963* (New York: Henry Holt, 2000), 4, 196, 250–51, 262.

65. Du Bois, *Autobiography*, 30.

66. W. E. B. Du Bois, "Human Rights for All Minorities," in *W. E. B. Du Bois Speaks: Speeches and Addresses, 1920–1963*, ed. Philip S. Foner (New York: Pathfinder Press, 1960), 181, 189.

67. Du Bois, *Autobiography*, 285, 43; Du Bois, "The Revelation of Saint Orgne the Damned," in *W. E. B. Du Bois Speaks*, 111; Lewis, *W. E. B. Du Bois: Fight for Equality*, 306, 307.

68. Du Bois, *Autobiography of W. E. B. Du Bois*, 305; W. E. B. Du Bois, "The Negro and Socialism," in Du Bois, *W. E. B. Du Bois Speaks*, 307.

69. Lewis, *W. E. B. Du Bois: Fight for Equality*, 496–98, 526, 555; Du Bois, "Negro and Socialism," 309, 299.

Chapter 4

1. Peniel E. Joseph, *Stokely: A Life* (New York: Basic Civitas, 2014), 15, NOOK; Stokely Carmichael, *Ready for Revolution: The Life and Struggles of Stokely Carmichael (Kwame Ture)*, with Ekwueme Michael Thelwell (New York: Scribner, 2003), 74, 100–1.

2. Harvard Sitkoff, *The Struggle for Black Equality, 1954–1992*, rev. ed. (New York: Hill and Wang, 1993), 8–16; On the "long civil rights movement," see Jacquelyn Dowd Hall, "The Long Civil Rights Movement and the Political Uses of the Past," *Journal of American History* 91, no. 4 (March 2005): 1233–63; and Glenda Elizabeth Gilmore, *Defying Dixie: The Radical Roots of Civil Rights* (New York: W. W. Norton, 2008), 2.

3. Sitkoff, *Struggle for Black Equality*, 21–51; Thomas C. Holt, *Children of Fire: A History of African Americans* (New York: Hill and Wang, 2010), 293–99.

4. James M. Washington, "Martin Luther King, Jr., Martyred Prophet for a Global Beloved Community of Justice, Faith, and Hope" in James M. Washington, ed. *A Testament of Hope: The Essential Writings and Speeches of Martin Luther King, Jr.* (New York: HarperCollins, 1986), xvi–xvii; Sitkoff, *Struggle for Black Equality*, 56–57.

5. Clayborne Carson, *In Struggle: SNCC and the Black Awakening of the 1960s* (Cambridge, Mass.: Harvard University Press, 1981), 10–13, 14, 19.

6. Barbara Ransby, *Ella Baker and the Black Freedom Movement: A Radical Democratic Vision* (Chapel: University of North Carolina Press, 2003), 1, 4, 6; Charles M. Payne, *I've Got the Light of Freedom: The Organizing Tradition and the Mississippi Freedom Struggle* (Berkeley: University of California Press, 1995), 67–68, 83, 92.

7. Ransby, *Ella Baker and the Black Freedom Movement*, 239, 245, 244.

8. Carson, *In Struggle*, 22, 23.

9. Carson, *In Struggle*, 31, 46, 51.

10. Carson, *In Struggle*, 31, 43.

11. James Forman, *The Making of Black Revolutionaries* (1972; repr., Seattle: University of Washington Press, 1997), 24, 29.

12. Forman, *Making of Black Revolutionaries*, 55.

13. Forman, *Making of Black Revolutionaries*, 82.

14. Forman, *Making of Black Revolutionaries*, 83.

15. Forman, *Making of Black Revolutionaries*, 105, 106.

16. James Forman, "Control, Conflict and Change: The Underlying Concepts of the Black Manifesto," in Robert S. Lecky and H. Elliott Wright, eds. *Black Manifesto: Religion, Racism, and Reparations* (New York: Sheed and Ward, 1969), 37, 38, 50–51.

17. Forman, "Control, Conflict and Change," 114, 118.

18. Forman, "Control, Conflict and Change," 120–22, 124.

19. Forman, *Making of Black Revolutionaries*, 457, 456.

20. Timothy B. Tyson, "Robert F. Williams, 'Black Power,' and the Roots of the African American Freedom Struggle," *Journal of American History* 85, no. 2 (September 1998): 541, 549, 565.

21. Malcom X, "Who Taught You to Hate Yourself?" excerpt of speech given in Los Angeles in 1962, YouTube, December 2, 2014, video, 1:07, https://www.youtube.com/watch?v=18Ern-fNEb4. For more on the Nation of Islam, see Edward E. Curtis IV, *Black Muslim Religion in the Nation of Islam, 1960–1975* (Chapel Hill: University of North Carolina Press, 2006).

22. Peniel Joseph, *Waiting 'Til the Midnight Hour: A Narrative History of Black Power in America* (New York: Holt Paperbacks, 2006), 19, 127–29, 8.

23. Joseph, *Stokely: A Life*, 1–13; Carmichael, *Ready for Revolution*, 87, 90–91, 92.

24. Carmichael, *Ready for Revolution*, 86, 93.

25. Carmichael, *Ready for Revolution*, 93, 94.

26. Joshua Bloom and Waldo E. Martin Jr. *Black against Empire: The History and Politics of the Black Panther Party* (Berkeley: University of California Press, 2013), 2, 21, 31, 32.

27. "The Ten Point Platform and Program of the Black Panther Party, 1966," in *The Modern African American Political Thought Reader: From David Walker to Barack Obama*, ed. Angela Jones (New York: Routledge, 2013), 282–84; Huey P. Newton, *Revolutionary Suicide* (1973; repr., New York: Penguin, 2009) 156, Kindle.

28. Newton, *Revolutionary Suicide*, 9, 11, 35, 36–37.

29. Newton, *Revolutionary Suicide*, 68, 37, 58; Thomas R. Flynn, *Existentialism: A Very Short Introduction* (Oxford: Oxford University Press, 2006), 67–72.

30. Huey P. Newton, "On the Relevance of the Church: May 19, 1971," in *To Die for the People: The Writings of Huey P. Newton* (New York: Random House, 1972), 64, 65.

31. Newton, *Revolutionary Suicide*, 178, 179–80; Amiri Imamu Baraka, "The Legacy of Malcolm X and the Coming of the Black Nation," in *By These Hands: A Documentary History of African American Humanism*, ed. Anthony Pinn (New York: New York University Press, 2001), 246.

32. Newton, *Revolutionary Suicide*, 70; Elaine Brown, *A Taste of Power: A Black Woman's Story* (New York: Pantheon Books, 1992), 136.

33. Robyn C. Spencer, *The Revolution Has Come: Black Power, Gender, and the Black Panther Party in Oakland* (Durham, N.C.: Duke University Press, 2016), 30–31; E. Brown, *A Taste of Power*, 135.

34. Joseph, *Waiting 'Til the Midnight Hour*, 219–20, 227, 221; Bloom and Martin, Jr., *Black against Empire*, 310–11.

35. Eldridge Cleaver, *Soul on Ice* (New York: Dell, 1968), 18, 19.

36. Cleaver, *Soul on Ice*, 41, 43–44, 61, 65.

37. David Hilliard and Lewis Cole, *This Side of Glory: The Autobiography of David Hilliard and the Story of the Black Panther Party* (Chicago: Lawrence Hill Books, 1993), 70, 113, 115.

38. Hilliard and Cole, *This Side of Glory*, 113–14; Newton, "On the Relevance of the Church," 74.

39. Kuwasi Balagoon et al., *Look for Me in the Whirlwind: The Collective Autobiography of the New York 21* (New York: Random House, 1971), 111, 237.

40. Balagoon et al., *Look for Me in the Whirlwind*, 241, 264, 265.

41. Sarah Webster Fabio, "Free by Any Means Necessary," *Black Panther*, May 18, 1968, quoted in Philip S. Foner, ed. *The Black Panthers Speak* (New York: Da Capo Press, 1995), 21.

42. Evette Pearson, "In White America Today," *Black Panther*, January 4, 1969, quoted in Foner, *Black Panthers Speak*, 25, 26.

43. Spencer, *Revolution Has Come*, 95.

44. Spencer, *Revolution Has Come*, 97–98; Donna Jean Murch, *Living for the City: Migration, Education, and the Rise of the Black Panther Party in Oakland, California* (Chapel Hill: University of North Carolina Press, 2010), 177–78; Eldridge Cleaver, "Message to Sister Erica Huggins of the Black Panther Party," *Black Panther*, July 5, 1969, in Foner, *Black Panthers Speak*, 98; E. Brown, *Taste of Power*, 3–5.

45. Spencer, *Revolution Has Come*, 85; Murch, *Living for the City*, 169; "Why the Free Breakfast?" *Black Panther*, October 4, 1969, in Foner, *Black Panthers Speak*, 169.

46. World Health Organization, *Constitution of the World Health Organization*, October 2006, http://www.who.int/governance/eb/who_constitution_en.pdf; Alondra Nelson, *Body and Soul: The Black Panther Party and the Fight against Medical Discrimination* (Minneapolis: University of Minnesota Press, 2011), 11, 12, 15, 51.

47. Newton, *Revolutionary Suicide*, 20; Murch, *Living for the City*, 180; *Black Panther*, February 7, 1970, 7.

48. Murch, *Living for the City*, 181, 182.

49. James H. Cone, *For My People: Black Theology and the Black Church* (Maryknoll, N.Y.: Orbis Books, 1984), 32, 5, 53; For eighteenth- and nineteenth-century black theology, see Cornel West, *Prophesy Deliverance! An Afro-American Revolutionary Christianity*, anniversary ed. (Louisville: Westminster John Knox Press, 2002), 101–4.

50. James H. Cone, *A Black Theology of Liberation* 2nd ed. (Maryknoll, N.Y.: Orbis Books, 1986), 23–33, 63; Anthony B. Pinn, *Introducing African American Religion* (New York: Routledge, 2013), 186, 188.

51. Henry James Young, "Black Theology: Providence and Evil," *Duke Divinity School Review* 40, no. 2 (Spring 1975): 95; Pinn, *Introducing African American Religion*, 186; Cone, *For My People*, 117–18.

52. Pinn, *Introducing African American Religion*, 191, 194–95.

53. Lewis R. Gordon, "Remembering William R. Jones (1933–2012): Philosopher and Freedom Fighter," *LRG Blog*, accessed February 8, 2019, http://www.lewisrgordon.com/sketches/remembering-william-r-jones.html; Unitarian Universalist Ministers Association, "In Memory of . . . William R. Jones (1933–2012)," *Remembering the Living Tradition* (blog), August 15, 2012, https://www.uuma.org/blogpost/569858/147952/In-Memory-of----William-R-Jones-1933-2012.

54. William R. Jones, *Is God a White Racist? A Preamble to Black Theology* (1973; Boston: Beacon Press, 1998), vii, viii, ix, x–xi.

55. W. Jones, *Is God a White Racist?*, 4–7, 11, 20–21, 22, 71.

56. W. Jones, *Is God a White Racist?*, 185–88, 193, 195, 197.

57. Virginia C. Fowler, *Nikki Giovanni: A Literary Biography* (Santa Barbara, Calif.: Praeger, 2013), 27–28.

58. Ben Keppel, *The Work of Democracy: Ralph Bunche, Kenneth B. Clark, Lorraine Hansberry, and the Cultural Politics of Race* (Cambridge, Mass.: Harvard University Press, 1995), 23–24, 26; Anne Cheney, *Lorraine Hansberry* (Boston: Twayne Publishers, 1984), 6–7; Lorraine Hansberry, *To Be Young, Gifted, and Black: Lorraine Hansberry in Her Own Words*, ed. Robert Nemiroff (New York: Signet, 1969), 51.

59. Keppel, *Work of Democracy*, 189; Cheney, *Lorraine Hansberry*, 14, 33; Cheryl Higashida, "To Be(come) Young, Gay, and Black: Lorraine Hansberry's Existentialist Routes to Anticolonialism" *American Quarterly* 6, no. 4 (December 2008): 899–900; Lorraine Hansberry, "Simone de Beauvoir and *The Second Sex*: An American Commentary," in *Words of Fire: An Anthology of African-American Feminist Thought*, ed. Beverly Guy-Sheftall (New York: New Press, 1995), 129, 137.

60. Lorraine Hansberry, *A Raisin in the Sun* (New York: Vintage Books, 1959), 50, 51.

61. Robert Nemiroff, ed. *Lorraine Hansberry Speaks Out: Art and the Black Revolution* (New York: Caedmon Records, 1972); Hansberry, *To Be Young, Gifted, and Black*, 195, 197.

62. Hansberry, *Raisin in the Sun*, 57; Higashida, "To Be(come) Young, Gay, and Black," 900.

63. Hansberry, *Raisin in the Sun*, 117–18; Harold Cruse, *The Crisis of the Negro Intellectual* (New York: New York Review Books, 1967), 283; Keppel, *Work of Democracy*, 179.

64. Hansberry, *Raisin in the Sun*, 119; Keppel, *Work of Democracy*, 22; Lloyd W. Brown, "Lorraine Hansberry as Ironist: A Reappraisal of 'A Raisin in the Sun,'" *Journal of Black Studies* 4, no. 3 (March 1974): 240–41; Michelle Gordon, "'Somewhat Like War': The Aesthetics of Segregation, Black Liberation and 'A Raisin in the Sun,'" in "Representing Segregation," special issue, *African American Review* 42, no. 1, (Spring 2008):124, 122.

65. Andrew Shin and Barbara Judson, "Beneath the Black Aesthetic: James Baldwin's Primer of Black American Masculinity," *African American Review* 32, no. 2 (Summer 1998): 250; James Campbell, *Talking at the Gates: A Life of James Baldwin* (New York: Penguin Books, 1991), 3–10.

66. James Baldwin, *The Fire Next Time* (New York: Vintage International, 1962), 15, 28, 29, 30–31; Campbell, *Talking at the Gates*, 8.

67. Baldwin, *Fire Next Time*, 31–32, 34–36, 37–38; James Baldwin, *Notes of a Native Son* (Boston: Beacon Press, 1955), 108.

68. Baldwin, *Fire Next Time*, 38–39.

69. Baldwin, *Fire Next Time*, 40, 47.

70. Baldwin, *Fire Next Time*, 33; Soyica Diggs Colbert, "Go Tell It on the Mountain: Baldwin's Sermonic," in *The Cambridge Companion to James Baldwin*, ed. Michele Elam (New York and Cambridge: Cambridge University Press, 2015), 56, 58.

71. Trudier Harris, introduction to *New Essays on "Go Tell It on the Mountain"* ed. Trudier Harris (Cambridge: Cambridge University Press, 1996), 1; Campbell, *Talking at the Gates*, 29–30; James Baldwin, *Go Tell It on the Mountain* (New York: Dell, 1952), 11–13, 88, 144.

72. Baldwin, *Go Tell It on the Mountain*, 88, 36, 145; Clarence E. Hardy III, *James Baldwin's God: Sex, Hope, and Crisis in Black Holiness Culture* (Knoxville: University of Tennessee Press, 2003), x, 7, 10, 20.

73. James Baldwin, *Blues for Mister Charlie* (New York: Dial Press, 1964), xv.

74. Baldwin, *Blues for Mister Charlie*, 4.

75. Baldwin, *Blues for Mister Charlie*, 4.

76. Baldwin, *Blues for Mister Charlie*, 19.

77. Shin and Judson, "Beneath the Black Aesthetic," 248; Baldwin, *Go Tell It on the Mountain*, 13, 194–95; Campbell, *Talking at the Gates*, 32–33; Hardy, *James Baldwin's God*, 64, 63.

78. Campbell, *Talking at the Gates*, 71; Cleaver, *Soul on Ice*, 101, 106; Sondra A. O'Neale, "Fathers, Gods, and Religion: Perceptions of Christianity and Ethnic Faith in James Baldwin," in *Critical Essays on James Baldwin*, ed. Fred L. Standley and Nancy V. Burt (Boston: G. K. Hall, 1988), 140; T. Harris, introduction to *New Essays on "Go Tell It on the Mountain,"* 21–23.

79. James Baldwin and Nikki Giovanni, *A Dialogue* (Philadelphia: J. B. Lippincott, 1973), 24, 35, 36; Virginia C. Fowler, ed. *Conversations with Nikki Giovanni* (Jackson: University Press of Mississippi, 1992), 4.

80. Nikki Giovanni, *Gemini: An Extended Autobiographical Statement on My First Twenty-Five Years of Being a Black Poet* (Indianapolis: Bobbs-Merrill, 1971), 130, 131.

81. Giovanni, *Gemini*, 50.

82. Nikki Giovanni, "The True Import of Present Dialogue, Black vs. Negro (For Peppe, Who Will Ultimately Judge Our Efforts)," in *Black*

Feeling, Black Talk/Black Judgment (1968; repr., New York: Morrow Quill Paperbacks, 1978), 19–20.

83. Cheryl Clarke, *"After Mecca": Women Poets and the Black Arts Movement* (New Brunswick, N.J.: Rutgers University Press, 2005), 16, 47.

84. Clarke, "After Mecca," 2.

85. Florynce "Flo" Kennedy, "Nobody Ever Died from a Blow Job, 1976," in A. Jones, *Modern African American Political Thought Reader*, 330; Florynce "Flo" Kennedy, "A Comparative Study: Accentuating the Similarities of the Societal Position of Women and Negroes," in Guy-Sheftall, *Words of Fire*, 105.

Afterword

1. Octavia Butler, *Dawn* (New York: Warner Books, 1987); Octavia Butler, "The Evening and the Morning and the Night," in *Dark Matter: A Century of Speculative Fiction from the African Diaspora*, ed. Sheree R. Thomas (New York: Warner Books, 2000), 172; For a discussion of the "nondogmatic belief system" that Butler constructed in some of her novels, see Philip H. Jos, "Fear and the Spiritual Realism of Octavia Butler's Earthseed," *Utopian Studies* 23, no. 2 (2012): 408–29.

2. Octavia Butler, "The Monophobic Response" in Thomas, *Dark Matter*, 415, 416.

3. Alice Walker, "Recommendation Letter for Staughton Lynd for the Danforth Foundation, January 1966," box 2, folder 5, Alice Walker Papers, Emory University Manuscripts and Rare Books Library, Atlanta (hereafter cited as Walker Papers).

4. Alice Walker, *In Search of Our Mother's Gardens: Womanist Prose* (San Diego: Harcourt Brace Jovanovich, 1983), 265; Alice Walker, "The Only Reason You Want to Go to Heaven is That You Have been Driven Out of Your Mind," in Anthony B. Pinn, ed., *By These Hands: A Documentary History of African American Humanism* (New York and London: New York University Press, 2001), 290, 293, 297.

5. Alice Walker, "The Diary of an African Nun," in *The Black Woman: An Anthology*, ed. Toni Cade (New York: New American Library, 1970), 39, 41; Alice Walker Leventhal to John Henrik Clarke, 1968, box 2, folder 7, Walker Papers.

6. Alice Walker, *The Third Life of Grange Copeland* (New York: Harcourt Brace Jovanovich, 1970), 12–13, 131, 132.

7. Alice Walker, *The Color Purple* (Orlando: Harcourt, Inc., 1982); Steven Spielberg, dir., *The Color Purple* (1985; Burbank, Calif.: Warner

Home Video, 2007), DVD; "William Ferris Interview with Alice Walker, 1994," in William Ferris, *The Storied South: Voices of Writers and Artists* (Chapel Hill: University of North Carolina Press, 2013), 70.

8. Rudolph P. Byrd, ed. *The World Has Changed: Conversations with Alice Walker* (New York: New Press, 2010), 27, 30–31.

9. Walker, *In Search of Our Mother's Gardens*, xi, xii; Melanie L. Harris, *Gifts of Virtue, Alice Walker, and Womanist Ethics* (New York: Palgrave Macmillan, 2010), 1, 4–5.

10. Anthony B. Pinn, *Varieties of African American Religious Experience* (Minneapolis: Augsburg Fortress Publishers, 1998), 2, 3; Anthony B. Pinn, *The End of God-Talk: An African American Humanist Theology* (Oxford: Oxford University Press, 2012), 5, 9–11; Anthony B. Pinn, *Writing God's Obituary: How a Good Methodist Became a Better Atheist* (Amherst, N.Y.: Prometheus Books, 2014).

11. Anthony B. Pinn, *Introducing African American Religion* (London: Routledge, 2013), 239–42.

12. "An African-American Humanist Declaration" *Free Inquiry* 10, no. 2 (Spring 1990): 14–15.

13. Pinn, *Introducing African American Religion*, 243; Black Nonbelievers, "About Us," accessed February 9, 2019, https://blacknonbelievers.wordpress.com.

14. Black Skeptics of Los Angeles, "Our Mission," accessed February 9, 2019, http://blackskepticsla.org/our-mission/; Black Skeptics of Los Angeles, "Our Work," accessed February 9, 2019, http://blackskepticsla.org/our-work/; Sikivu Hutchinson, *Moral Combat: Black Atheists, Gender Politics, and the Values Wars* (Los Angeles: Infidel Books, 2011), 251.

15. Pinn, *Introducing African American Religion*, 245; Pew Research Center Religious Landscape Study, "Atheists," accessed July 30, 2017, http://www.pewforum.org/religious-landscape-study/religious-family/atheist/; Pew Research Center Religious Landscape Study, "Agnostics," accessed February 24, 2019, http://www.pewforum.org/religious-landscape-study/religious-family/agnostic/; Pew Research Center Religious Landscape Study, "The Unaffiliated," accessed February 24, 2019, http://www.pewforum.org/religious-landscape-study/religious-tradition/unaffiliated-religious-nones/. This and the next paragraph are adapted from Christopher Cameron, "Black Atheists Matter: How Women Freethinkers Take On Religion," *Aeon*, December 1, 2016, https://aeon.co/ideas/black-atheists-matter-how-women-freethinkers-took-on-religion.

16. Hutchinson, *Moral Combat*, 247.

BIBLIOGRAPHY

Manuscript Collections

Atlanta, Georgia

Emory University Manuscripts, Archives, and Rare Book Library
  Louise Thompson Patterson Papers
  Alice Walker Papers

New Haven, Connecticut

Beinecke Rare Books and Manuscript Library
  Claude McKay Papers
  James Weldon Johnson Collection

New York, New York

Egbert Ethelred Brown Papers, Schomburg Center for Research in Black
  Culture
Hermina Dumont Huiswood Papers, Tamiment Library and Robert F.
  Wagner Labor Archives

Washington, D.C.

Alain Locke Papers, Moorland-Springarn Research Center

Newspapers and Periodicals

Amsterdam News (New York)
The Black Panther

Boston Investigator
Christian Century
Christian Recorder
The Crisis: A Record of the Darker Races
The Crusader
Freethought
Free Inquiry
Lutheran Herald and Journal of the Fort Plain, N.Y., Franckean Synod
Messenger
The Nation
New Masses
New York Call
New York Times
Opportunity
Truth Seeker

Books, Journals, and Other Published Sources

Adams, Catherine, and Elizabeth H. Pleck. *Love of Freedom: Black Women in Colonial and Revolutionary New England*. Oxford: Oxford University Press, 2010.

Akers, Charles W. *Called unto Liberty: A Life of Jonathan Mayhew, 1720–1766*. Cambridge, Mass.: Harvard University Press, 1964.

Alexander, Nathan. *Race in a Godless World: Atheism, Race, and Civilization in Britain and the United States, c. 1850–1914*. New York and Manchester: New York University Press and Manchester University Press, 2019.

Allen, Norm Jr., ed. *The Black Humanist Experience: An Alternative to Religion*. Amherst, N.Y.: Prometheus Books, 2003.

Anderson, Jervis. *A. Philip Randolph: A Biographical Portrait*. 1972. Reprint, Berkeley: University of California Press, 1986.

Aptheker, Herbert. "An Unpublished Frederick Douglass Letter." In Pinn, *By These Hands*, 77–80.

Baraka, Amiri Imamu. "The Legacy of Malcolm X and the Coming of the Black Nation." In Pinn, *By These Hands*, 237–48.

Balagoon, Kuwasi et al. *Look for Me in the Whirlwind: The Collective Autobiography of the New York 21*. New York: Random House, 1971.

Baldwin, Davarian. *Chicago's New Negroes: Modernity, The Great Migration, and Black Urban Life*. Chapel Hill: University of North Carolina Press, 2007.

Baldwin, Davarian, and Minkah Makalani, eds. *Escape from New York: The New Negro Renaissance Beyond Harlem.* Minneapolis: University of Minnesota Press, 2013.

Baldwin, James. *Blues for Mister Charlie.* New York: Dial Press, 1964.

———. *The Fire Next Time.* New York: Vintage International, 1962.

———. *Go Tell It on the Mountain.* New York: Dell, 1952.

———. *Notes of a Native Son.* Boston: Beacon Press, 1955.

Baldwin, James, and Nikki Giovanni. *A Dialogue.* Philadelphia: J. B. Lippincott, 1973.

Ball, Charles. *Slavery in the United States: A Narrative of the Life and Adventures of Charles Ball, a Black Man, Who Lived Forty Years in Maryland, South Carolina and Georgia, as a Slave Under Various Masters, and was One Year in the Navy with Commodore Barney, During the Late War.* New York: John S. Taylor, 1837. http://docsouth.unc.edu/neh/ballslavery/ball.html.

Barbera, Donald R. *Black and Not Baptist: Nonbelief and Freethought in the Black Community.* New York: iUniverse, 2003.

Best, Wallace D. *Langston's Salvation: American Religion and the Bard of Harlem.* New York: New York University Press, 2017.

———. *Passionately Human, No Less Divine: Religion and Culture in Black Chicago, 1915–1952.* Princeton, N.J.: Princeton University Press, 2005.

Bibb, Henry. *Narrative of the Life and Adventures of Henry Bibb, an American Slave, Written by Himself; With an Introduction by Lucius C. Matlack.* New York: printed by the author, 1849. http://docsouth.unc.edu/neh/bibb/bibb.html.

Black Nonbelievers. "About Us." Accessed February 9, 2019. https://blacknonbelievers.wordpress.com.

Black Skeptics of Los Angeles. "Our Mission." Accessed February 9, 2019. http://blackskepticsla.org/our-mission/.

———. "Our Work." Accessed February 9, 2019. http://blackskepticsla.org/our-work/.

Bloom, Joshua, and Waldo E. Martin Jr. *Black against Empire: The History and Politics of the Black Panther Party.* Berkeley: University of California Press, 2013.

Brown, Elaine. *A Taste of Power: A Black Women's Story.* New York: Pantheon Books, 1992.

Brown, Lloyd W. "Lorraine Hansberry as Ironist: A Reappraisal of A Raisin in the Sun." *Journal of Black Studies* 4 (March 1974): 237–47.

Brown, William Wells. *Clotel or, The President's Daughter.* 1853. Reprint, New York: Penguin Books, 2004.

———. *Narrative of William W. Brown, a Fugitive Slave. Written by Himself.* Boston: American Anti-Slavery Society, 1847. Reprinted in *I Was Born a Slave: An Anthology of Classic Slave Narratives.* Volume 1, *1772–1849.* Edited by Yuval Taylor. Chicago: Lawrence Hill Books, 1999.

Buck, Christopher. *Alain Locke: Faith and Philosophy.* Los Angeles: Kalimát Press, 2005.

Buell, Lawrence, ed. *The American Transcendentalists: Essential Writings.* New York: Modern Library, 2006.

Burleigh, Michael. *Sacred Causes: The Clash of Religion and Politics, from the Great War to the War on Terror.* New York: HarperCollins, 2007.

Butler, Octavia. *Dawn.* New York: Warner Books, 1987.

———. "The Evening and the Morning and the Night." In Thomas, *Dark Matter,* 171–98.

———. "The Monophobic Response." In Thomas, *Dark Matter,* 415–16.

Bynum, Cornelius L. "'An Equal Chance in the Race for Life': Reverdy C. Ransom, Socialism, and the Social Gospel Movement, 1890–1920." *Journal of African American History* 43 (Winter 2008): 1–20.

Byrd, Rudolph P. *The World Has Changed: Conversations with Alice Walker.* New York: New Press, 2010.

Callahan, Allen Dwight. *The Talking Book: African Americans and the Bible.* New Haven, Conn.: Yale University Press, 2006.

Cameron, Christopher. "Black Atheists Matter: How Women Freethinkers Take On Religion." *Aeon,* December 1, 2016. https://aeon.co/ideas/black -atheists-matter-how-women-freethinkers-took-on-religion.

———. "Slavery and African American Irreligion." *Journal of Southern Religion* 18 (2016): jsreligion.org/vol18/cameron.

———. *To Plead Our Own Cause: African Americans in Massachusetts and the Making of the Antislavery Movement.* Kent, Ohio: Kent State University Press, 2014.

———. "Zora Neale Hurston, Freethought, and African American Religion." *Journal of Africana Religions* 4 (2016): 236–44.

Campbell, James. *Talking at the Gates: A Life of James Baldwin.* New York: Penguin Books, 1991.

Carmichael, Stokely. *Ready for Revolution: The Life and Struggles of Stokely Carmichael (Kwame Ture).* With Ekwueme Michael Thelwell. New York: Scribner, 2003.

Carson, Clayborne. *In Struggle: SNCC and the Black Awakening of the 1960s.* Cambridge, Mass.: Harvard University Press, 1981.

Casanova, José. "The Secular, Secularizations, Secularisms." In *Rethinking Secularism*, edited by Craig Calhoun, Mark Juergensmeyer, and Jonathan Vanantwerpen, 54–74. Oxford: Oxford University Press, 2011.

Channing, William E. *Slavery*. Boston: James Munroe, 1835.

Chauncy, Charles. *Twelve Sermons on the Following Seasonable and Important Subjects* . . . . Boston: Kneeland, 1765.

Cheney, Anne. *Lorraine Hansberry*. Boston: Twayne Publishers, 1984.

Chilcoat, Julius J. "From a Colored Physician." *Liberal Review* 1, no. 1 (February 1904): 58.

Chireau, Yvonne. *Black Magic: Religion and the African American Conjuring Tradition*. Berkeley: University of California Press, 2003.

Clarke, Cheryl. *"After Mecca": Women Poets and the Black Arts Movement*. New Brunswick, N.J.: Rutgers University Press, 2005.

Cleaver, Eldridge. *Soul on Ice*. New York: Dell, 1968.

Colaiaco, James A. *Frederick Douglass and the Fourth of July*. New York: Palgrave Macmillan, 2006.

Colbert, Soyica Diggs. "Go Tell It on the Mountain: Baldwin's Sermonic." In *The Cambridge Companion to James Baldwin*, edited by Michele Elam, 56–69. New York: Cambridge University Press, 2015.

Cone, James H. *A Black Theology of Liberation*. 2nd ed. Maryknoll, N.Y.: Orbis Books, 1986.

———. *For My People: Black Theology and the Black Church*. Maryknoll, N.Y.: Orbis Books, 1984.

Cruse, Harold. *The Crisis of the Negro Intellectual*. New York: New York Review Books, 1967.

Curtis, Edward E. IV. *Black Muslim Religion in the Nation of Islam, 1960–1975*. Chapel Hill: University of North Carolina Press, 2006.

———. *Muslims in America: A Short History*. Oxford: Oxford University Press, 2009.

Davis, Thadious M. *Nella Larsen, Novelist of the Harlem Renaissance: A Woman's Life Unveiled*. Baton Rouge: Louisiana State University Press, 1994.

Degras, Jane, ed. *The Communist International 1919–1943 Documents*. Vol. 2, *1923–1928*. London: Oxford University Press, 1960.

Demerath, N. J. "Irreligion, A-Religion, and the Rise of the Religion-Less Church: Two Case Studies in Organizational Convergence." *Sociological Analysis* 30 (1969): 191–203.

Diedrich, Maria. *Love across Color Lines: Ottilie Assing and Frederick Douglass*. New York: Hill and Wang, 1999.

Douglass, Frederick. *Narrative of the Life of Frederick Douglass, An American Slave, Written by Himself.* Boston: American Anti-Slavery Society, 1845. http://docsouth.unc.edu/neh/douglass/douglass.html.

————. *The Frederick Douglass Papers. Ser. 2, Autobiographical Writings.* Vol. 2, *My Bondage and My Freedom.* Edited by John W. Blassingame, John R. McKivigan, and Peter P. Hinks. New Haven, Conn.: Yale University Press, 2003.

————. "What to the Slave Is the Fourth of July?" in *Narrative of the Life of Frederick Douglass, An American Slave: Written by Himself, with Related Documents.* 2nd ed. Edited by David W. Blight. Boston: Bedford/St. Martin's, 2003.

Du Bois, W. E. B. *The Autobiography of W. E .B. Du Bois: A Soliloquy on Viewing My Life from the Last Decade of Its First Century.* New York: International Publishers, 1968.

————. *Du Bois on Religion.* Edited by Phil Zuckerman. Walnut Creek, Calif.: AltaMira Press, 2000.

————. *W. E. B. Du Bois Speaks: Speeches and Addresses, 1920–1963.* Edited by Philip S. Foner. New York: Pathfinder Press, 1960.

duCille, Ann. *The Coupling Convention: Sex, Text, and Tradition in Black Women's Fiction.* New York: Oxford University Press, 1993.

Durant, Will. *The Story of Philosophy: The Lives and Opinions of the Greater Philosophers.* New York: Simon and Schuster, 1951.

Emerson, Ralph Waldo. *Nature.* In *The American Transcendentalists: Essential Writings,* ed. Lawrence Buell, 3–67. New York: Modern Library, 2006.

Evans, Curtis J. *The Burden of Black Religion.* Oxford: Oxford University Press, 2008.

Executive Sessions of the Senate Permanent Subcommittee on Investigations of the Committee on Government Operations. Vol. 2, *Eighty-Third Congress: First Session, 1953.* Washington, D.C.: U.S. Government Printing Office, 2003.

Fabre, Michel. *The Unfinished Quest of Richard Wright.* 1973. Reprint: Urbana: University of Illinois Press, 1993.

Ferguson, Jeffrey B., ed. *The Harlem Renaissance: A Brief History with Documents.* Boston: Bedford/St. Martin's, 2008.

Ferris, William. *The Storied South: Voices of Writers and Artists.* Chapel Hill: University of North Carolina Press, 2013.

Feuerbach, Ludwig. *The Essence of Christianity.* London: John Chapman, 1854. https://archive.org/details/a581696600feneuoft.

Finkelman, Paul, ed. *Defending Slavery: Proslavery Thought in the Old South, A Brief History with Documents.* Boston: Bedford/St. Martin's, 2003.

Fischer, Kirsten. *Suspect Relations: Sex, Race, and Resistance in Colonial North Carolina*. Ithaca, N.Y.: Cornell University Press, 2002.

Floyd-Thomas, Juan M. *The Origins of Black Humanism in America: Reverend Ethelred Brown and the Unitarian Church*. New York: Palgrave Macmillan, 2008.

Flynn, Thomas R. *Existentialism: A Very Short Introduction*. Oxford: Oxford University Press, 2006.

Foner, Philip S., ed. *The Black Panthers Speak*. New York: Da Capo Press, 1995.

Forbes, Robert Pierce. *The Missouri Compromise and Its Aftermath: Slavery and the Meaning of America*. Chapel Hill: University of North Carolina Press, 2007.

Forman, James. "Control, Conflict and Change: The Underlying Concepts of the Black Manifesto." In *Black Manifesto: Religion, Racism, and Reparations*, edited by Robert S. Lecky and H. Elliott Wright, 34–51. New York: Sheed and Ward, 1969.

—————. *The Making of Black Revolutionaries*. 1972. Reprint, Seattle: University of Washington Press, 1997.

Forson, Psyche A. Williams. "'Suckin' the Chicken Bone Dry': African American Women, Fried Chicken, and the Power of a National Narrative." In *Cooking Lessons: The Politics of Gender and Food*, ed. Sherrie A. Inness, 169–92. Lanham, Md.: Rowman and Littlefield, 2001.

Fountain, Daniel L. *Slavery, Civil War, and Salvation: African American Slaves and Christianity, 1830–1870*. Baton Rouge: Louisiana State University Press, 2010.

Fowler, Virginia C., ed. *Conversations with Nikki Giovanni*. Jackson: University Press of Mississippi, 1992.

—————. *Nikki Giovanni: A Literary Biography*. Santa Barbara, Calif.: Praeger, 2013.

Free Religious Association. *The Free Religious Association: Proceedings at the Forty-sixth Annual Meeting*. Boston: Free Religious Association, 1913.

Freud, Sigmund. *The Future of an Illusion*. 1927. Reprint, New York: W. W. Norton, 1989.

Frey, Sylvia, and Betty Wood. *Come Shouting to Zion: African American Protestantism in the American South and British Caribbean to 1830*. Chapel Hill: University of North Carolina Press, 1998.

Gates, Henry Louis Jr. Afterword to Hurston, *Their Eyes Were Watching God*, 195–200.

Gates, Henry Louis Jr., and A. K. Appiah, eds. *Zora Neale Hurston: Critical Perspectives Past and Present*. New York: Amistad, 1993.

Gates, Henry Louis Jr., and Nellie Y. McKay, eds. *The Norton Anthology of African American Literature.* New York: W. W. Norton, 1997.

Gilmore, Glenda Elizabeth. *Defying Dixie: The Radical Roots of Civil Rights.* New York: W. W. Norton, 2008.

Ginzberg, Lori D. "'The Hearts of Your Readers Will Shudder': Fanny Wright, Infidelity, and American Freethought." *American Quarterly* 46 (1994): 195–226.

Giovanni, Nikki. *Black Feeling, Black Talk/Black Judgment.* 1968. Reprint, New York: Morrow Quill Paperbacks, 1978.

―――――. *Gemini: An Extended Autobiographical Statement on My First Twenty-Five Years of Being a Black Poet.* Indianapolis: Bobbs-Merrill, 1971.

Glaude, Eddie S. Jr. *Exodus! Religion, Race, and Nation in Early Nineteenth-Century Black America.* Chicago: University of Chicago Press, 2000.

Gomez, Michael. *Exchanging Our Country Marks: The Transformation of African Identities in the Colonial and Antebellum South.* Chapel Hill: University of North Carolina Press, 1998.

Gordon, Lewis R. "Remembering William R. Jones (1933–2012): Philosopher and Freedom Fighter." *LRG Blog.* Accessed February 8, 2019. http://www.lewisrgordon.com/sketches/remembering-william-r-jones.html.

Gordon, Michelle. "'Somewhat Like War': The Aesthetics of Segregation, Black Liberation and 'A Raisin in the Sun.'" In "Representing Segregation." Special issue, *African American Review* 42 (Spring 2008): 121–33.

Gorham, Candace R. M. *The Ebony Exodus Project: Why Some Black Women Are Walking Out on Religion—and Others Should Too.* Durham, NC: Pitchstone Publishing, 2013.

Grasso, Christopher. *Skepticism and American Faith: From the Revolution to the Civil War.* New York: Oxford University Press, 2018.

―――――. "Skepticism and American Faith: Infidels, Converts, and Religious Doubt in the Early Nineteenth Century." *Journal of the Early Republic* 22 (2002): 465–508.

Greenspan, Ezra. *William Wells Brown: An African American Life.* New York: W. W. Norton, 2014.

Grossman, James R. *Land of Hope: Chicago, Black Southerners, and the Great Migration.* Chicago: University of Chicago Press, 1989.

Guild, June Purcell. *Black Laws of Virginia: A Summary of the Legislative Acts of Virginia Concerning Negroes from Earliest Times to the Present.* Richmond: Whittet and Shepperson, 1936.

Gura, Philip F. *American Transcendentalism: A History*. New York: Hill and Wang, 2008.

Guy-Sheftall, Beverly, ed. *Words of Fire: An Anthology of African-American Feminist Thought*. New York: New Press, 1995.

Hahn, Steven. *A Nation under Our Feet: Black Political Struggles in the Rural South from Slavery to the Great Migration*. Cambridge, Mass.: Harvard University Press, 2003.

Hakutani, Yoshinobu, ed. *Critical Essays on Richard Wright*. Boston: G. K. Hall, 1982.

Hall, Jacquelyn Dowd. "The Long Civil Rights Movement and the Political Uses of the Past." *Journal of American History* 91 (March 2005): 1233–63.

Hansberry, Lorraine. *A Raisin in the Sun*. New York: Vintage Books, 1959.

————. "Simone de Beauvoir and *The Second Sex*: An American Commentary." In Guy-Sheftall, *Words of Fire*, 128–42.

————. *To Be Young, Gifted, and Black: Lorraine Hansberry in Her Own Words*. Edited by Robert Nemiroff. New York: Signet, 1969.

Hardy, Clarence E. III. *James Baldwin's God: Sex, Hope, and Crisis in Black Holiness Culture*. Knoxville: University of Tennessee Press, 2003.

Harris, LaShawn. "Running with the Reds: African American Women and the Communist Party during the Great Depression." *Journal of African American History* 94 (Winter 2009): 21–43.

Harris, Leonard, ed. *The Philosophy of Alain Locke: Harlem Renaissance and Beyond*. Philadelphia: Temple University Press, 1989.

Harris, Melanie L. *Gifts of Virtue, Alice Walker, and Womanist Ethics*. New York: Palgrave Macmillan, 2010.

Harris, Trudier. Introduction to *New Essays on "Go Tell It on the Mountain,"* edited by Trudier Harris, 1–28. The American Novel series. Cambridge: Cambridge University Press, 1996.

Harrison, Hubert. *A Hubert Harrison Reader*. Edited by Jeffrey B. Perry. Middletown, Conn.: Wesleyan University Press, 2001.

————. *When Africa Awakes: The "Inside Story" of the Stirrings and Strivings of the New Negro in the Western World*. New York: Porro Press, 1920.

Harvey, Paul. *Through the Storm, Through the Night: A History of African American Christianity*. Lanham, Md.: Rowman and Littlefield, 2011.

Hatch, Nathan O. *The Democratization of American Christianity*. New Haven, Conn.: Yale University Press, 1989.

Haywood, Harry. *Black Bolshevik: Autobiography of an Afro-American Communist*. Chicago: Liberator Press, 1979.

Hecht, Jennifer Michael. *Doubt: A History*. San Francisco: HarperCollins, 2003.

Heyrman, Christine Leigh. *Southern Cross: The Beginnings of the Bible Belt*. Chapel Hill: University of North Carolina Press, 1997.

Higashida, Cheryl. "To Be(come) Young, Gay, and Black: Lorraine Hansberry's Existentialist Routes to Anticolonialism." *American Quarterly* 6 (December 2008): 899–924.

Hill, Ruth Edmonds, ed. *The Black Women Oral History Project*. Westport, Conn.: Meckler, 1991.

Hilliard, David, and Lewis Cole. *This Side of Glory: The Autobiography of David Hilliard and the Story of the Black Panther Party*. Chicago: Lawrence Hill Books, 1993.

Holifield, E. Brooks. *Theology in America: Christian Thought from the Age of the Puritans to the Civil War*. New Haven, Conn.: Yale University Press, 2003.

Holland, Frederic May. *Frederick Douglass: The Colored Orator*. Rev. ed. New York: Haskell House, 1969.

Holmes, A. T. "The Duties of Christian Masters (1851)." In Finkelman, *Defending Slavery*, 106.

Holt, Thomas C. *Children of Fire: A History of African Americans*. New York: Hill and Wang, 2010.

Honderich, Ted, ed. *The Oxford Guide to Philosophy*. Oxford: Oxford University Press, 2005.

Horowitz, Helen Lefkowitz. *Rereading Sex: Battles over Sexual Knowledge and Suppression in Nineteenth-Century America*. New York: Alfred A. Knopf, 2002.

Howe, Daniel Walker. *What Hath God Wrought: The Transformation of America, 1815–1848*. Oxford: Oxford University Press, 2007.

Hughes, Langston. *The Big Sea*. New York: Hill and Wang, 1940.

———. *Selected Poems of Langston Hughes*. New York: Vintage, 1990.

Hunter, Tera W. *To 'Joy My Freedom: Southern Black Women's Lives and Labors after the Civil War*. Cambridge, Mass.: Harvard University Press, 1997.

Hurston, Zora Neale. *Folklore, Memoirs, and Other Writings*. New York: Library of America, 1995.

———. *Their Eyes Were Watching God*. 1937. Reprint, New York: HarperCollins, 2006.

Hutchins, Zachary McLeod. "Rejecting the Root: The Liberating, Anti-Christ Theology of Douglass's *Narrative*." *Nineteenth-Century Literature* 68, no. 3 (December 2013): 292–322.

Hutchinson, Sikivu. *Godless Americana: Race and Religious Rebels*. Los Angeles: Infidel Books, 2013.

————. *Moral Combat: Black Atheists, Gender Politics, and the Values Wars*. Los Angeles: Infidel Books, 2011.

Ingersoll, Robert G. *The Works of Robert G. Ingersoll, in Twelve Volumes*. Vol. 7, Dresden ed., *Interviews*. New York: Dresden Publishing, 1908.

Jackson, Roy. *The God of Philosophy: An Introduction to the Philosophy of Religion*. 2nd ed. Durham, U.K.: Acumen, 2011.

Jacobs, Harriet. *Incidents in the Life of a Slave Girl, Written by Herself*. Edited by Lydia Maria Child. Boston: printed by the author, 1861. http://docsouth.unc.edu/fpn/jacobs/jacobs.html.

Jacoby, Susan. *Freethinkers: A History of American Secularism*. New York: Owl Books, 2004.

————. *The Great Agnostic: Robert Ingersoll and American Freethought*. New Haven, Conn.: Yale University Press, 2013.

James, Winston. *A Fierce Hatred of Injustice: Claude McKay's Jamaica and His Poetry of Rebellion*. London: Verso, 2000.

————. *Holding Aloft the Banner of Ethiopia: Caribbean Radicalism in Early Twentieth-Century America*. London: Verso, 1998.

Jea, John. *The Life, History, and Unparalleled Sufferings of John Jea, the African Preacher, Compiled and Written by Himself*. Portsea, England, 1811.

Johnson, Brian L. *W. E .B. Du Bois: Toward Agnosticism, 1868–1934*. Lanham, Md.: Rowman and Littlefield, 2008.

Johnson, Walter. *Soul by Soul: Life Inside the Antebellum Slave Market*. Cambridge, Mass.: Harvard University Press, 1999.

Jones, Angela, ed. *The Modern African American Political Thought Reader: From David Walker to Barack Obama*. New York: Routledge, 2013.

Jones, Charles C. *The Religious Instruction of the Negroes: In the United States*. Savannah: Thomas Purse, 1842.

Jones, William R. *Is God a White Racist? A Preamble to Black Theology*. 1973. Reprint, Boston: Beacon Press, 1998.

Jos, Philip H. "Fear and the Spiritual Realism of Octavia Butler's Earthseed." *Utopian Studies* 23 (2012): 408–29.

Joseph, Peniel E. *Stokely: A Life*. New York: Basic Civitas, 2014. NOOK.

————. *Waiting 'Til the Midnight Hour: A Narrative History of Black Power in America*. New York: Holt Paperbacks, 2006.

Kahn, Jonathan S., and Vincent W. Lloyd, eds. *Race and Secularism in America*. New York: Columbia University Press, 2016.

Kelley, Robin D. G. *Hammer and Hoe: Alabama Communists during the Great Depression*. Chapel Hill: University of North Carolina Press, 1990.

Kennedy, Florynce "Flo." "A Comparative Study: Accentuating the Similarities of the Societal Position of Women and Negroes." In Guy-Sheftall, *Words of Fire*, 102–6.

———. "Nobody Ever Died from a Blow Job, 1976," in A. Jones, *Modern African American Political Thought Reader*, 329–31.

Keppel, Ben. *The Work of Democracy: Ralph Bunche, Kenneth B. Clark, Lorraine Hansberry, and the Cultural Politics of Race*. Cambridge, Mass.: Harvard University Press, 1995.

Kerste, Andrew E., and Clarence Lang, eds. *Reframing Randolph: Labor, Black Freedom, and the Legacies of A. Philip Randolph*. New York: New York University Press.

Kierkegaard, Søren. "Truth Is Subjectivity." In *Philosophy of Religion: Selected Readings*, 2nd ed., edited by Michael Peterson, William Hasker, Bruce Reichenbach, and David Basinger, 94–97. New York: Oxford University Press, 2001.

Kirkley, Evelyn A. *Rational Mothers and Infidel Gentlemen: Gender and American Atheism, 1865–1915*. Syracuse, N.Y.: Syracuse University Press, 2000.

Kornweibel, Theodore Jr. *No Crystal Stair: Black Life and the Messenger, 1917–1928*. Westport, Conn.: Greenwood Press, 1975.

———. *"Seeing Red": Federal Campaigns against Black Militancy, 1919–1925*. Bloomington: Indiana University Press, 1998.

Kulikoff, Allan. "How Africans Became African Americans." In *Major Problems in African-American History*, vol. 1, *From Slavery to Freedom, 1619–1877*, edited by Thomas C. Holt and Elsa Barkley Brown, 182–93. Boston: Wadsworth, 2000.

Lackey, Michael. *African American Atheists and Political Liberation: A Study of the Sociocultural Dynamics of Faith*. Gainesville: University Press of Florida, 2007.

Lamb, Daniel Smith. *Howard University Medical Department: A Historical, Biographical and Statistical Souvenir*. Washington, D.C.: R. Beresford, 1900.

Lamont, Corliss. *The Philosophy of Humanism*. 1949. Reprint, New York: Continuum, 1990.

Larsen, Nella. *Quicksand*. 1928. Mineola, N.Y.: Dover, 2006.

Lenin, V. I. "Socialism and Religion." In *Collected Works*, vol. 10, *November 1905–June 1906*, edited and translted by Andrew Rothstein. Moscow: Foreign Languages Publishing House, 1962.

Lewis, David Levering, ed. *The Portable Harlem Renaissance Reader*. New York: Penguin Books, 1994.

————. *W. E. B. Du Bois: Biography of a Race, 1868–1919.* New York: Henry Holt, 1993.

————. *W. E. B. Du Bois: The Fight for Equality and the American Century, 1919–1963.* New York: Henry Holt, 2000.

————. *When Harlem Was in Vogue.* New York and Oxford: Oxford University Press, 1979.

Lippy, Charles H. *Introducing American Religion.* London: Routledge, 2009.

Locke, Alain. "Moral Training in Elementary Schools." *Teacher* 8 (April 1904): 96–97.

————, ed. *The New Negro: Voices of the Harlem Renaissance.* 1925. Reprint, New York: Simon and Schuster, 1992.

————. "Pluralism and Intellectual Democracy." In Leonard Harris, *Philosophy of Alain Locke,* 51–66.

————. "Unity through Diversity: A Bahá'í Principle." In Leonard Harris, *Philosophy of Alain Locke,* 133–38.

Locke, Alain, Mordecai W. Johnson, Leon A. Ransom, and Doxie A. Wilkerson. "Is There a Basis for Spiritual Unity in the World Today?" *Town Meeting: Bulletin of America's Town Meeting of the Air* 8 (June 1, 1942): 5–10.

Makalani, Minkah. "Internationalizing the Third International: The African Blood Brotherhood, Asian Radicals, and Race, 1919–1922." *Journal of African American History* 96 (Spring 2011): 151–78.

Malcolm X. "Who Taught You to Hate Yourself?" Excerpt of speech given in Los Angeles in 1962. YouTube, December 2, 2014. Video, 1:07. https://www.youtube.com/watch?v=18Ern-fNEb4.

Marable, Manning. "A. Philip Randolph and the Foundations of Black American Socialism." *Radical America* 14 (March–April 1980): 7–29.

Martin, Waldo E. Jr. *The Mind of Frederick Douglass.* Chapel Hill: University of North Carolina Press, 1984.

Masur, Louis P., ed. *The Autobiography of Benjamin Franklin, with Related Documents.* Boston: Bedford/St. Martin's, 2003.

Mather, Cotton. *The Negro Christianized: An Essay to Excite and Assist that Good Work, the Instruction of Negro-Servants in Christianity.* Boston: B. Green, 1706.

May, Henry F. *The Enlightenment in America.* Oxford and New York: Oxford University Press, 1976.

Mayhew, Jonathan. *Seven Sermons Upon the Following Subjects; viz. The Difference betwixt Truth and Falshood, Right and Wrong. The Natural Ability of Men for Discerning these Differences. The Right and Duty of*

Private Judgment. Objections Considered. The Love of God. The Love of Neighbors. The First and Great Commandment, &c. Boston: Rogers and Fowle, 1749.

McDuffie, Erik S. *Sojourning for Freedom: Black Women, American Communism, and the Making of Black Left Feminism.* Durham, N.C.: Duke University Press, 2011.

McKay, Claude. *A Long Way from Home.* New York: Lee Furman, 1937.

———. "A Negro Poet." In *The Passion of Claude McKay.* Edited by Wayne Cooper. New York: Schocken Books, 1973.

———. *My Green Hills of Jamaica and Five Jamaican Short Stories.* Edited by Mervyn Morris. Kingston, Jamaica: Heinemann Educational Book (Caribbean), 1979.

McKivigan, John R. *The War against Proslavery Religion: Abolitionism and the Northern Churches, 1830–1865.* Ithaca, N.Y.: Cornell University Press, 1984.

McLellan, David. *Marxism and Religion: A Description and Assessment of the Marxist Critique of Christianity.* New York: Harper and Row, 1987.

Miller, Sally. "For White Men Only: The Socialist Party of America and Issues of Gender, Ethnicity and Race." In "New Perspectives on Socialism I." Special issue, *Journal of the Gilded Age and Progressive Era* 2 (July 2003): 283–302.

Moore, Richard B. "Hubert Henry Harrison." In *Dictionary of American Negro Biography.*, ed. Rayford W. Logan and Michael R. Winston, 292–93. New York: W. W. Norton, 1982.

Morais, Herbert M. *Deism in Eighteenth Century America.* 1934. Reprint, New York: Russell and Russell, 1960.

Morris, Aldon. *The Scholar Denied: W. E. B. Du Bois and the Birth of Modern Sociology.* Oakland: University of California Press, 2015.

Murch, Donna Jean. *Living for the City: Migration, Education, and the Rise of the Black Panther Party in Oakland, California.* Chapel Hill: University of North Carolina Press, 2010.

Naison, Mark. *Communists in Harlem during the Depression.* Urbana: University of Illinois Press, 1983.

Nelson, Alondra. *Body and Soul: The Black Panther Party and the Fight against Medical Discrimination.* Minneapolis: University of Minnesota Press, 2011.

Nemiroff, Robert, ed. *Lorraine Hansberry Speaks Out: Art and the Black Revolution.* New York: Caedmon Records, 1972.

Newman, Michael. *Socialism: A Very Short Introduction.* Oxford: Oxford University Press, 2005.

Newton, Huey P. *Revolutionary Suicide*. 1973. Reprint, New York: Penguin, 2009. Kindle.

————. *To Die for the People: The Writings of Huey P. Newton*. New York: Random House, 1972.

Nietzsche, Friedrich. *Beyond Good and Evil: Prelude to a Philosophy of the Future*. 1886. Translated by Walter Kaufmann. Reprint, New York: Vintage Books, 1989.

Northup, Solomon. *Twelve Years a Slave. Narrative of Solomon Northup, A Citizen of New-York, Kidnapped in Washington City in 1841, and Rescued in 1853, from a Cotton Plantation Near the Red River, in Louisiana*. Auburn, N.Y., 1854.

O'Neale, Sondra A. "Fathers, Gods, and Religion: Perceptions of Christianity and Ethnic Faith in James Baldwin." In *Critical Essays on James Baldwin.*, edited by Fred L. Standley and Nancy V. Burt, 125–43. Boston: G. K. Hall, 1988.

Ottanelli, Fraser M. *The Communist Party of the United States: From the Depression to World War II*. New Brunswick, N.J.: Rutgers University Press, 1991.

Paine, Thomas. *The Age of Reason*. 1794. Reprint, New York: Barnes and Noble, 2006.

————. *Common Sense and Related Writings*. Edited by Thomas P. Slaughter. Boston: Bedford/St. Martin's, 2001.

Palmer, Elihu. *The Examiners Examined; Being a Defence of the Age of Reason*. New York: L. Wayland and J. Fellows, 1794.

Paul, Nathaniel. "Emancipation Address." In *Jim Crow New York: A Documentary History of Race and Citizenship, 1777–1827*, ed. David N. Gellman and David Quigley, 227–32. New York: New York University Press, 2003.

Payne, Charles M. *I've Got the Light of Freedom: The Organizing Tradition and the Mississippi Freedom Struggle*. Berkeley: University of California Press, 1995.

Payne, Daniel. *Recollections of Seventy Years*. Nashville: A. M. E. Sunday School Union, 1888. http://docsouth.unc.edu/church/payne70/payne.html.

Perry, Jeffrey B. *Hubert Harrison: The Voice of Harlem Radicalism, 1883–1918*. New York: Columbia University Press, 2009.

Pew Research Center Religious Landscape Study. "Agnostics." Accessed February 24, 2019. http://www.pewforum.org/religious-landscape-study/religious-family/agnostic/.

————. "Atheists." Accessed January 19, 2019. http://www.pewforum.org/religious-landscape-study/religious-family/atheist/.

————. "Racial and Ethnic Composition." Accessed January 19, 2019. http://www.pewforum.org/religious-landscape-study/racial-and-ethnic -composition/.

————. "The Unaffiliated." Accessed February 24, 2019. http://www .pewforum.org/religious-landscape-study/religious-tradition/unaffiliated -religious-nones/.

Pinn, Anthony B. *By These Hands: A Documentary History of African American Humanism*. New York: NYU Press, 2001.

————. *The End of God-Talk: An African American Humanist Theology*. Oxford: Oxford University Press, 2012.

————. *Introducing African American Religion*. London: Routledge, 2013.

————. *Varieties of African American Religious Experience*. Minneapolis: Augsburg Fortress Publishers, 1998.

————. *Writing God's Obituary: How a Good Methodist Became a Better Atheist*. Amherst, N.Y.: Prometheus Books, 2014.

Putnam, Samuel P. *400 Years of Freethought*. New York: Truth Seeker, 1894.

Raboteau, Albert J. *Slave Religion: The "Invisible Institution" in the Antebellum South*. Oxford: Oxford University Press, 1978.

Rampersad, Arnold. *The Life of Langston Hughes*. Vol. 1, *1902–1941: I, Too, Sing America*. New York: Oxford University Press, 1986.

Rampersad, Arnold, and David Roessel, eds. *The Collected Poems of Langston Hughes*. New York: Vintage, 1994.

Randolph, Peter. *Sketches of Slave Life: Or, Illustrations of the "Peculiar Institution."* Boston: printed by the author, 1855.

Ransby, Barbara. *Ella Baker and the Black Freedom Movement: A Radical Democratic Vision*. Chapel Hill: University of North Carolina Press, 2003.

Richardson, Robert D. *Emerson: The Mind on Fire*. Berkeley: University of California Press, 1995.

Robinson, Cedric J. *Black Marxism: The Making of the Black Radical Tradition*. Chapel Hill: University of North Carolina Press, 1983.

Ross, Jack. *The Socialist Party of America: A Complete History*. Lincoln: University of Nebraska Press, 2015.

Scharfman, Rachel. "On Common Ground: Freethought and Radical Politics in New York City, 1890–1917." Ph.D. diss., New York University, 2005.

Schlereth, Eric R. *An Age of Infidels: The Politics of Religious Controversy in the Early United States*. Philadelphia: University of Pennsylvania Press, 2013.

Schmidt, Leigh Eric. *Village Atheists: How America's Unbelievers Made Their Way in a Godly Nation*. Princeton, N.J.: Princeton University Press, 2016.

Scott, Bonnie Kime, ed. *The Gender of Modernism: A Critical Anthology*. Bloomington: Indiana University Press, 1990.

Sernett, Milton C. *Bound for the Promised Land: African American Religion and the Great Migration*. Durham, N.C.: Duke University Press, 1997.

Service, Robert. *Comrades!: A History of World Communism*. Cambridge, Mass.: Harvard University Press, 2010.

Shin, Andrew, and Barbara Judson. "Beneath the Black Aesthetic: James Baldwin's Primer of Black American Masculinity." *African American Review* 32 (Summer 1998): 247–61.

Shore, Elliot. *Talkin' Socialism: J. A. Wayland and the Role of the Press in American Radicalism, 1890–1912*. Lawrence: University Press of Kansas, 1988.

Singer, Peter. *Marx: A Very Short Introduction*. Oxford: Oxford University Press, 2000.

Sitkoff, Harvard. *The Struggle for Black Equality, 1954–1992*. Rev. ed. New York: Hill and Wang, 1993. First published 1981.

Smith, Peter. *An Introduction to the Baha'i Faith*. Cambridge: Cambridge University Press, 2008.

Sobel, Mechal. *Trabelin' On: The Slave Journey to an Afro-Baptist Faith*. Princeton, N.J.: Princeton University Press, 1979.

Solomon, Mark. *The Cry Was Unity: Communists and African Americans, 1917–1936*. Jackson: University Press of Mississippi, 1998.

Sorrett, Josef. *Spirit in the Dark: A Religious History of Racial Aesthetics*. New York: Oxford University Press, 2016.

Spencer, Robyn C. *The Revolution Has Come: Black Power, Gender, and the Black Panther Party in Oakland*. Durham, N.C.: Duke University Press, 2016.

Spielberg, Steven, dir. *The Color Purple*. 1985; Burbank, Calif.: Warner Home Video, 2007. DVD.

Steward, Austin. *Twenty-Two Years a Slave, and Forty Years a Freeman; Embracing a Correspondence of Several Years, while President of Wilberforce Colony, London, Canada West*. Rochester: William Alling, 1857. http://docsouth.unc.edu/fpn/steward/steward.html.

Stringfellow, Thornton. "The Bible Argument: Or, Slavery in the Light of Divine Revelation (1860)." in Finkelman, *Defending Slavery*, 123.

Taylor, Charles. *A Secular Age*. Cambridge, Mass.: Harvard University Press, 2007.

Taylor, Cynthia. A. *Philip Randolph: The Religious Journey of an African American Labor Leader*. New York: New York University Press, 2006.

Thomas, Sheree R., ed. *Dark Matter: A Century of Speculative Fiction from the African Diaspora*. New York: Warner Books, 2000.

Turner, James. *Without God, Without Creed: The Origins of Unbelief in America*. Baltimore: Johns Hopkins University Press, 1985.

Turner, Joyce Moore. *Caribbean Crusaders and the Harlem Renaissance*. Urbana: University of Illinois Press, 2005.

Turner, W. Burghardt, and Joyce Moore Turner, eds. *Richard B. Moore, Caribbean Militant in Harlem: Collected Writings, 1920–1972*. Bloomington: Indiana University Press, 1988.

Tyson, Timothy B. "Robert F. Williams, 'Black Power,' and the Roots of the African American Freedom Struggle." *Journal of American History* 85 (September 1998): 540–70.

Unitarian Universalist Ministers Association. "In Memory of . . . William R. Jones (1933–2012)." *Remembering the Living Tradition* (blog). August 15, 2012. https://www.uuma.org/blogpost/569858/147952/In-Memory -of----William-R-Jones-1933-2012.

Van Deburg, William L. "Frederick Douglass: Maryland Slave to Religious Liberal." In Pinn, *By These Hands*, 83–100.

Walker, Alice. *The Color Purple*. Orlando: Harcourt Inc., 1992.

———. "The Diary of an African Nun." In *The Black Woman: An Anthology*, ed. Toni Cade, 38–41. New York: New American Library, 1970.

———. "The Only Reason You Want to Go to Heaven Is That You Have Been Driven Out of Your Mind." In Pinn, *By These Hands*, 287–98.

———. *In Search of Our Mother's Gardens: Womanist Prose*. San Diego: Harcourt Brace Jovanovich, 1983.

———. *The Third Life of Grange Copeland*. New York: Harcourt Brace Jovanovich, 1970.

Wall, Cheryl A. "Mules and Men and Women: Zora Neale Hurston's Strategies of Narration and Visions of Female Empowerment." *Black American Literature Forum* 23 (Winter 1989): 661–80.

———. "Passing for What? Aspects of Identity in Nella Larsen's Novels." *Black American Literature Forum* 20, no. 1–2 (Spring–Summer 1986): 97–111.

Walters, Kerry. *Revolutionary Deists: Early America's Rational Infidels*. New York: Prometheus Books, 2011.

Warren, Sidney. *American Freethought, 1860–1914*. New York: Gordian Press, 1966.

Washington, James M., ed. *A Testament of Hope: The Essential Writings and Speeches of Martin Luther King, Jr.* New York: HarperCollins, 1986.

Weinfeld, David. "Isolated Believer: Alain Locke, Baha'i Secularist." In *New Perspectives on the Black Intellectual Tradition*, ed. Keisha Blain et al., 83–98. Evanston, Ill.: Northwestern University Press, 2018.

Weisenfeld, Judith. "On Jordan's Stormy Banks: Margins, Center, and Bridges in African American Religious History." In *New Directions in American Religious History*, edited by Harry S. Stout and D. G. Hart, 417–44. New York: Oxford University Press, 1997.

West, Cornel. *Prophesy Deliverance! An Afro-American Revolutionary Christianity.* Anniversary ed. Louisville: Westminster John Knox Press, 2002. First published 1982.

Whitted, Qiana J. *"A God of Justice?" The Problem of Evil in Twentieth-Century Black Literature.* Charlottesville: University of Virginia Press, 2009.

Wilkerson, Isabel. *The Warmth of Other Sons: The Epic Story of America's Great Migration.* New York: Vintage, 2010.

Williamson, Scott C. *The Narrative Life: The Moral and Religious Thought of Frederick Douglass.* Macon, Ga.: Mercer University Press, 2002.

Willis, John C. "From the Dictates of Pride to the Paths of Righteousness: Slave Honor and Christianity in Antebellum Virginia." In *The Edge of the South: Life in Nineteenth-Century Virginia.*, ed. Edward L. Ayers and John C. Willis, 37–55. Charlottesville: University Press of Virginia, 1991.

Wilmore, Gayraud S. *Black Religion and Black Radicalism: An Interpretation of the Religious History of African Americans.* Maryknoll, N.Y.: Orbis Books, 1973.

Wilson, C. A. *Men with Backbone: And Other Pleas for Progress.* 2nd ed. Kingston, Jamaica: Educational Supply Company, 1913.

Wilson, Robert J. III. *Benevolent Deity: Ebenezer Gay and the Rise of Rational Religion in New England, 1696–1787.* Philadelphia: University of Pennsylvania Press, 1984.

Wintz, Cary D., and Paul Finkelman, eds. *Encyclopedia of the Harlem Renaissance.* 2 vols. New York and London: Routledge, 2004.

Wood, Gordon S. *Empire of Liberty: A History of the Early Republic, 1789–1815.* Oxford: Oxford University Press, 2009.

World Health Organization. *Constitution of the World Health Organization.* October 2006. http://www.who.int/governance/eb/who_constitution_en.pdf.

Wright, George Frederick. *The Logic of Christian Evidences*. Andover, Mass.: Warren F. Draper, 1883.

Wright, Richard. *Black Boy (American Hunger)*. 1945. Reprint, New York: HarperCollins, 1998.

———. "Blueprint for Negro Writing." In Gates and McKay, *Norton Anthology of African American Literature*, 1380–88.

———. *Native Son*. 1940. Reprint, New York: HarperCollins, 1993.

———. Review of *Their Eyes Were Watching God*, by Zora Neale Hurston. *New Masses*, October 5, 1937, 22–23.

———. *The God That Failed*. Edited by Richard H. Crossman. New York: Harper and Row, 1949.

Young, Henry James. "Black Theology: Providence and Evil." *Duke Divinity School Review* 40 (Spring 1975): 87–96.